War Pictures

WORLD WAR II: THE GLOBAL, HUMAN, AND ETHICAL DIMENSION

G. Kurt Piehler, series editor

War Pictures

Cinema, Violence, and Style in Britain, 1939–1945

Kent Puckett

Fordham University Press | New York 2017

Fordham University Press also publishes its books in a variety of electronic formats. Some content that appears in print may not be available in electronic books.

Visit us online at www.fordhampress.com.

Library of Congress Cataloging-in-Publication Data available online at http://catalog.loc.gov.

Printed in the United States of America
19 18 17 5 4 3 2 1
First edition

Contents

Preface

> My father fought a hard war. He fought Hitler, prosecuting the war with a violence that proved uncontainable. I don't know how to solve that, but without men like my father the war would not have been won!
>
> —Derek Jarman, *The Last of England* (1987)

I began to think about the arguments presented in this book in 2003 when the beginning of war in Iraq made it hard not to see war everywhere. I found that the books I read, the records I listened to, and the films and shows I watched all seemed to be *about* war even when they had evidently little to do with war. In ways both necessary and helplessly trivial, I felt that I saw war everywhere and that seeing war was maybe what interpretation was for. But why? What made looking for evidence of war where it apparently wasn't seem like a necessity? Why was it that war seemed to touch objects and ideas so distant from it? Was this creeping significance a matter of my imagination—maybe even my guilt—or was it rather evidence of something larger, a shift in how one thinks during a conflict that was imagined as open-ended and exceptional? How did a war, which was only barely about itself, manage to make everything else about war, too? With these questions in mind, I began with my colleague Alan Tansman to prepare graduate and undergraduate courses on war and representation. We paired texts that addressed particular wars with contemporary novels, poems, or films that seemed to have little or nothing to do with their wars, that is, with texts that held their wars "at a distance."[1] How did representations work differently as they drifted across the porous border between texts that treated war and its consequences directly and those that addressed them obliquely or not at all? *The Iliad* is about war and so is *All Quiet on the Western Front* (1929). Although they don't address their wars directly, there is little doubt that Ford Madox Ford's *The Good Soldier* (1915), Sam Peckinpah's *The Wild Bunch* (1969), and Erich Auerbach's *Mimesis* (1946) are also about war. But what about examples where the relation is more tenuous but maybe no less real: what about *Singin' in the Rain* (1952) or *The Theory of the Novel* (1920) or *Salem's Lot* (1975)? Both Laurence Olivier's and Kenneth Branagh's *Henry V* (1944 and 1989, respectively) are of course about their wars, but what about David Lean's *Brief Encounter* (1945) or his *Great Expectations* (1946)? War seems in some of these cases to be exactly where it is not; although neither allegorized nor referred to, war feels like an invisible and obscure but no less animating spirit in these and other wartime examples.

In addition to reminding us of its own presence, weight, and pathos, war can thus reveal what's always strained about *aboutness*, a quality that can and perhaps needs to mean several things at once. To be *about* is, according to the *Oxford English Dictionary*, to be "all over or around," "at large," "without any definite purpose," "on the move," "to one side, aside, away," "in circumference," "around the outside," "in every direction," "approximately," "more or less," "with regard to," and, finally, "to have as a subject matter, to be concerned with." As a number of critics have recently suggested, war can highlight the essentially impacted nature of aboutness. Alex Woloch argues that George Orwell's war writing "is (oddly) 'about' intentionality, 'about' about-ness. It doesn't merely seek to transmit this intention but to dramatize it."[2] Marina MacKay writes that "modernist writing produced between 1914 and 1918 stretched the concept of 'aboutness' almost to its breaking point in its approach to the war that saw its publication."[3] Mary Favret suggests that, at least since the late eighteenth century, war has become as much a shared, qualifying, and ambient idea about the world as a quantifiable state of affairs: "War becomes an object of knowledge, a universalizing abstraction; indeed, in wartime it threatens to become all you know."[4] Kate McLoughlin writes that, in many of the best cases, war texts succeed because they fail "to write about war, writing instead about the difficulties of its representation."[5] In each of these cases, these critics take the scope, the inclusiveness, and the violence of war as a challenge to representation, reference, and aboutness; because modern wars tend to colonize everything else at the level of the experience and the concept, because they are traumatic, because they undermine the difference between civilian and soldier, private and public, inside and outside, it is hard from within the ambit of a war to say that anything is simply and directly *about* anything else. Aboutness, like metaphor, relies on difference, which is itself one of modern war's less obvious casualties.

Beginning with the fraught relation between war and representation I turned to a few films made in Britain during World War II that to me seem to call particular attention to problems that war posed for aesthetic representation: *The Life and Death of Colonel Blimp* (1943), *Henry V* (1944), and *Brief Encounter* (1945). What did it mean practically to shoot and to edit a film in the context of total mobilization? In what ways can the form and the content of cinema specifically respond to the concept of total war? Was everything that fell within the assertively capacious frame of total war somehow *about* war? How did World War II's avowed status as a war for national survival put pressure on the cinematic treatment of everyday life and national character? How, as the war progressed, did filmmakers deal with anxieties that came not only with war but also with the anticipated approach of war's end, with the idea of life lived after the transformative social dislocations of war? What would viewers who were living or who had lived through years of blackout, bombing, rationing, and dislocation have seen, heard, and felt when they bought a ticket, entered a darkened cinema, and saw a film more or less about war? More to the point, how might these particular films help us to see a more general relation between total war and cinematic representation and thus to understand the limits of aesthetic representation when faced with organized violence?

There are, of course, many ways to approach these questions. One could write a more or less comprehensive history of filmmaking during the war years and look at how the nuts and bolts of war administration intersected with the film industry; one could work to prepare an atlas or glossary of films made during the war in order to isolate themes, motifs, and ideas that correspond with this or that phase of the war as it unfolded: the Phoney War, the Battle of Britain, the Battle of the Atlantic, the opening of the Eastern Front, and so on; or one could proceed biographically, looking at the ways that directors, actors, cinematographers, producers, and others brought individual experiences to their various attempts to represent and to understand World War II. These approaches are variously represented in a number of important books on the British cinema, including Anthony Aldgate and Jeffrey Richards's *Britain Can Take It: British Cinema and the Second World War* (1994), James Chapman's *The British at War: Cinema, State and Propaganda, 1939–1945* (1998), Charles Drazin's *The Finest Years: British Cinema of the 1940s* (2007), Antonia Lant's *Blackout: Reinventing Women for Wartime British Cinema* (1991), S. P. MacKenzie's *British War Films: 1939–1945* (2006), Robert Murphy's *British Cinema and the Second World War* (2000), and Neil Rattigan's *This Is England: British Film and the People's War, 1939–1945* (2001).

While I draw often on these writers and others, I employ a more speculative method. A reader of an early draft suggested that what follows is not film studies but rather *film writing*. Though meant as criticism, the distinction is probably a good one. I try to write on, through, and *about* these films not from within the terms of one or another field but rather as aesthetic objects whose significance, complexity, and pathos exceed their status as evidence for or against the value of this or that methodology. In this my work comes closer (in intent if not quality) to recent examples of historically charged aesthetic writing about war such as Alexander Nemerov's *Icons of Grief: Val Lewton's Home Front Pictures* (2005), T. J. Clark's *The Sight of Death: An Experiment in Art Writing* (2006), Leo Mellor's *Reading the Ruins: Modernism, Bombsites and British Culture* (2011), and Sarah Cole's *At the Violet Hour: Modernism and Violence in England and Ireland* (2012). In each of these cases, novels, paintings, and films are taken not only as evidence within a historical record but also as a problematic kind of history, as forms in which the tension, pressure, or paradox of history as a process is at least partially embodied or encoded. Consequently, I also look back to a long and idiosyncratic strain of historical thinking differently represented by figures such as Marc Bloch, Norbert Elias, Simone Weil, Walter Benjamin, and Johann Huizinga, all of whom are writers I look to and write about in what follows. To my mind, these figures share a sense that art and culture can, at their best, not only embody or represent a moment in time but also disrupt assumptions about the present's relation to the past and undo or at least reveal tricks we play on ourselves in order to forget what we owe that past. As they bring the past into rough contact with the present, art and culture lead, for better or worse, into the future. It is no coincidence that Bloch, Elias, Weil, Benjamin, and Huizinga wrote about war during and—if they were lucky—after war, a fact that forces us to confront ways in which, as Marina MacKay writes in an essay on the wartime origins of Ian Watt's *The Rise of the Novel*, "critical writing is subject to the same historical and biographical contingencies as those traditionally admitted with respect to other forms of writing."[6]

I am most interested here in how the experience of war's violence came together with political ambivalences that were particular to the British scene before and during the war to put a productive pressure on film style and specifically cinematic modes of representation. Such an object of study indeed makes a strong, close, and sometimes intuitive kind of reading necessary. Put differently, the enormity of the violence of World War II, its avowed conceptual status as a total war, and the complex emotional and ethical responses that the war elicited produced a situation in which connotations that unfurl across the levels of film form, film content, and film style demand interpretation in the strongest sense; as Roland Barthes writes, "to interpret a text is not to give it a (more or less justified, more or less free) meaning, but on the contrary to appreciate what *plural* constitutes it."[7] Because I want to look to the films themselves in order to ask what war-weary filmmakers and audiences might have seen, thought, and felt when they made or watched films that were more and less about war during a time of war, I take for granted the possibility that these films possess a formal and aesthetic complexity—a semantic plurality—that exceeds good and necessary empirical questions about institutional history, influence, and intention. I have, in other words, to think about *aboutness* as an occasion not for declaration but, crucially, for connotation, association, and suggestion.

If we cannot say for sure what the past thought about itself, we can at least identify some of those thoughts' overlapping and sometimes incommensurate conditions of possibility; maybe that's what history or, perhaps, historicity is: a shifting conceptual horizon against or through which we try to see and understand each other and ourselves. It is a field of hopes, beliefs, good and bad ideas, practices, dispositions, and habits that makes other beliefs, ideas, and practices possible but almost never necessary. I want both to understand how cinema became an especially appropriate and enormously popular medium through which to think about the nature of violence during World War II and to understand how it resulted from and contributed to history understood as that field of conceptual possibility. How did resources specific to the cinematic medium—cutting, casting, color, sound design—allow filmmakers and audiences to engage with the difficulties of thinking about total war?[8] The different but related temporalities—the specific historicity—of war and cinema come together to make these questions especially vital. While popular memory tends to treat World War II as a single period, people living through it experienced particular years, seasons, months, and weeks as periods distinct in and of themselves. The early days of the Phoney War were felt as different in kind from the Battle of Britain, which was itself felt as different in kind from everything that followed. We can see this accelerated process of auto-periodization at work in journals and diaries. For instance, Hugh Trevor-Roper was able in 1942 to look back to 1940 with real nostalgia, which is to say to look at that year as a time really different from his present; he writes about reading his journal from that other year: "I read through again the chronicle of that memorable year in our history, and was astonished at the serene, effortless confidence with which we accepted, and reacted to, the most colossal disasters. Had we paused to think, we would have seen that we had been defeated, and that the value of further resistance was questionable; but this intellectual process never occurred to us, and we survived."[9]

This sense of wartime as an internally fractured set of distinct periods had a particular significance for filmmakers, particularly those who were committed in one way or another to cinema as a form of democratic propaganda. Because, in other words, it takes a long time to make a film, the specific problems that wartime films try to address (guilt over appeasement, anticipation of invasion, the experience of the Blitz, wariness about the nature of Anglo-American relations, worry about social life after wartime, etc.) were often already out-of-date by the time the films in fact appeared. "The feature film," writes Nicholas Reeves, "is too unwieldy a weapon to deploy in these kind of propaganda campaigns and, almost without exception, films that were designed to play a part in such particular, time-specific campaigns failed to meet their original objectives."[10] We need, in that case, to see that a film made in 1942 and released in 1943 would have been reacting to problems that were maybe most alive in 1941, a fact that, given the compressed and internally differentiated nature of Britain's wartime, made each film into an especially volatile mix of residual, dominant, and emergent ideas about a war that was changing all the time.[11]

What's conceptually difficult and even paradoxical about World War II thus takes several forms in *War Pictures*. It was, for instance, said again and again both in films and in other contexts that, because World War II was a total war, the British had to suspend values that had seemed to define the national character in order to protect those values from destruction at the hands of Hitler and the Nazis. In order to save civilization, civilization had to be sacrificed; values had to be suspended in order to protect those same values; immoral methods had to be adopted so as to overcome immorality. Following the proverbial logic of "it takes a thief to catch a thief," the paradoxical and dispiriting idea that "it takes a fascist to fight a fascist" was everywhere during the war years, finding fraught expression in journals, diaries, political speeches, opinions about the war captured by Mass-Observation, as well as in novels, poems, documentaries, and feature films.[12] For reasons that I'll describe in what follows, I take this dilemma—that it takes a fascist to fight a fascist—to be both necessary to the British experience of total war and a structuring formal impetus behind some of the best British films of those years. In this regard, *War Pictures* is in conversation with a number of recent books about the culture and society of the British home front, works that attempt both to address the broad ambivalences and ambiguities of World War II and look to ways in which the specific fact or fantasy of total war put pressure on local experiences of class, gender, national identity, and empire; I'm thinking here of Adam Piette's *Imagination at War: British Fiction and Poetry 1939–1945* (1995), Karen Schneider's *Loving Arms: British Women Writing the Second World*

War (1997), Mark Wollaeger's *Modernism, Media, and Propaganda: British Narrative from 1900 to 1945* (2006), Lyndsey Stonebridge's *The Writing of Anxiety: Imagining wartime in Mid-Century British Culture* (2007), Patrick Deer's *Culture in Camouflage* (2009), Kristine A. Miller's *British Literature of the Blitz: Fighting the People's War* (2009), Marina Mackay's *Modernism and World War II* (2010), Susan R. Grayzel's *At Home and Under Fire: Air Raids and Culture in Britain from the Great War to the Blitz* (2012), Gill Plain's *Literature of the 1940s: War, Postwar and "Peace"* (2013), and Paul Saint-Amour's *Tense Future: Modernism, Total War, Encyclopedic Form* (2015).

In addition to thinking through some political and strategic paradoxes immanent to the British experience of total war, I'll also argue that the films on which I focus engage with an even more difficult wartime idea. Where from a certain view one can imagine that particular wars are responsible for particular periods of conflict and violence—that wars cause violence—the films I discuss entertain, largely at the level of style, the sobering possibility that an essential human tendency toward violence and aggression might in fact stand as a more general cause of this or that war: this is instead to imagine that violence—original, human, intransigent—causes war. In this way, these films echo and anticipate arguments about the precedence of violence and aggression found in Hobbes and de Maistre, Freud and Lacan, Walter Burkert's *Homo Necans: The Anthropology of Ancient Greek Sacrificial Ritual and Myth* (1983) and Lawrence Keeley's *War Before Civilization: The Myth of the Peaceful Savage* (1996).[13] This idea, that human aggression might precede and thus exceed even the totalizing damage of total war, is one that these films approach delicately, obliquely, and formally. The notion that wars are in some sense natural and inevitable—and thus that no war could end all or any wars—is a difficult, dispiriting one to make in the midst of a costly, draining campaign. Part of the aesthetic brilliance of these films comes from their willingness to make—at the level of cinematic technique and film style—so unhappy but so important an argument about war and its violence.

War Pictures

Introduction

> One really has to rack one's brains to find anything to say about a British film. One wonders why. But that's the way it is. And there isn't even an exception to prove the rule.
>
> —Jean-Luc Godard, review of J. Lee Thompson's *Woman in a Dressing-Gown* (1958)

> Before continuing with our diagnosis it becomes necessary to have a definition of style.
>
> —Cyril Connolly, *Enemies of Promise* (1938)

I first saw *The Life and Death of Colonel Blimp* (1943) years ago when a friend lent me an old, much-played VHS tape of its shortened and badly recut American release.[1] Even washed-out, wobbly, and stripped of its all-important flashback structure, the film struck me as odd, willful, beautiful, and—to use a word often associated with the British cinema—*eccentric.* The story of a bluff and romantic old soldier as he fought, lived, and found and lost love in three wars (the Boer War and World Wars I and II), *Colonel Blimp* seemed both whimsical and cynical, nostalgic and pragmatic, cosmopolitan and patriotic. Although unquestionably a war film, it also felt to me like something other, something more than a war film. As it turns out, that first, dimly remembered and mixed-up impression of the film was more or less right: like several of the films I discuss in this book, *Colonel Blimp* is a committed work of propaganda that nonetheless embraces a thematic and aesthetic complexity that would otherwise seem antithetical to propaganda.

C. A. Lejeune, a film critic for the *Observer* in 1943, wrote this about *Blimp*: "It is a handsome piece. It is frequently a moving piece. But what is it about?"[2] We might say provisionally that *Colonel Blimp* is about two very different things: while the film sometimes seems to suggest that Britain had to move beyond the old decencies, beyond the "sporting-club rules" that underwrote earlier wars, at other times it seems to suggest that Britain was fighting in order to preserve exactly those decencies, exactly those old rules. It is in these conflicted terms that the film offers both a criticism and an unexpectedly sincere defense of Clive Candy, the film's out-of-touch old soldier and its titular "Blimp."[3] Essentially ambivalent, *Colonel Blimp* both accepts and deplores the all-in tactics of modern total war; and, because its ideological ambivalence is matched with a superbly excessive visual style—with bravura formal experiments in color, cutting, and composition—the film seems willfully to undermine even as it pursues its practical aims as wartime propaganda.

If *Colonel Blimp* is eccentric, it is at least decisively so (in the words of British film critic Raymond Durgnat, the film's director, Michael Powell, "reveres eccentricity"[4]). Like an uncertain satellite, the film follows an erratic, wavering, or hyperbolic path around its own official ideas about war and violence.[5] This is one way to picture its striking inability or unwillingness to be about any one thing, its inability or unwillingness to center in on a single argument or coherent theme. In charting its eccentric but nonetheless committed course in relation to war, *Colonel Blimp* manages to be propaganda while also resisting the ideological and aesthetic simplifications that a war-weary British public had come to expect from propaganda.[6] Committed and complex, the cinematic eccentricity of *Colonel Blimp* enabled Powell and Pressburger to have their bellicose cake and eat it, too.[7] It allowed them, in other words, to manage what was almost impossible about their war.

War Pictures argues for a kind of tactical cinematic eccentricity that allowed some important British wartime films to respond to political and social contradictions characteristic of the British home front between 1939 and 1945. Seen at one and the same time as a characteristic national virtue and as an implicit and maybe unruly kind of critique, the idea of eccentricity helped the British to navigate some political and ethical contradictions necessary to the experience of total mobilization and total war. In particular, the tactical ambivalence these British war films display allowed audiences to confront—if not necessarily to overcome—the disturbing, paradoxical, and maybe self-defeating possibility that a commitment to a total war against totalitarianism was perhaps also a commitment to totalitarianism, and that to fight a fascist you maybe had to become a fascist. In that case, we can look to the specific demands that total war made on a few British filmmakers in order to see and to consider something more general about aesthetic style and its relation to violence during and after World War II. In other words, looking at the stylistic eccentricity of British war cinema will both reveal some local paradoxes that shaped British thinking about combat, commitment, and the home front during World War II and lend us a broader sense of how aesthetic objects can stand as an answer to and expression of history and its violence.

The Concept of Cinematic Eccentricity

Written between the wars, Edith Sitwell's *English Eccentrics* casts eccentricity as a distinctively English expression of "attitude, rigidity, protest, or explanation."[8] "Any dumb but pregnant comment on life, any criticism of the world's arrangement, if expressed by only one gesture, and that of sufficient contortion, becomes eccentricity."[9] For Sitwell, eccentricity happens when a personal or attitudinal difference is strategically embraced, sharpened, and turned into a gesture of tacit defiance. Sitwell's interwar sense of eccentricity as an essential, exaggerated, and fully lived "criticism of the world's arrangement" thus recalls and intensifies John Stuart Mill's more mild observations about the eccentricities of the English in *On Liberty* (1859): "That so few now dare to be eccentric, marks the chief danger of the time."[10] Although most of Mill's great work is dedicated to identifying shared discursive norms that could best preserve individual liberties within a whole national community, he carves out a counterintuitive but necessary place for the eccentric, for the person whose value derives from his or her essential inability to conform to shared discursive norms: "Precisely because the tyranny of opinion is such as to make eccentricity a reproach, it is desirable, in order to break through that tyranny, that people should be eccentric."[11] More than a quirk of character, eccentricity was for Mill and later for Sitwell a kind of immanent critique, a lived rejoinder to what both understood as an increasingly homogenous mass culture: "Eccentricity," according to Mill, "has always abounded when and where strength of character has abounded; and the amount of eccentricity in a society has generally been proportional to the amount of genius, mental vigour, and moral courage which it contained."[12] Eccentricity is thus a practical answer to what, following Sitwell, we might call the melancholy of the given: "we may seek in our dust-heap for some rigid, and even splendid, attitude of Death, for some exaggeration of the attitudes common to Life."[13] Published in 1933, *English Eccentrics* stands as an odd and oddly prescient argument against totalization, and, as we will see, echoes of her anxious feel for the endangered but necessary eccentricity of the English returned again and again as the British home front tried to think its way through the putative totality of total war.[14]

Eccentricity understood as a form of tacit resistance brings to mind another close, contemporary, but differently classed concept to mind: a *vulgarity* that is also sometimes associated with the British cinema. For instance, after saying that there was nothing to say about British films, Jean-Luc Godard goes on nonetheless to say something harsh about all that was wrong with them: "From beginning to end [*Woman in a Dressing-Gown*] is an incredible debauch of camera movements as complex as they are silly and meaningless. . . . May the English lose the Middle East soon if the loss of their political power could restore their sense of beauty, if not efficiency."[15] For Godard the provincial clumsiness of the British cinema is an effect of its pushing technical virtuosity toward and past a limit. This resistance to too much technique recalls the critic Jean Queval's earlier complaint that the British cinema's "most consecrated director," David Lean, "seems to be only interested in those exceptional subject matters that flatter the super-technician."[16] Similarly, Durgnat observes that, to some, Michael Powell "seemed a stylist and a rhetorician, camouflaging an absence of idea by a weakness for the grandiose, out-of-context effect"; he was, in other words, "an 'eccentric technician.'"[17] Writing about *Brief Encounter*, Richard Dyer acknowledges, "many people find the whole film too deliberate, too crafted."[18] The US critic Dwight Macdonald struck a related note when he asserted that "the British . . . douse their movies with close-ups the way people with defective taste buds use ketchup."[19] For each of these critics, British cinematic virtuosity threatens to fall into vulgarity when it tries too hard and goes too far, when it fails to subordinate the social and material and thus partial presence of filmmaking-as-technique to the finished film as a whole. "It is," writes the art historian T. J. Clark, "an advantage of the term 'vulgar'. . . that discursively it points two ways: to the object itself, to some abjectness or absurdity in its very make-up (some tell-tale blemish, some atrociously visual quality which the object will never stop betraying however hard it tries); and to the object's existence in a particular social world, for a set of tastes and styles of individuality which have still to be defined, but are somewhere there, in the world even before it is deployed."[20] For Clark, vulgarity is not only a flaw but also a form of protest because, like Sitwell's eccentricity, it reveals limits immanent to "a particular social world."[21]

We could say, then, that eccentricity and vulgarity are what happens when style reaches a limit, a limit that Paul Valéry similarly approached when he cast style as an aesthetic effort that, as it reaches hopelessly toward universality, must instead stop just short of "extravagance and eccentricity": "A personality . . . acquires the interest of an original, of a unique specimen which stands out from among the collection of similar beings that is the human race; it becomes a kind of *deviation toward the ideal* [emphasis mine]."[22] Roland Barthes, drawing on Valéry, similarly sees style as a "crude" encounter between the ideal and the concrete: "Whatever its sophistication, style has always something crude about it: it is a form with no clear destination, the product of a thrust, not an intention, and, as it were, a vertical and lonely dimension of thought . . . it is the writer's 'thing,' his glory and his prison, it is his solitude."[23] Closer to home, Durgnat maintains: "Personal style is the content which the artist contributes, intuitively, to every subject with which he deals. Inevitably, it is frequently the deepest, the determinant part of the content."[24] For Durgnat as for Clark, personal style is that "which the object will never stop betraying however hard it tries"; it is that which is the truth of a work's content even though it is not properly of that content. Because eccentricity and vulgarity name aspects of style that cannot be willed or unwilled, because they represent style's thing, they can perhaps reveal a potential for political resistance latent in all style.

Style, vulgarity, eccentricity: a film like *Colonel Blimp* is, it seems to me, unthinkable without them. Although undoubtedly a film of wartime, which is to say a film that emerges from and responds to an especially totalizing social situation, *Colonel Blimp* is also a film whose style as style seems somehow at odds with that situation. At the same time that the film explicitly supports measures necessary to total war, it seems also to reject the concept of totality upon which total war depends. Consider, for example, its persistent but apparently unmotivated use of the color red, a color that cuts through and against particular shots with an almost feral insistence. There is the red that punctuates the humid, bustling interior of Cafe Hohenzollern when Candy visits Berlin in 1902; the red of the crosses that mark exhausted nurses' uniforms as they rest in a repurposed French church during World War I; the red that illuminates Deborah Kerr's face as she waits for a traffic light to shift in the midst of World War II's blacked-out London. Because these irruptions of red feel unmotivated and thus related more to one another than to any aspect of the film's narrative, they suggest an aleatory order of significance that works independently of narrative or plot or natural causality.[25] The red of one war doesn't just recall or remind us of the red of another; it is, rather, exactly the same red, a fact that both calls attention to the film's rich and deliberate use of Technicolor and turns film style into a figure for the mysterious and eternal recurrence of war, violence, and love. The simple but profound stylistic repetition of the color red across three wars thus recalls the trivial Proustian miracle that occurs when Marcel realizes that the taste of a cookie dipped in tea is exactly what it was decades before; insofar as the taste is a straightforward because perfectly full repetition, it cuts across history making different, counterintuitive, and critical modes of analysis possible. Red works both as an aesthetic or affective intensity to be enjoyed for its own sake and as a tacit and embodied argument against narrative's or, indeed, history's capacity to explain why some feelings, images, or events seem inevitably to recur. Because the red is an assertion of a director's will, it is an element of style; because it is a little garish, it is perhaps vulgar; and, because it is a detail that refuses to attend to the film's putative political, thematic, or narrative center, it is richly and technically eccentric.

Throughout *War Pictures*, I'll return to instances of stylistic or technical eccentricity that put different kinds of pressure on the whole and, as it were, official work of these films. I'm interested, in other words, in how their objects, ideas, images, and figures can appear as concentrated moments of ambivalence, as points of instability—Jacques Lacan calls them "anamorphic ghosts"—that serve as hinges between different and sometimes opposed ways of looking at the world and at war.[26] Light that seems impossibly to stream across the threshold of a flashback in David Lean's *Brief Encounter*; a stray allusion—to an old song, a famous painting, or to Donald Duck—that means two radically different things in two equally available historical contexts; a cut (or, in *Colonel Blimp*, the conspicuous absence of a cut) that calls attention to disparate but equally viable systems of aesthetic value; contrapuntal casting decisions that overload the intrinsic narrative significance of a character with the excessive and extrinsic charisma of the character actor; willful anachronisms—in Laurence Olivier, Lean, and, later, Derek Jarman—that appear to force the present into rough, inconclusive contact with the past.

I take these moments of conceptual ambivalence or impaction as instances of what Antoine de Baecque has recently called "cinematographic forms of history"; they are moments that index "the irruption of history" into the flow of an official discourse that would have us rather forget the past: "A few filmmakers have tried to capture this sense of irruption, or at least have striven, through a particular *mise-en-scène*, to give form to history, whether the history of the past or the history unfolding before their eyes."[27] More recently, D. A. Miller has pointed to the "hidden pictures" that seem to interrupt Alfred Hitchcock's films, to instances "in which a strongly narrativized image has been fashioned to conceal something that—if ever seen—would not enhance its coherence, but explode it."[28] The films I look at are marked with these images, objects, "moments of irruption," and "hidden pictures," with forms that push style to and past a limit in order to produce a tactical eccentricity specific to the political pressures of wartime. Indeed, as I argue in relation to David Lean's *Brief Encounter* (see chapter 3), these moments of cinematic eccentricity not only call attention to the fraught or contradictory conditions particular to World War II but also trouble the very idea of a war as a discrete, bound, or narratable period; insofar as they upset ordinary or "natural" cinematic temporality, they help us also to see how war's violence can run excessively past or over war's official beginnings and ends, blurring the conceptual and narrative lines that would allow us to separate times of peace from times of war.[29]

Casting cinematic eccentricity in these terms will remind some readers of Kristin Thompson's classic essay on "the concept of cinematic excess" in which she states: "Style is the use of repeated techniques which become *characteristic* of the work; these techniques are foregrounded so that the spectator will notice them and create connections between their individual uses. Excess does not equal style, but the two are closely linked because they both involve the material aspects of the film. Excess forms no specific patterns which we could say are characteristic of the work. But the formal organization provided by style does not exhaust the material of the filmic techniques, and a spectator's attention to style might well lead to a noticing of excess as well."[30] In other words, if style characterizes a work, excess or eccentricity push that character toward and maybe past a limit, toward the raw and indigestible condition of the film's or the image's thing. Just as Sitwell and Clark respectively saw eccentricity and vulgarity as inchoate attitudes of protest against the melancholy homogeneity of a social given—the monotony of the "dust-heap"—so does Thompson see cinematic excess both as an expression of the essential materiality of film and as an incomplete relation that exists between individual details and the ostensibly homogenous or totalizing systems they both rely on and resist. She quotes Stephen Heath: "Homogeneity is haunted by the material practice it represses and the tropes of that repression, the forms of continuity, provoke within the texture of the film the figures—the edging, the margin—of the loss by which it moves: permanent battle for the resolution of that loss on which, however, it structurally depends, mediation between image and discourse, narrative can never contain the whole film which permanently exceeds its fictions."[31]

In *Colonel Blimp* certain aspects of the film—its regular and unmotivated use of the color red, the larger-than-life fact of Clive Candy's smooth and sweating head, the oddly balletic energy of the motorcyclists racing through its opening scene—are excessive because they appear to resist resolution into a larger thematic or narrative unity, because they gesture with eccentric or vulgar insistence toward modes of being that will not be made to make sense. These impacted, difficult, or aberrant instances of cinematic style assert themselves against the thematic, aesthetic, or politicial unities that would seem otherwise to organize the film; they remain distinct, compelling, incommensurate, and indigestible despite otherwise reasonable demands of taste, plot, or ideology. We might say that part of what made it so hard to see in 1943 what *Colonel Blimp* was about was exactly its excessive, eccentric, and maybe vulgar insistence on the self-evident force and value of film style, its unwillingness or inability to subordinate aesthetic character to the demands of one or another social, political, or narrative system.

A People's War

Of course, suggesting that a film as big and accomplished as *Colonel Blimp* is marked with moments of cinematic excess will seem uncontroversial if not passé.[32] However, what remains striking and specific about the aesthetic ambition of *Colonel Blimp* is how its particular form of excess works within an avowed work of political propaganda made during a time of total mobilization. For, while it is more or less obvious to our post-poststructuralist sensibilities that bodies, affects, or things will never be entirely absorbed within one or another social, aesthetic, or narrative totality, something else must be at stake when that excess appears in a propaganda film made self-consciously in the midst of what was taken almost universally as a total and thus totalizing war. Powell and Pressburger were indeed explicit about their film's tactical relation to the putative totality of total war: "Englishmen," they wrote in a memo prepared for Brendan Bracken's Ministry of Information, "are by nature conservative, insular, unsuspicious, believers in good sportsmanship and anxious to believe the best of other people. These attractive virtues, which are, we hope, unchanging, can become absolute vices unless allied to a realistic acceptance of things as they are, in modern Europe and in Total War."[33] They thus sold their film as a film about total war and, more to the point, about the need to put British audiences in a position clearly and simply to see and thus to accept "things as they are" in total war. However, as I discuss at length in chapter 1, the ministry wasn't convinced and it ultimately withheld its support from Powell and Pressburger's film, suggesting in an internal memorandum that, instead of clarifying the nature and stakes of total war, the film rather confused matters: its "overcomplication of ideas" was "dangerous."[34]

Confusing instead of clarifying, yes, but maybe not their fault. As Paul K. Saint-Amour has recently pointed out, "total war" has always been maybe too fuzzy, maybe too capacious a concept to be all that useful as either a military or a historical term of art:[35]

> [T]he range of meanings clustered under the expression "total war" can be profoundly at odds with one another. It makes a great difference whether you

> ascribe the targeting of civilians to the rise of certain weapons technologies, to an exterminatory war of ideas, or to the emergence of a certain kind of state or military-industrial complex. Scholars who write of total war must choose between incompatible options—between viewing it, for instance, as an expanded conflict (e.g., from fronts to areas) versus an intensified one (e.g., from defeating to eliminating an enemy). Or they must content themselves with all-of-the-above arguments. As a concept, total war has become at once so comprehensive and so self-contradictory that even those who remain committed to it must repeatedly justify their use of the term.[36]

Seen in these terms, total war is maybe less a coherent and thus representable material or historical situation than an academic or imaginative problem, an idea that indexes interpretive contradictions, anxieties, and aspirations that follow from the fraught and bewildering experience of war pursued on a global scale.[37] "If," as Jan Mieszkowski suggests, "total war was explicitly understood as an ideal that might never be realized in practice, this has not prevented several generations of historians from debating which previous wars . . . are most genuinely deserving of the title, suggesting that another cultural 'achievement' of the First World War was the way in which it pitted theoretical and historical analyses of modern militarism against one another, a rift that has yet to be resolved."[38]

That said: if it is hard, given the fundamental looseness of the term, to say why or how one war was at last more total than another, it is nonetheless clear that total war was an enormously powerful, specific, and starkly immediate *idea* for those living through World War II—a war that did, after all, turn on the way it practically undermined conceptual differences between soldier and civilian; in other words, turn on "the central significance of civilians in the conflict, the indispensable roles that they played in the war's outcome, as well as the vulnerabilities that they shared, as a direct consequence, with the soldiers."[39] Kristine A. Miller writes: "The Blitzkrieg on the United Kingdom during World War II was the most direct attack on civilians in British history. As London and other British cities came under siege beginning in September 1940, the common cause of national defense seemed to reduce distance between soldiers and civilians, to resolve differences between men and women, and to repair divisions between leisured and working classes."[40] Thanks, then, to what Eric Hobsbawm calls "the strange democratization of war," millions of people between 1939 and 1945 had to think about the reach and consequence of their everyday experience in the terrifying, leveling, and nonetheless highly abstract terms of total war.[41] How else were you to think of a war that seemed to touch everyone and everything? Put differently, whatever its status as material reality or logistical fact, the *concept* of total war allowed ordinary people to understand or to imagine or to feel their local experience as meaningfully related to the war as a whole: "What was happening," writes Elizabeth Bowen, "was out of all proportion to our faculties of knowing, thinking and checking up."[42] This is what Mieszkowski takes as total war's specifically conceptual necessity: war becomes "total only once it had to be imagined as such."[43]

It was thus the idea of total war that allowed the British to experience and to cast their war as a "People's War" or as an everyday, everyone kind of epic. Drawing on Hegel's lectures on fine art, Saint-Amour writes:

> [B]oth national holism and its signature literary genre are galvanized by war: "conflict in a state of war [is, writes Hegel,] the situation most suited to epic. For in war it is precisely the whole nation which is set in motion and which experiences a fresh stimulus and activity in its entire circumstances, because here the whole has an inducement to answer for itself." A hundred years before the expression's first use, something like total war is presupposed in Hegel's characterization of epic: a nation wholly animated by war produces epic accounts of itself as an integrated, self-identical, self-fulfilling totality.[44]

Thinking about life on the blitzed home front as a kind of all-in, quotidian, kitchen-sink epic depended on taking even the dullest details of ordinary life as a necessary part of a whole war effort. Going to work, saving money, spending money, caring for family, eating, not eating, planting a garden, turning lights off or on, boiling just enough water for tea: in the avowed terms of total war, these behaviors can be understood merely, if perversely, as various means to a single strategic end. Everything counted; every part had its role to play in the whole. And indeed, once one accepted the fully motivated totality of total war, one had more or less to reject the very idea of excess; in a total war, there is simply no such thing. As Barthes puts it in a different context: "Even were a detail to appear irretrievably insignificant, resistant to all functionality, it would nonetheless end up with precisely the meaning of absurdity or uselessness: everything has a meaning, or nothing has."[45] Taken to its logical limit, the concept of total war reveals the experience of excess as either impossible or unpatriotic.

This is, perhaps, why so much domestic propaganda focused on the idea of reducing or repurposing waste; in addition to making the most of resources, campaigns against the idea of everyday waste allowed ordinary people to affirm the conceptual totality of war again and again and again.[46] Cleaning one's plate, flipping a switch, drinking tea, going to the cinema thus became personal, daily, and ritual ways in which to accede in both practice and belief to the more or less unimaginable scale of a truly global mechanized war. Taken together, these minor commitments add up to what Adam Piette calls "the war in the mind," to an idea about totality that underwrote and sometimes even supplanted the real experience of war.[47] In *Tense Future* Saint-Amour goes on to discuss a number of "texts of interwar modernism"—including *Ulysses* and *Parade's End*—that rely on an "encyclopedic" style to undermine the epic totality of total war: "Set beside such an epic premise, the fragmentariness and internal fissuring of long modernist fictions begin to look less like the flaws through which a longed-for totality seeped away and more like a critical refusal of epic's all-too-vital political logic. These distended interwar works, that is, did not decline from epic but simply declined it, refusing to embrace its renewed contemporaneity."[48] The films I consider also take up something like this act of "critical refusal," this immanent, formal rejection of the idea of totality. Insofar as they rely on impacted moments of stylistic excess or eccentricity, they quietly refuse the concept of totality, calling attention to the particular and the uncounted as political, ethical, and aesthetic values. Cinematic eccentricity allowed some wartime filmmakers to imagine or to embody experiences or beliefs that might exceed or escape the otherwise restricted economy of total war.

That is, however, only part of the story. For, if the British were in fact encouraged to understand their war as epic, as whole, as total, they were also asked explicitly to see it as a war for the preservation of more or less unassimilable particulars. If, in other words, eccentricity could stand as a tacit argument against totality, it was also often imagined as exactly and paradoxically that which the British were fighting for. Although World War II was a total war, it was nonetheless cast again and again as a defense of national, regional, and even personal idiosyncrasy. As we will see, British propagandists such as J. B. Priestley sometimes struggled to present World War II as a distinctively and, perhaps, oxymoronically "English epic," as, in other words, a very big war fought to protect a democratic jumble of very small but very precious things: for Priestley, the war was being fought for little people, for little "ham-and-egg teas," and for the "fussy little steamers" at Dunkirk.[49] Angus Calder writes: "If Churchill evoked Henry V and Thomas Babbington Macaulay, Priestley's heroes were Falstaff and Sam Weller. He depicted the 'little man,' who preserved the spirit of English comedy within himself."[50] In other words, the British were forced to find ways to preserve ideologically the little or the particular or the eccentric as a civilizational value while also accepting the large, totalizing terms of total mobilization;

they had to strain somehow to see particularity as a reason to wage a total war against totalitarianism.

This Sceptered Isle

This is why eccentricity seems to me so useful a concept with which to capture the British cinema's complex wartime emphasis on style. Although eccentricity had long been understood as an especially English national value, it took on a special significance immediately before and during the war.[51] Reviewing Sitwell's volume in 1933, E. M. Forster agreed, noting anxiously: "[E]ccentricity ranks as a national asset, and . . . so long as it is respected there is some hope that our country will not go mad as a whole. Madness, today, is becoming a State-monopoly, beneath whose death-dealing wings the standardized individuals march to their doom."[52] Sir Ernest Barker, in a 1947 volume on *The Character of England*, defined eccentricity as an expression of the essentially heterogeneous disposition of English, "may we say, less subtly, that most of us are mixtures, unreconciled mixtures, and that elements of freakishness, disconcertingly mixed with the element of form, can make disconcerting appearance?"[53] Cyril Connolly's 1938 *Enemies of Promise*, a book that appeared in the midst of the Munich crisis, takes pains both to defend and to adapt what Connolly identifies as "the Mandarin style," an "eccentric, unpractical, untidy" but perfectly civilized mode that he wanted to preserve not as an alternative to war but rather as a motivated and tellingly, if inadvertently, imperial justification for war: "Civilization—the world of affection and reason and freedom and justice—is a luxury which must be fought for, as dangerous to possess as an oil-field or an unlucky diamond."[54] In each of these cases and, indeed, in much of the period's propaganda, English eccentricity is cast not only as a specific and defining national quality but also as an endangered national value. "Under threat of extinction," writes Karen Schneider, "the British way of life cried out for preservation, warts and all."[55] Seen thus in relation to both Britain's war with totalitarianism and its long transition from "empire to welfare state," eccentricity thus begins to emerge as an index of a larger cultural outlook that Jed Esty refers to as "becoming minor": "If there was an Anglocentric and anthropological turn among intellectuals bent on remaking England into a knowable community, it was a largely discursive event, even a fantasy. But the nature of that Anglocentrism remains important, not only because we need to understand and remember the baleful effects of nativism, but also because the reconsolidation of Englishness seems so intertwined with the broadening definition of culture in the period."[56]

This effort to become minor is visible in repeated and imprecise wartime efforts to present Britain not as a vast, morally compromised, and culturally homogenizing global empire but rather as a confined, Shakespearean, and "scepter'd isle," as, in other words, the little island home of a rugged, honest, and idiosyncratic people. It is in these terms that the war could be imagined as "a defense," writes Marina Mackay, "of the small and particular against the undemocratically homogenizing."[57] For Adam Piette, "Fear of invasion transformed Britain in the minds of its subjects into a tiny island."[58] Victoria Stewart writes, "Eccentricity often goes alongside ingenuity, an ability to think beyond existing paradigms and, implicitly, in a Second World War context, to counter what was perceived as the stereotypically German approach."[59] Jeremy Havardi argues that eccentricity is one of the myths informing what we think we "know" about the English and their war: "they prefer eccentricity, improvisation, guile and ingenuity to mechanized efficiency."[60] C. P. Snow, reflecting on "the tightness" and "extreme homogeneity" of British officialdom during the war, observes: "It is perfectly true that the English unconsciously adopt all sorts of devices for making their population, genuinely small by world standards, seem a good deal smaller than it really is."[61] And we might think again of Priestly's celebration of the paradoxically epic littleness of the civilian ships that brought so many British troops back from Dunkirk: "But here at Dunkirk is another English epic. And to my mind what was most characteristically English about it—so typical of us, so absurd and yet so grand and gallant that you hardly know whether to laugh or to cry when you read about them—was the part played in the difficult and dangerous embarkation—not by the warships, magnificent though they were—but by the little pleasure-steamers."[62] We can also see this effort at work in a number of propaganda films that saw the large experience of war expressed in the little lives of ordinary, embodied, funny, sometimes sad, socially specific, and entirely eccentric characters, films like *The Lion Has Wings* (1939), *In Which We Serve* (1942), *A Canterbury Tale* (1944), and *The Volunteer* (1944). In each case, a longstanding association between England and eccentricity was used to make Britain's opposition to totalitarianism into a matter of not only political circumstance but also national character in the deepest sense; understood—however factitiously—as minor, idiosyncratic, and little, Britain could position itself as not only a strategic but also an ethical and existential antithesis to the totalitarian ethos of Hitler's Germany.[63]

This Is England

Some of the best examples of this opposition between democratic particularity and totalitarian homogeneity appear in several films that Humphrey

Jennings made for the Crown Film Unit during the war; films such as *London Can Take It!* (1940), *Words for Battle* (1941), *Listen to Britain* (1942), and *Fires Were Started* (1943) use cinematic technique (montage in particular) to imagine Britain as an internally differentiated and democratic totality, as, in other words, a collection of distinct and idiosyncratic fragments, images, and perspectives that both added up to and yet managed nonetheless to exceed a shared social whole. Jennings, himself a notable eccentric, pursued his long commitment to the idea of Britain as an internally differentiated and nontotalitarian whole in his early association with I. A. Richards and William Empson at Cambridge, in his work with the British Surrealist Group in the mid-thirties, in *Pandemonium*, his unfinished "imaginative history" of the Industrial Revolution, as well as in the war films he made under what we might call the weak influence of John Grierson.[64] In each case, Jennings uses techniques of collage, montage, conceptual juxtaposition, and the chance encounter in order to capture the feel of particulars that both add up to and critically exceed a particular aesthetic, social, or historical whole.[65] If, however, the effort to think between the part and the national whole runs through all his work, its most developed and influential expression appears in a handful of wartime films that directly inspired the filmmakers I look at in in this book. Consider, for example, *London Can Take It!* The film, which Jennings made with Harry Watt, is built out of shots of ordinary people going to work, navigating a partially ruined city, and waiting for nightfall and the inevitable reappearance of bombers during the London Blitz. Individual images—of people walking, sleeping, shopping, talking, stepping through a shattered storefront, clearing away rubble—produce a sense not only of London's ability to "take it" but also of its sheer democratic variety. Jennings's London is full, chaotic, tense, funny, and open; and, although it seems to teeter on the verge of chaos, its parts—like the images that add up to the whole of Jennings's film—somehow add up without losing their individual character.[66]

Charles Madge, who was, with Jennings, one of the founders of Mass Observation, wrote: "I think it may help to understand [Jennings] if one reconsiders what he meant by 'the image.' It was a meaning personal to himself and bound up with his early researches into poetry and painting. His use of 'image' is not far off from the way it is used in psychology, in literary criticism and in surrealist theory, but it is not quite identical with any of these. It has resemblances to the psychological concept of the gestalt: 'the combination of many effects, each utterly insensible alone, into one sum of fine effect.'"[67] Crucially, this juxtaposition of images or fragments is almost entirely specific to the cinema: "Jennings—amongst a host of

London can take it!

other avant-garde film makers—recognized how technical advances in film could be used to expand the image space and the promise of modernity to the masses: the possibility of combining collective activity with individual agency into free identity."[68] Seen in these terms, Jennings's films are maybe the best because the richest expression of what we might think of as an *official eccentricity*, of minorness strategically cast as an ideological alternative to totalitarianism; they are instances of eccentricity—a free identity—put to work for the collective activity of national propaganda.[69] Jennings made the difference between his local, regionally specific, and recalcitrant propaganda and that of the Nazis explicit: "In a BBC broadcast, Jennings told listeners that [his film] *The Silent Village* portrayed 'the clash of two types of culture,' what he called 'this new-fangled, loudspeaker, blaring culture invented by Dr. Goebbels' against 'the ancient, Welsh, liberty-loving culture which has been going on in those valleys way, way back into the days of King Arthur.'"[70]

However, if imagining England as an honest, recalcitrant, and minor island nation is an example of official eccentricity at work, we can also see traces of a more difficult, more anarchic and *unofficial eccentricity* in British war culture, modes of aesthetic and political excess that, while they may have worked against totalitarianism, also called attention to compromises, obfuscations, and modes of violence that the British had both to embrace and to disavow in the service of total mobilization. Adam Piette's *Imagination at War* offers one undeniable account of how unofficial, private experiences threatened official, public accounts of the war: "These public stories turn out to be hopelessly charged with broken, complex and dark feeling once read at the raw level the mind living through them."[71] We can see this unruly political attitude in George Orwell's observation that "everything in our age conspires to turn the writer, and every other kind of artist as well, into a minor official, working on themes handed to him from above and never telling what seems to him the whole of the truth."[72] This official bad faith was for Orwell most evident in the hard truth of wartime Britain's willingness to look away from the "vaster injustice" of empire: "[H]ow can we 'fight Fascism' except by bolstering up a far vaster injustice? For of course it *is* vaster. What we always forget is that the overwhelming bulk of the British proletariat does not live in Britain, but in Asia and Africa. . . . This is the system which we all live on and which we denounce when there seems to be no danger of its being altered. Of late, however, it has become the first duty of a 'good anti-Fascist' to lie about it and help to keep it in being."[73] A similarly unofficial take on the official demands that war made on the mind appears in E. M. Forster's celebration of Milton's *Areopagitica* as a prescient and intransigent argument against wartime censorship: "We are willing enough to praise freedom when she is safely tucked away in the past and cannot be a nuisance. In the present, amidst dangers whose outcome we cannot foresee, we get nervous about her, and admit censorship."[74] It is there as well in the comic despair of Evelyn Waugh's *Put Out More Flags*: "War in the air, war of attrition, tank war, war of nerves, war of propaganda, war of defense in depth, war of movement, people's war, total war, indivisible war, war infinite, war incomprehensible, war of essence without accidents or attributes, metaphysical war, war in time-space, war eternal . . . all war is nonsense, thought Ambrose."[75] And, indeed, something like this unofficial energy at work in the unpretentious but no less difficult surrealism that cuts through and threatens to exceed the official war aims of Jennings's films, in cuts and combinations that accentuate and even exaggerate contradictions immanent to the concept of total mobilization.

This dark, unruly current is also there in Olivier's otherwise obviously patriotic *Henry V*. As I argue in chapter 2, although the film is rightly remembered as one of the critical triumphs of wartime propaganda, Olivier's decision to foreground the recalcitrant and minor presence of both Falstaff and Ancient Pistol stands as a quiet and maybe inchoate rebuke to any and all forms of authority, even Merry England's. In the case of Falstaff, Olivier's decision to begin his film with an image of a dying, diminished Falstaff—a scene that appears nowhere in Shakespeare—forces us to consider what energies had to be lost in order at last to secure the marital glory of Henry, Agincourt, and, perhaps, Churchill himself. Put differently, insofar as Falstaff is one of Shakespeare's great figures of wit, pleasure, and life, Olivier's startling invention of Falstaff's death scene uses a moment of cinematic excess in order to mourn excess, to acknowledge the degree to which an English total war must threaten or sacrifice values that had seemed most English. In the case of Pistol, Olivier's tacit suggestion is even more difficult; that is, although Pistol's continued role in both the play and the film offers a sort of weak compensation for Falstaff's disappearance earlier in the Henriad, his lingering, sloppy appearance at the end of Olivier's film suggests something sour about the divergent ends of war. For, while the battle was won, Pistol—as played by Robert Newton, a great and wasted actor—looks at last directly into the camera, promising, "To England will I steal, and there I'll steal." Running quite against Henry's image of an ideologically consistent "band of brothers," Pistol instead evokes the image of a veteran ruined by war, a figure whose experience bars him from a community for which he had fought. In these terms, the hard eccentricity of Ancient Pistol represents the degree to which the dilemma of total war and the creep of its necessary totalitarianism threatened to unleash fundamentally antisocial forces during and after the war. Seen in light of increasingly pronounced home front anxieties about what years of war would have done to British soldiers about to come home, the English eccentric stands less as a workable part of a propaganda program and more as a fundamental and lingering rebuke to the very idea of a postwar society to come.

It Takes a Fascist . . .

Participants returned to this unofficial, critical sense of moral compromise or contradiction again and again during the war, often enacting or referring explicitly to what we might call the double bind of total war, the real and practical imperative to fight and to destroy totalitarianism whatever the cost. "Total war against a totalitarian state had," writes Angus Calder, "a logic of its own, a logic, one might say, of the *Catch-22* variety, which overrode qualms."[76] This is why Churchill made sure (after Chamberlain, Norway, and the fall of France) to cast the war as a civilizational struggle: "Here in this strong City of Refuge which enshrines the title-deeds of human progress and is of deep consequence to Christian civilization; here, girt about by the seas and oceans where the Navy reigns; shielded from above by the prowess and devotion of our airmen—we await undismayed the impending assault."[77] According to Michael Walzer, after Czechoslovakia, Poland, and France, it had become clear "that Nazism was an ultimate threat to everything decent in our lives, an ideology and a practice of domination so murderous, so degrading even to those who might survive, that the consequences of its final victory were literally beyond calculation, immeasurably awful."[78] Churchill thus cast the war as a "supreme emergency," a quasi-legal designation that paved the way to total mobilization and, later, to the recognized illegalities of strategic bombing: "Our task is not only to win the battle—but to win the war. After this battle in France abates its force, there will come the battle for our Island—for all that Britain is, and all that Britain means. That will be the struggle. In that supreme emergency we shall not hesitate to take every step, even the most drastic, to call forth from our people the last ounce and the last inch of effort of which they are capable."[79] For Walzer, Churchill's phrase "supreme emergency" implies "that there is a fear beyond ordinary fearfulness . . . of war, and a danger to which that fear corresponds, and that this fear and danger may well require exactly those measures that the war convention bars."[80] It was thus in the almost-technical terms of the supreme emergency that the British understood the need to suspend exactly those values for which they needed also to fight.[81]

The concept of the "supreme emergency" will no doubt remind some readers of what Giorgio Agamben, following Carl Schmitt, refers to as the "state of exception," a juridical logic that grounds the law's sovereign authority in its ability paradoxically to suspend itself as law: "if the law employs the exception—that is the suspension of law itself—as its original means of referring to and encompassing life, then a theory of the state of exception is the preliminary condition for any definition of the relation that binds and, at the same time, abandons the living being to law."[82] Indeed, the passage of the Emergency Powers (Defence) Acts of 1939 and 1940, which I discuss in chapter 2, did much to blur the line between totalitarianism and democracy in wartime Britain, a fact that aligns Churchill's government with what Agamben takes as contradictions broadly characteristic of the modern state: "This transformation of a provisional and exceptional measure into a technique of government threatens radically to alter—in fact, has already palpably altered—the structure and meaning of the traditional distinction between constitutional forms. Indeed, from this perspective, the state of exception appears as a threshold of indeterminacy between democracy and absolutism."[83] That said, although this model does help to account for some aspects of the double bind of total war, I am more interested in seeing how things worked at a less stark and more local level of abstraction. In other words, what seems essential to Agamben's model is the fact that, because the state of exception occurs at the threshold or limit of political consciousness ("a zone of indifference, where inside and outside do not exclude each other but rather blur with each other"), it tends to appear within ordinary, everyday thought as a return of the repressed, as a distorted, disguised, or symptomatic expression of a more fundamental and thus more obscure contradiction.[84] Because the state of exception is one of thought's structural preconditions, it cannot, as it were, be thought directly.

I want to argue that the British experience of the wartime state of exception worked differently. What is striking about the British experience of paradox is that it was experienced as a known, conscious, quotidian, but no less painful, thing. The shared and mind-bending sense that cherished values would have to be suspended in order to protect exactly those values was not an unconscious or distorted or latent content during the war. It was—and this is the most remarkable thing I learned while writing this book—what a lot of ordinary people thought and said to one another about the war while it was happening. As opposed, then, to following Agamben and seeing the double bind of total war as a kind of structuring and preconditional secret, as wartime Britain's political unconscious, I want rather to understand what it meant that so difficult a paradox could and did circulate as the articulate and confounding stuff of everyday life during the war. In these terms, we might look less to the gothic designs of Schmitt or Agamben and more to the wistful and pragmatic compromises that William Empson took as characteristic of Britain's war: "You see," he said of the hero he thought this war demanded, "he's willing to do more than get himself killed. He's willing to cripple his own personality for the sake of a cause he believes in."[85] I want in what follows to try to capture the structure of this conceptual problem both as it shaped British thinking about the war and as it found aesthetic expression in some important wartime films. What, after all, does it mean or feel like to be both for and against a war at the same time? To be, as total mobilization demanded, both a civilian and a soldier? To know that one has to undermine one's values in order to preserve those values? What does it mean to need to imagine and indeed to work toward the end of a culture in order to find the strength to fight for that culture?

This entirely open and explicit but no less difficult ethical bind often took a similar proverbial form, something like "it takes a fascist to fight a fascist." Expressions of this "to catch a thief" logic appear in different but related forms throughout the war, in parliamentary debates, in essays and editorials about censorship and propaganda, in ordinary conversations overheard by members of Mass-Observation, in private letters, journals, diaries, novels, and poems, as well as in both documentary and feature films. Early on in the war, Churchill acknowledged that it might "seem a paradox that a war undertaken in the name of liberty and right should require, as a necessary part of its processes, the surrender for some time of so many of the dearly valued liberties and rights."[86] In *Why Britain Is at War*, Harold Nicolson wrote, "We may loathe the Nazi system from the very depths of our souls, yet it is a hard thought that we must ourselves adopt Nazi methods in order to defeat the thing that we dislike."[87] Later, while working at the Ministry of Information, he wrote in his diary: "At present the Ministry is too decent, educated and intellectual to imitate Goebbels. I cannot live by intelligence alone. We need crooks. Why I hate Hitler so much is that he has coined a new currency of fraudulence which he imposes by force. I am prepared to see the old world of privilege disappear. But as it goes, it will carry with it the old standards of honour."[88] For Cyril Connolly, it was "a war of which we are all ashamed and yet a war which has to be won."[89] Orwell put it bluntly: "to be corrupted by totalitarianism one does not have to live in a totalitarian country."[90] E. M. Forster wrote in 1939: "Sensitive people are having a particularly humiliating time just now. Looking at the international scene, they see, with a clearness denied to politicians, that if Fascism wins we are done for, and that we must become Fascist to win. There seems no escape from this hideous dilemma and those who face it most honestly often go jumpy. They are vexed by messages from contradictory worlds, so that whatever they do appears to them as a betrayal of something good."[91] Referring to this and to similar statements, Jed Esty observes, "As the decade wore on, fascist aggression made fervent nationalism both increasingly unappealing and increasingly necessary."[92]

As mentioned previously, a sharp and explicit version of the dilemma appears in *Colonel Blimp*. Indeed, in their memo to the Ministry of Information, Powell and Pressburger identify a set of English values—fairness, naïveté, honesty—before making their real case: "We think these are splendid virtues: so splendid that, in order to preserve them, it is worthwhile shelving them until we have won the war."[93] Insofar as the film's protagonist, Clive Candy, represents exactly these virtues, his experience over the course of the twentieth century and its wars represents not only the life and death of a particular image of Britain but also a set of structural problems that are built into the idea of a national character as such; in order to preserve one's character, that character must (at least for the duration) be suspended or "shelved." One reviewer wrote: "The moral of his career is left uncertain; with one voice the film censures his beliefs, with another protests that they are the beliefs of all upright men."[94] As I've been suggesting, the presence of these two voices isn't evidence of simple incoherence or bad faith; it is rather an effort to capture in cinematic form a contradiction necessary to the British experience of World War II. I'll look at the dilemma of *Colonel Blimp*—that it pits Englishness against Englishness in order to save Englishness—and examine how resources specific to cinematic form might offer ways to embody, to acknowledge, and perhaps to escape or to transcend that dilemma.

One can see other, less direct versions of the double bind at work within several of the war's pivotal moments. We can see it in something like its reverse form in the drama of appeasement played out between Chamberlain and Hitler in 1938. Instead of sacrificing values in order to preserve those same values, the attempt to appease Hitler at Munich was, as Churchill argued in his celebrated eulogy for Chamberlain, rather a last-ditch and hopeless effort to preserve English values that led nearly to their loss:

> It fell to Neville Chamberlain in one of the supreme crises of the world to be contradicted by events, to be disappointed in his hopes, and to be deceived and cheated by a wicked man. But what were these hopes in which he was disappointed? What were these wishes in which he was frustrated? What was that faith that was abused? They were surely among the most noble and benevolent instincts of the human heart—the love of peace, the toil for peace, the strife for peace, the pursuit of peace, even at great peril, and certainly to the utter disdain of popularity or clamour.[95]

It was, in other words, precisely because Chamberlain really embodied certain national values that he came close to seeing those values destroyed absolutely. What the war needed, Churchill implies, was someone willing not to embody but rather to suspend English virtues in the name of those same virtues; this was exactly what Churchill, acting in the name of the supreme emergency, was willing to do.[96] Chamberlain and Churchill thus represent mirror images of the same double bind; one almost destroyed the national character by trying to save it while the other saved it precisely by suspending it and, in time, maybe losing it altogether. We can see this same bind at work in the British public's ambivalent response to the figure of the commando (see chapters 2 and 3); says Alan Allport: "He was brave and skilled, but his style of fighting was unsportsmanlike, 'dirty,' suspiciously un-English. The name connoted a flirtation with illegality, an impatience with mere rules, a willingness to mete out justice with direct action regardless of the methods employed. The commando was a bit of a brute. He brought gangster values to the battlefield. Would he bring them home as well?"[97] The commando became one especially visible representative of a larger ambivalence around a war that was both necessary and regrettable. And finally, we can see the double bind again at the war's end in the growing sense that, for good or ill, total war had fundamentally altered the social fabric of Britain, its imperial ambitions and identity, as well as the basic terms in which it was able to imagine or to anticipate a future.

As we will see in relation to the weird, involute temporality of *Brief Encounter*, the pressures of wartime meant that, whatever else, ordinary life in Britain after the war would be different. On the one hand, the rhetoric and the reality of sacrifice shared across socio-economic classes made it impossible to return in the short term to conditions that existed before the war. This shift was anticipated in and shaped by the 1942 Report on Social Insurance and Allied Services, which was prepared by the economist William Beveridge and served as a rough blueprint for the postwar welfare state as implemented by Clement Attlee and the Labour Party after their surprise postwar victory in 1945. What's more, the fact of women's broad participation in the war effort—in factories, in the fire service, as members of the Women's Land Army, the Air Raid Precautions, the Women's Voluntary Services, the Auxiliary Territorial Service, the Women's Auxiliary Air Force, and elsewhere—made the idea of simply returning to an older model of the family and domestic life unlikely and, for many women, unwelcome. Independence, freedom, authority, and different ways of imagining the sexual division of labor in Britain were unintended consequences of years of total mobilization. The structural challenge of a total war against totalitarianism thus had immediate and lingering political consequences for the British sense of self.

Churchill's Black Dog

The double bind of total war, the fraught idea that "it takes a fascist to fight a fascist," deserves an even closer look. Taken to its limit, the dilemma that the British faced as a result of their encounter with the putatively anti-totalitarian totality of total mobilization begins to approach a concept of absolute and transitive aggression that Freud, Lacan, and others had begun to develop before, during, and after the war. Indeed, the specific transitivity of the phrase "it takes a fascist to fight a fascist" resembles a logic of identification and aggression that Lacan, for instance, took as essential to psychic life immediately after the war. In both "The Mirror Stage" (1949) and "Aggressiveness in Psychoanalysis" (1948), Lacan lays out an account of development that turns on what he sees as a fundamental narcissistic mistake. When the small child, who experiences his or her body as uncoordinated, broken, in fragments, sees the whole and apparently coordinated image of either another child or, indeed, his or her own reflection in a mirror, it installs in the ego a structuring desire for and an identification with the imaginary coordination, coherence, and wholeness of what Lacan calls "the Ideal-I." The child, jubilant at the potential represented by this image, reaches out toward that ideal reflection only to stumble and fall. This mix of jubilation and consequent disappointment, then, leads to what Lacan understands as a sort of primal jealousy, an essential and aggressive relation to the other that turns on the idea that, in order to become whole, one must make the other less so; that to become whole, one must tear the other to pieces. Left there, this would stand as one especially macabre moment in a larger story of psychic development.

Lacan, however, takes things a step further, suggesting that, because this moment of identification, jubilation, and jealousy is built on a mistake, one can never do enough to close the gap that stands between us and our ideals; one can't fix something that isn't really broken. As a result, the aggression that results from that founding error is directed outward at more and more of the world; because this first narcissistic wound must remain open, it bleeds out into and onto everything else, resulting in a version the world-killing aggression that both Lacan and Freud associate with the death drive. As Leo Bersani and Ulysses Dutoit write in their essay on Terrence Malick's *The Thin Red Line*: "In telling us that the greatest human happiness is exactly identical to the greatest human unhappiness, psychoanalysis at once 'explains' a violence that no individual or social transformations could eliminate, and renders superfluous any further explanations."[98]

Lacan's two essays on aggression were, of course, signs of their time. As Jacques-Alain Miller argues:

> You can understand why he took up the subject of aggression in 1948, because at that time it was a popular topic in psychoanalysis; it was what the ego psychology psychoanalysts considered acceptable in Freud's notion of the death instinct, that is, in his notion that there is not only libido, but also the death drive. After World War II, which seemed to have demonstrated the existence of some kind of death drive, after five years of world war, concentration camps, the atom bomb, etc., the idea that there might be such a thing as a death drive in humanity didn't seem so far-fetched.[99]

As we will see, a number of writers took up the idea of an essential and intractable violence before, during, and immediately after the war, including Walter Benjamin, Simone Weil, Johannes Huizinga, Norbert Elias, Marc Bloch, and others. Looking back on Britain's decision to firebomb German cities, Anthony Burgess wrote that it seemed "to arise from some mysterious human darkness, against the light of reason."[100] In 1940, Virginia Woolf wrote, "The young airman up in the sky is driven not only by the voices of loudspeakers; he is driven by voices in himself—ancient instincts, instincts fostered and cherished by education and tradition."[101] Anthony Storr speculates that Winston Churchill emerged as a hero partly because the particular terms of World War II satisfied his innate depressive's aggression—his "black dog"—in a way nothing else could: "Winston Churchill was often accused of being a warmonger, which he was not. But there is no doubt that fighting enemies held a strong emotional appeal for him, and that, when he was finally confronted by an enemy whom he felt to be wholly evil, it was a release which gave him enormous vitality. Hitler was such an enemy; and it is probable that Churchill was never happier than when he was fully engaged in bringing about Hitler's destruction. For here, at last, was an opportunity to employ the full force of his enormous aggressiveness."[102]

In her recent *At the Violet Hour,* Sarah Cole has written about the ways in which British and Irish culture between the wars attempted to capture the essential or primal excess of war's violence in aesthetic form; indeed, in her account, interwar culture was an ongoing and necessarily incomplete negotiation between an enchanted violence that promises structure and renewal and a disenchanted violence that refuses "that structure" and insists "on the bare, forked existence of the violated being, bereft of symbol."[103] She draws on Weil's "*The Iliad,* or the Poem of Force" in order to capture the feeling that, at best, our fragile world was and was only the presence of a few institutions straining weakly against the force of an essential violence: "Force is an entity that corresponds less to any given act or individual than to a broad compulsion with the capacity to constrain, strike, or even annihilate. More generally, force, as I am imagining it, is almost a condition of existence, a way of considering the swell of power that surrounds and can demolish the individual, even as, in some cases, it provides a sense of that individual's purpose (to resist, to rebel)—or, as Holocaust survivors tell it, to resist or rebel by the bare fact of remaining human."[104] Or, to put it in terms Forster used as he tried to say "What I Believe" in 1938: "So that is what I feel about force and violence. It is, alas! the ultimate reality on this earth, but it does not always get to the front. Some people call its absences 'decadence'; I call them 'civilization' and find in such interludes the chief justification for the human experiment."[105] For Forster, civilization isn't a natural state occasionally interrupted by eruptions of violence; it is itself an interruption, a welcome and ephemeral pause in an otherwise continuous history of violence.[106]

This brings us back to the relation between style and violence that I began to lay out earlier, to ways in which historically specific modes of eccentricity or vulgarity were mobilized in Britain during wartime; in other words, back to moments of accreted, impacted, or heightened style that seem to push the character of particular films toward and past an implicit limit. In addition to thinking of these moments either as an expression of Sitwellian protest or as a mode of specifically cinematic excess, one might think about Theodor Adorno's 1934 essay on Beethoven's "late style." Adorno takes issue with the fact that most commentary on the late works explains their difficult, knotty style in terms of the biographical fact of Beethoven's impending death: "The accepted explanation is that they are products of a subjectivity or, still better, of a personality ruthlessly proclaiming itself, which breaks through the roundedness of form for the sake of expression, exchanging harmony for the dissonance of its sorrow and spurning sensuousness charm under the dictates of the imperiously emancipated mind."[107] This explanation of the late works tries, in other words, "to gain awareness of death directly in the work of art," to see the individual impending death appear as content within a given work.[108] Adorno goes on to argue that this approach is misguided because art cannot in fact be about death in any direct sense: "If the legitimacy of art is abolished before death's reality, then death can certainly not be assimilated by the work of art as its 'subject.' It is imposed on creatures alone, and not on their constructions, and thus has always appeared in art in a refracted form: as allegory."[109] In other words, because the reality of one's own death is essentially unrepresentable, it doesn't make sense to say that any piece of music, a book, or a film is in fact *about* death, at least insofar as we take aboutness to mean a direct and referential relation between a form and its content.

That said, death does matter to the late works, and it matters precisely, if paradoxically, because it is unrepresentable; that is, insofar as the imperative to confront death forces a particular medium to confront its necessary representational limits, it makes itself felt in a work precisely in the moments when style, failing to get at what it feels it must address, ends up pointing back toward itself. The simultaneous need and inability to represent death thus allows style at last to break free from reference: "Touched by death, the masterly hand sets free the matter it previously formed. The fissures and rifts within it, bearing witness to the ego's finite impotence before Being, are its last work. . . . In this way, in late Beethoven, the conventions become expression in the naked depiction of themselves."[110] Death, in other words, makes itself felt in the late Beethoven work when style becomes clotted, excessive, or, to use my word, eccentric; it makes itself felt when forms express themselves as forms, when style is set free to be for itself. In his own self-consciously Adornian reflection on late style, Edward Said refers to the great and elderly Beethoven's work as "wayward and eccentric."[111]

The films that I discuss are not necessarily late in a chronological or biological sense, but they do, I think, share a relation to style that Adorno has in mind. That is, if what makes a style late is its need to deal with death, the films I discuss must deal with the fact of war, with an experience tied up not only with the widely, absurdly shared imminence of death but also with death's essential resistance to representation. If, as we have seen, the conceptual totality of total war resists representation, that resistance returns in these films in moments of impacted style, moments of aesthetic eccentricity or stylistic excess that give paradoxical expression to the fact of a war that, as a result of its scope, its intensity, and its approach toward totality, cannot be represented directly. Because the British experience of total war and total mobilization resisted representation, it freed the films I discuss to confront and to embody that resistance in moments of heightened, impacted, vulgar, wayward, excessive, or eccentric style.

Original Violence

I have begun to suggest that this whole and complex play of identification, form, force, aggression, eccentricity, and style is somehow contained within the historically specific and yet proverbial phrase, "it takes a fascist to fight a fascist." In other words, at the same time that the oft-repeated phrase captures some specific aspects of the British experience of World War II (the psychic legacy of appeasement, the gangster tactics of the commando, and the fear that the war had in one way or another broken the future), its barely managed mix of aggression toward the other and deferred but inevitable aggression toward the self stands as a real but tacit effort to register the nature of an unofficial violence that would both exceed and stand as a source of the local and official modes of violence imagined in and harnessed by total war. Aspects of the films and texts I address thus stand at a nearly subterranean level as efforts to explicate or unpack the tautological violence of that phrase; they make a tacit case about the sources and the depths of human violence that may have been let loose by the war but that seemed also to precede and to exceed it, to come from and to lead toward, as it were, some deeper, more mysterious, and technically eccentric place. And, indeed, the drive is, if nothing else, eccentric. That is, while the films discussed here might argue at the official level that wars cause violence and that we fight wars in order to put an end to violence, at the unofficial level they use moments of impacted, ironic, or exaggerated style in order to gesture toward a more disturbing argument about the nature of human violence; rather than seeing violence as an effect of this or that conflict, these films ask us to consider the possibility that an innate human tendency toward violence, what Johan Huizinga calls "original violence," had been revealed by the specific terms of modern total war: "As soon as one member or more of a community of States virtually denies the binding character of international law and, either in practice or in theory, proclaims the interests and power of its own group—be it nation, party, class, church or whatsoever else—as the sole norm of its political behaviour, not only does the last vestige of the immemorial play-spirit vanish but with it any claim to civilization at all. Society then sinks down to the level of the barbaric, and original violence retakes its ancient rights."[112] Thought of in these terms, the only way to mitigate or at least to face the violence of war is to confront its deepest sources.

In an effort to capture forms of ideological and historical ambivalence, these films thus foreground complicated relations between past and present both within the disorienting frame of wartime and between the war and what came before and what might come after. They thus put expressive pressure on the problem of wartime, a kind of time that, as Mary Favret sees it, "teeters," a kind of time that sees "past, present, and future all threaten to surrender to an obliterating violence."[113] As if to acknowledge exactly this pressure, the films I discuss employ complicated temporal structures that rely on flashbacks, nested narratives, and multiple aesthetic frames. Contemporary critics, in fact, noted the degree to which the flashback had become an almost pathological sign of the times; one wrote in 1941, "Lately I notice . . . a revival of the flashback to a degree which amounts almost to a mania."[114] In some cases, this strategy is tied to an evident desire to understand the present in relation to the past: *Colonel Blimp* begins with a conflict between a younger and an older man that leads the latter to reflect on how his past made him what he is in the present, on how youth somehow makes age: the synchronic becomes diachronic. *Brief Encounter* similarly begins at its end, with a middle-aged women thinking through the beginning, middle, and end of her brief and chaste affair with a man she met at a train station. And, while really being about the later days of World War II (1944), *Henry V* gives us the Battle of Agincourt (1415) as seen from the perspective of Shakespeare's present (1600); as a result, Olivier's film presents Britain's long history of violence as less a progressive line than a recursive knot.

More than satisfying a desire to understand how the present is the result of a past, these complicated designs trouble the stability of past, present, and future. And although we can, of course, identify a narratorial "present" in each of the films—1942 in *Colonel Blimp*, the end of the affair in *Brief Encounter*, 1600 in *Henry V*—they seem often to exaggerate or accentuate their structural complexities in order to make it difficult to measure accurately the difference between one time and another. In this, these films use the specificity of cinematic form—cuts, casting decisions, soundtracks, and close-ups—to make good on Benjamin's roughly contemporary hopes for historical materialism in *The Arcades Project*: "Historical materialism must renounce the epic element in history. It blasts the epoch out of the reified 'continuity of history.' But it also explodes the homogeneity of the epoch, interspersing it with ruins—that is, with the present."[115] In other words, these films reflect and foreground a temporal confusion essential to wartime, a confusion that makes it hard on the battlefield or in life to register the difference between cause and effect, before and after, past, present, and future; as a result, they use techniques specific to cinema in order to approach an eccentric history methodologically appropriate to thinking about the conceptual ambivalence of modern, total war.

Propaganda in a Tragic Key

In a recent essay, T. J. Clark calls for what he calls "politics in a tragic key." Central to this politics is the recognition that human aggression is both inevitable and terrible:

> It is a logical error of the left . . . to assume that a full recognition of the human propensity to violence—to blood-soaked conformity—closes off the idea of a radical reworking of politics. The question is: what root is it we need to get down to? And even a Hazlitt-type honesty about "a *hankering* after evil in the human mind" can perfectly well coexist (as it did in Hazlitt's post-Augustan generation) with a "By our own spirits we are deified." Human capacities may well be infinite; they have certainly been hardly explored, hardly been given their chance of flowering; but the tragic sense starts from an acknowledgment that the infinity (the unplumbable) is for bad as much as good.[116]

As they use eccentricities of cinematic style to imagine a past that did not escape but rather managed its original violence and as they compare that past to a present where violence appears to have broken all its bounds, the films I discuss work toward something like Clark's politics in a tragic key; it is precisely because they do not deny human violence that they are able or at least seek to imagine an alternative to one of its most spectacular and logically deranged forms: total war. Indeed, what's remarkable about these films is in part their ability formally to capture both the irreducible fact of that human violence and our necessary, limited, but also human efforts to escape or to manage that violence. This, to return to the beginning, is what I want to see as the specific and strategic eccentricity of the British cinema. Faced not only with the outsized practical and ethical demands of total war but also with the intimation of more absolute sources of violence, these films cultivate moments of aesthetic and formal eccentricity both in order to find expression for ideas that might resist more direct modes of argumentation and in order to protest violence's tendency to reduce exactly the kinds of difference that eccentricity seeks to preserve. These films embrace cinematic style in order to strike a Sitwellian pose in the face of death. And although they are not late works in his sense, these films nonetheless share a quality that Adorno took as an effect of style's confrontation with death: "The force of subjectivity in late works is the irascible gesture with which it leaves them. . . . Touched by death, the masterly hand sets free the matter it previously formed."[117] The artist's encounter with death, a previously private encounter that had become all too public during the years of World War II, works not to personalize the work but rather to set stylistic aspects immanent to the medium free; and just as the musical material of Beethoven's late quartets reveals limits to both public and private modes of significance, so do the medium-specific eccentricities of the British cinema come to the surface as a tacit and stubborn—and maybe vulgar—answer to an official ideology that would subordinate life's particulars to one and only one form: total war. In this these films work toward an ideal that, in another piece, Clark has seen at work in Poussin's *Landscape with a Man Killed by a Snake* (1648): "Will any picture of the world that aims to *contain* the powers of blackness necessarily look forced—putting death at too great a distance, letting light win out predictably over dark, squaring and immobilizing its objects, faring and truing? Can some pictures show the necessity—the naturalness—of that stilling and containment? Show it happening as part of the agony?"[118] What I see in these films is something like this: both an attempt to contribute something to a war that had to be won and a necessarily eccentric effort to imagine the limits of a violence that, like a snake with its tail in its mouth, seems always to find its way home.

Snapshots of *War Pictures*

Chapter 1 examines the exemplary case of *The Life and Death of Colonel Blimp*, a film that Winston Churchill and the Ministry of Information sought actively to undermine. Whereas the government saw it as counterproductive, Powell and Pressburger held that the film was, in fact, a successful argument in favor not only of war but also of a specifically *total* war. In order to assess the relation between these different claims, I look at how the form of the film—particularly its relation to montage—allows it to embody a complex and necessary argument about the nature and necessity of war. The film allowed Powell and Pressburger to articulate or rather to embody a paradoxical idea that I take as characteristic of British thinking about the war, the idea that it might "take a fascist to fight a fascist," that, in other words, Britain strategically would have to suspend exactly the values for which it understood itself to be fighting. This leads to some larger claims about what we might call the practical historiography of World War II, to claims both about the film's engagement with the theory of war in the wake of Clausewitz and about the ways in which this film and other wartime texts rely on an imagined pastoral past in order to understand and to deal with the violence of the present. The film thus embodies a historical self-consciousness that characterized some of the most important aesthetic responses to the war.

Chapter 2 looks at Olivier's *Henry V* (1944), a film that, as opposed to Colonel Blimp, was taken immediately as a critical and political triumph. Rather than accept the film's status as unproblematically good propaganda, I see Olivier's accomplishment in relation to the larger context of thinking about Shakespeare during the war. Shakespeare's plays and *Henry V* in particular were mobilized popularly and by a number of prominent scholars during and for the war. Olivier's film thus appears as part of a moment in British cultural history that continues to inform our understanding of Shakespeare, his play, and the twentieth-century history of literary criticism. I look at this context in order to see how Olivier's film both supports and undermines its own apparent patriotism. In order to make this case, I bring together the film's complicated representation of British history, its use of a particular type of tracking shot, and, most importantly, its use of casting, type-casting, and casting against type. In particular, I consider the tacitly critical presence of the great and alcoholic character actor Robert Newton as Ancient Pistol in order to reflect on Olivier's canny and hitherto unnoticed take on the ethical complexities of war. Newton, who was both a great actor and what we might call today a train wreck, stands in the film as a figure for another, more complicated argument about the human costs and the consequences of total war.

Chapter 3 considers a film that would seem to have little to do with a war to which it never refers: David Lean's *Brief Encounter* (1945). Although the film never names the war, it was made during, set before, and released after the war, an odd historical situation that makes Lean's film almost perfectly, if obliquely, "about" war. I look at aspects of the film—its use of a particular kind of light, differently significant fashions, and a reference to Donald Duck—that would have meant entirely different things before and after war. As a result of putting pressure on the very significance of things as they drift across the representational divide between before and after, the film emerges as a powerful and engaged form of historical reckoning. I then turn to an image that seems exemplary in this regard: a recurrent shot of the actor Celia Johnson's face. Seeing the face as a form of history allows me both to connect Lean's film to a broader tradition of European art cinema and to argue for the film's complex thinking about what the world might have held in store for men and women after war. Looking at Celia Johnson's face looking off into the distance activates a series of identifications and reversals that get to the heart of what was fraught about the last days of total war. More particularly, I work to understand Celia Johnson's face in relation to the transformative pressures that total mobilization put on the British experience of sex and gender during and after the war. *Brief Encounter* thus emerges as a film with crucial comments about the social legacy of World War II, a legacy that, I argue, continues to be felt in British culture and the British cinema.

In the Epilogue, I argue that Jarman was one the first postwar filmmakers in Britain to recognize what was at stake in these earlier films. Indeed, both his historical distance from the war and his political and personal commitments as a gay artist working in Thatcher's England made it possible for him to see those films not simply as a past against which to react but rather as an intensely critical cinema: "There is only one English feature director whose work is in the first rank. Michael Powell is the only director to make a clear political analysis in his films, his work is unequalled. *The Life and Death of Colonel Blimp* is the finest English feature, and *A Canterbury Tale* and *A Matter of Life and Death* are not far behind."[119] Powell's clear-sighted and tacitly political appreciation of what it took to make a film during wartime partly inspired Jarman to make his own bracing, wildly intelligent films. As Jarman recognized, this hard-won and necessarily incomplete confrontation with war and history reveals these eccentric works of wartime propaganda as films, indeed, as art of the very highest order.

1 "But what is it about?"
The Life and Death of Colonel Blimp

The cheat or the spoil-sport shatters civilization itself.

—Johan Huizinga, *Homo Ludens* (1938)

He did not cease to complain . . . that the war was being carried on contrary to all the rules—as if there were any rules for killing people.

—Leo Tolstoy, *War and Peace* (1869)

When *The Life and Death of Colonel Blimp* appeared in 1943, it looked to many like a good movie that made for bad propaganda; if it was beautiful, moving, often funny, it seemed also too willful, too complicated, too weird, too eccentric to help its audiences know what to think and feel about the war. The *Monthly Film Bulletin* wrote that its "message may be obscure, but its emotional appeal is high."[1] The *Tribune* claimed that, although the film was "excellent entertainment . . . no-one decided *exactly* what they wanted to say with it."[2] The *Manchester Guardian* said that it "contradicts itself, mixes its motives, and never seems quite to settle down."[3] *The Daily Mail* wrote that "to depict British officers as stupid, complacent, self-satisfied, and ridiculous may be legitimate comedy, but it is disastrously bad propaganda in the time of war."[4] These mostly mixed responses to the film's apparently mixed motives are more or less representative. Molly Haskell writes: "When it opened, audiences were enthusiastic about the performances but disconcerted by the ambivalence toward war."[5] To be fair, the film did ask a lot from its first, war-weary viewers: instead of offering comfort or selling the war, it embraced formal complexity almost for its own sake. Its protagonist, a benighted but lovable English gentleman, stands both as a manifestly good man and as an implicit rebuke to Britain's backward-looking military establishment; the film takes care not only to feature a "good German" but also to make that German its most eloquent and, indeed, its most recognizably "English" spokesman; and the film overlays its very modern story of Britain's twentieth-century wars with a quasi-mystical tale of romantic eternal recurrence: disappointed in love, Clive Candy—the "Blimp" of the film's title—is haunted across decades by the appearance and reappearance of his feminine ideal, a figure played in each case by the same actor, Deborah Kerr. As opposed to sending a clear message about war, the film embraced, says Ian Christie, an "often skittish, playfully allegorical" tone that seemed self-consciously to distance it from other, more obviously instrumental war movies, films that were "championed for their realistic qualities, which, in the terms of the dominant critical discourse of the time, meant sober, unsensational narratives with believable characterizations and a prevailing sense of stoicism and emotional restraint."[6] Oddly romantic, gently surreal, often sweetly funny, the film appears to distance itself from the expected and perhaps necessary pragmatism of wartime propaganda. In a line I have already quoted, C. A. Lejeune, film critic for *The Observer*, summed up the film's attractive and playful incoherence in a word: "It is a handsome piece. It is frequently a moving piece. But what is it *about*?"[7]

Aesthetic complexity is one thing; aesthetic complexity in a time of war is quite another, a fact that became apparent as several members of government weighed in against the idea, the production, and at last the international distribution of *Colonel Blimp*. In a 1942 memo to Churchill, Sir James Grigg, secretary of state for war, wrote, "I think it of the utmost importance to get [*Colonel Blimp*] stopped."[8] A Ministry of Information report on an early draft of the film's script anticipated the critics' confusion, arguing that its complexity was not only ineffective propaganda but also a possibly active hindrance to the war effort: "The over-complication of ideas is . . . dangerous."[9] Churchill himself became involved and wrote to Minister of Information Brendan Bracken, asking him: "[P]ropose to me the measures necessary to stop this foolish production before it gets any further. I am not prepared to allow propaganda detrimental to the morale of the Army."[10] Although rightly unwilling to suppress the film (to do so "would have been a politically insensitive move in a democracy at war"), Bracken and the Ministry of Information did turn down Powell and Pressburger's request that Laurence Olivier be given leave from the Navy's Fleet Air Arm to play Candy; did deny them access to locations, vehicles, uniforms, and so on; and, in time, did interfere with the film's international distribution. *Colonel Blimp* did not play in the United States until later and, even then, it appeared in bowdlerized versions: by the 1950s it was circulating as *The Loves and Adventures of Colonel Blimp*; its all-important flashback structure had been stripped away; it had been cut from 163 to some 90 minutes;

and it was being marketed not as a war film but rather as a kind of "mad, mad, mad, mad" madcap romp: "The lusty lifetime of a gentleman who was sometimes quite a rogue! Dueling—hunting big game—pretty girls—life's a grand adventure with Colonel Blimp!"[11]

If the sense that the film was not good propaganda feels right enough (the film, we might want to agree, is too good to be good propaganda), Powell and Pressburger nonetheless responded to government reservations with alacrity, making a surprising case for the film's value as propaganda. Not at all complicated, they said, *Colonel Blimp* was an explicit argument not only in support of the war but also about the peculiar nature and necessary demands of total war: "Englishmen are by nature conservative, insular, unsuspicious, believers in good sportsmanship and anxious to believe the best of other people. These attractive virtues, which are, we hope, unchanging, can become absolute vices unless allied to a realistic acceptance of things as they are, in modern Europe and in Total War."[12] Their argument is at once clear and oddly involved: Englishmen must change to stay the same; because the war is a war for national survival, Britain needs to suspend exactly the aspects of its national character that it wants most to preserve; it has to embrace the "all-in" tactics of total war in order to protect values that would consider those tactics as repugnant. This paradox—that one needs to undo Englishness in order to save Englishness—is central to the film's form and content and is, as we shall see, a concentrated expression of a contradiction immanent to the British experience of World War II, one I have already tried to capture with the phrase, "it takes a fascist to fight a fascist." In the build-up to the film's release, the industry periodical *Kinematograph Weekly* restated Powell and Pressburger's case even more directly: "The film's vital theme that we must forget chivalry and sportsmanship to fight the enemy successfully and its dedication to the new aggressive spirit of the Allied Armies is a challenge to those among the democratic peoples who are only just awakening to the meaning of total war."[13] Years later, Powell reiterated this position, remembering the film as an argument about the suspension of the English past in the service of the present crisis, an argument against "British procrastination and British regard for tradition and all the things which we knew and which were losing the war."[14]

One can of course see why Grigg, Bracken, and Churchill were unconvinced despite Powell and Pressburger's several assurances. *Colonel Blimp* lacks battle scenes; it is ambivalent, to say the least, about the means and ends of each of the three wars it represents (the Boer War, World War I, and World War II); it is often remembered more for its hoary sentiment than for its bellicosity; it both recommends and preemptively mourns the loss of tradition—"all the things which we knew"—as it asks us both to forget and to remember "chivalry and sportsmanship"; it is a profound and moving embodiment of nostalgia for the English past as well as a steely rejection of nostalgia as fundamentally inappropriate to the tactical presentism of total war. Read through the distinctly mixed terms of its first reception, the film emerges as an ideal case of what (after Gestalt psychology, Wittgenstein, and E. H. Gombrich) is sometimes referred to as "multistability," a quality of some images that, according to W. T. J. Mitchell, "illustrate the co-existence of contrary or simply different readings in a single image."[15] Like the Necker cube, the "Double Cross," and the "Duck-Rabbit," *The Life and Death of Colonel Blimp* forces a viewer to confront the only apparently absurd possibility of a single object that coherently manages and contains ontologically opposed orders of significance: life *and* death, past *and* present, the love of tradition *and* the rejection of tradition. The film thus offers an ideal case for thinking about what makes a film more or less—more *and* less—about war.[16]

I want to see the this-and-that multistability of *Colonel Blimp* as an expression of another related and equally ambivalent wartime phenomenon, the official and unofficial desire to develop an effective, democratic, and layered alternative to Nazi propaganda. Faced with the bad but apparently effective example of Goebbels's Ministry of Propaganda, the Ministry of Information struggled early on in the war to balance apparently incommensurate goals: the goal of maintaining a strong relation to democratic values of openness, thoughtfulness, and critique and the goal of producing a coherent and persuasive propaganda apparatus that could compete with the Nazis' less scrupulous output.[17] F. C. Bartlett, the Cambridge psychologist who had been commissioned by the Ministry of Information to address exactly this issue, sought to bring these maybe incompatible goals together in the form of what he called "democratic propaganda," an open, self-conscious, and yet no less effective form of media persuasion that he opposed to the iron fist of "dictator propaganda":

> It does not go all out to short-circuit reason, as the dictator propaganda does. It recognizes that men act where their affections, sentiments, and emotions are concerned, but that these must and can be led by intelligence without losing their strength. It knows that the stability of a social order does not depend upon everybody's saying the same things, holding the same opinions, feeling the same feelings, but upon a freely achieved unity which, with many sectional and individual differences, is nevertheless able to maintain an explaining and consistent pattern of life.[18]

On the one hand, the virtues of Bartlett's idea are obvious enough; his proposed or rather hoped-for mix of argument, persuasion, and belief fit well with a broader set of cherished and, one might even say, Churchillian values: tolerance, directness, irony, and so on. On the other hand, Bartlett has a difficult time sustaining his good-faith effort both to imagine the wartime state as "a freely achieved unity" (a body both really free and highly organized) and to imagine such a condition as anything other than naive wish fulfillment; what, after all, is the practical difference between a freely achieved unity and unity imposed from beyond, between a spontaneously mobilized democracy and totalitarianism, between freedom as such and the freedom to obey?[19] One is reminded here of what Kant identified long ago as a paradox fundamental to enlightenment: "Argue as much as you will, and about what you will, but obey!"[20] Years after the war, Jacques Ellul, who had fought with French Resistance, wrote: "[T]here is . . . no 'democratic' propaganda. Propaganda made by democracies is ineffective, paralyzed, mediocre."[21]

Bartlett's hopeful and Ellul's negative assessments of the democratic possibilities of propaganda need both to be seen in relation to the larger fate of state propaganda before, during, and after the war. Mark Wollaeger writes: "By the forties, when the propaganda techniques pioneered by the British had been refined and deployed around the world for over two decades, propaganda seemed inescapable, and the sinister connotations it had begun to gather by the twenties were firmly established. For the Western world, Soviet domestic propaganda had begun to blur distinction between propaganda and education, and the Nazi campaign added associations with obfuscation and systematic deception."[22] Propaganda, in other words, was already antithetical to democracy by the time Powell and Pressburger made their film. An achieved "democratic propaganda" would thus have seemed to many like a fantasy.

This, I think, is the political and aesthetic challenge of *Colonel Blimp*. Even though it would have been clear to them that democratic propaganda was impossible, Powell and Pressburger went ahead and made democratic propaganda anyway; they made a film that both supported and questioned the war and, in so doing, embraced a paradox immanent to total war; in other words, they made *The Life and Death of Colonel Blimp*. I argue that *Colonel Blimp* is a great war film precisely because it embraces and embodies a salutary and politically necessary contradiction that sits differently at the heart of democratic propaganda and total mobilization; the film uses cinematic style to reveal total war as a necessary response to a supreme emergency even as it registers the civilizational loss represented by the passage from a productively neurotic culture of fair play to the generalized psychosis of total war.

War Starts at Midnight

Colonel Blimp begins in 1942 with a quarrel between Second Lieutenant "Spud" Wilson, a young and ambitious officer, and Clive "Sugar" Wynne-Candy, an elderly Major General and the "Blimp" of the film's title.[23] Spud, having been ordered to make it "like the real thing," initiates a mock military exercise between the Army and the Home Guard—Operation Beer Mug—hours before its officially scheduled start. He and his men capture Clive, who, lobster red and wrapped in only a towel, is caught napping among other old officers in the Turkish baths. Set against the tacky orientalist backdrop of the baths, the scene establishes a set of visual contrasts that will inform much of the film; as opposed to the young, good-looking, clean-shaven uniformity of Spud and his nearly identical men, the appearance of the older officers is characterized exactly by its rich, decaying, and almost florid particularity: the old gentlemen wear gaudy or plain robes, solid or striped towels wrapped loosely or tightly around bodies portly or thin. Some wear thick glasses; one sports a monocle. Clive himself, his aging body assertively human and dotted with beads of perspiration, stands not only as spokesman for the older generation but also as something wholly and almost aggressively itself; as opposed to the stereotyped, black-and-white image familiar from David Low's comic, the physical presence and particularity of Roger Livesy's Colonel Blimp is almost grossly visceral; it is flesh, facial hair, strained veins, popping eyes, sweat, and spittle.

Once confronted, Clive gives Spud a Blimpish dressing-down: "But you damned young idiot, war starts at midnight! Haven't you been told!"[24] Spud, in turn, tries to teach old Clive a new trick about winning at modern war: if the Nazis don't follow the rules of the game, why should we? "When I joined the Army, the only agreement I entered into was to defend my country by any means at my disposal, not only by National Sporting Club Rules but by every means that has existed since Cain slugged Abel!"[25] Clive finally snaps when Spud claims to know not only what Clive is but also what he was forty years ago:

> CANDY: You're an extremely impudent young officer, sir. But let me tell you that in forty years' time you'll be an old gentleman, too. And if your belly keeps pace with your head, you'll have a bigger one than any of us!

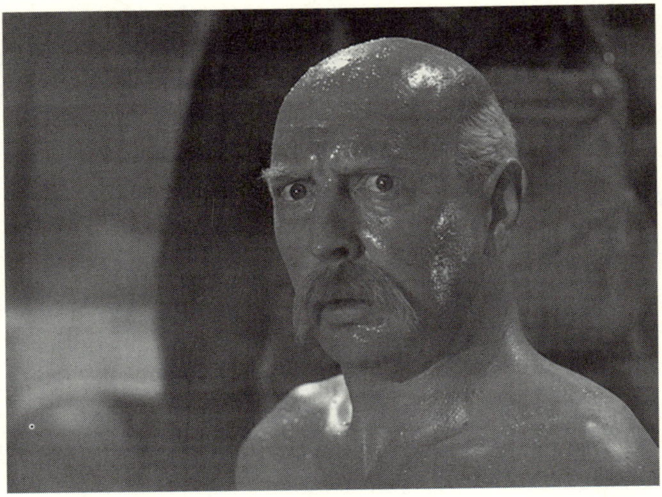

"I am Major General Clive Wynn-Candy."

SPUD: Maybe I shall. In forty years. But I doubt it. And I doubt if I'll have time to grow a mustache like yours, sir. But at least in 1983 I'll be able to say I was a fellow of enterprise.[26]

Clive then tosses Spud in and, as they sink beneath the water's surface, he continues to lecture the younger man, saying several times that the latter can't know what things were like "forty years ago": "You laugh at my big belly, but you don't know how I got it! You laugh at my mustache, but you don't know why I grew it! How do you know what sort of man I was—when I was as young as you are—forty years ago . . . forty years ago . . . *forty years ago*."[27] The words "forty years ago" hang, says the script, "in the air, like the thick clouds of steam" as the camera executes a slow tracking shot past Spud and Clive and on toward the far end of the pool.[28] With nothing but that spooky auditory cue to index the temporal shift, the film then flashes forty years back as a much younger Clive Candy emerges from the pool into which the elder Clive fell: the Clive who went into the pool was an old, walrus-faced man; the Clive who emerges from the water is a young and handsome career officer, recently awarded a Victoria Cross for his service in South Africa. From this point on, the film works to show what Spud cannot know: what difference forty years make. It follows Clive over the course of its three hours as he moves through life, three different wars, and three iterations of his great love, each again played by Deborah Kerr. The film then ends more or less where it began on the day following Spud's taking

"Forty years ago!"

of the Turkish baths, with Clive grimly—and then gamely—accepting his obsolescence now that times and wars have changed.[29]

Clive's drift into the past is not marked with a cut or edit or dissolve or wipe; it is not, in fact, marked with much of anything that could cinematically indicate a shift of scene or time. The camera instead tracks simply and smoothly from one side of the pool to the other, moving in the process from one time into another. Without a cut to mark the shift, the film's present in 1942 seems thus to flow imperceptibly into its past, an effect reinforced by the camera's patient attention to the limpid play of light across the gently churning surface of the narrow pool's water. It is, of course, odd that the film does not cut but instead tracks back from 1942 to 1902. In the classic cinematic grammar, even "slight lapses in time" are usually signaled with some kind of cut (or wipe, dissolve, fade, etc.)[30] In this instance, however, the film is not clear; past and present are brought together in a single, continuous tracking shot, a fact that makes it difficult—at least for a moment—to know where in the film we are; the tracking shot holds us suspended for a long moment in the space between two different moments in time.[31] This is all the more striking given the film's investment in the difference between the past and the present. In other words, whereas much of the film accentuates the hard difference between old and new wars, the lack of a cut appears instead to run past and present together, to imagine cinema as a medium conceptually capacious enough to contain or to superimpose or to blur two very different moments in time.

To cut or not to cut was of course a significant stylistic question for the cinema in 1943. The cut was, thanks to John Grierson's Soviet-inspired statements about the centrality of montage to documentary realism, an especially charged aspect of British as well as European thinking about cinematic technique, one that brought together his interest in cinema as a form of philosophical revelation (a cut between different things could, Grierson argued, reveal the presence of the *real* at work behind the merely *actual*) and his political commitment to an ideally centralized state (an ideal he referred to, with some sense of provocation, as a "good totalitarianism").[32] Aspects of these theories had, as I pointed out in the previous chapter, already been mobilized for the war effort in Humphrey Jennings's several influential propaganda films. The decision either to cut or not to cut was also at the heart of a broader set of questions about the historical potential and responsibilities of cinema in Europe during and after World War II, questions asked most influentially and controversially by André Bazin. For Bazin, the turn taken by Orson Welles and Jean Renoir away from a logic of montage associated with Griffith and Eisenstein (as well as with Grierson and Jennings) toward depth-of-field cinematography was significant both because it showed that cinema was not, as some critics had claimed, reducible to montage and because it introduced what he understood as an essential historical complexity into filmmaking. Whereas montage makes arguments about the relation between people and things, filming continuously in deep space implies a different kind of understanding, introducing the challenge of existential uncertainty into cinema: "The uncertainty in which we find ourselves as to the spiritual key or the interpretation we should put on the film is built into the very design of the image."[33] Put differently, because depth-of-field cinematography can make visible the relations between things in space and time, it can say more and more honestly than montage about what holds or doesn't hold a complex world together; it shows rather than tells. For Bazin, it was a more appropriate and rigorous form of history; or, as Raymond Durgnat puts it, "In the gospel according to Bazin, God invented the cine-camera, but the devil created scissors."[34]

In this light, Powell and Pressburger's decision to track and not to cut should be understood in the context of film history as well as history as such. As Bazin might have put it, where a cut could have simplified the film's historical argument about the past's relation to the present (and would at least have been logistically easier to execute), the tracking shot makes the very idea of historical development, progress or causality into a palpable problem; and, because the shot forces us to consider the meaning of a cut in its felt and phantom absence (it is a *no-cut*, a shot where a cut might and maybe should have been), it encourages us to see the film in terms of both a history of cinematic style and a history of violence that Bazin saw as an impetus behind that stylistic shift.[35] Clive Candy's uncut and fluid movement through and into the past is, in other words, another instance of what I call cinematic eccentricity. It is an almost viscous moment of cinematic style that refers both back to itself and, as I will argue, out toward some problems essential to the British experience of total war.

Brute Force and Ruddy Ignorance

Why put so much stylistic pressure on bathetic conflict between Clive Candy and Spud Wilson? Why track when it would have been easier and cleaner and clearer to cut? The shot, I maintain, is partly a response both to the immediate and adolescent violence of Clive's encounter with Spud and to the more serious and far-reaching political violence that Spud both embraces and represents. Rushing into the Turkish baths, Spud shouts out, "Brute force and ruddy ignorance!"[36] The cry is, on the one hand, a sign of Spud's youthful enthusiasm; as we see in early scenes, he and his men prepare for and pursue war with an adolescent's reckless and feckless intensity. On the other hand, read in terms of the film's larger message and some of his other statements, "brute force and ruddy ignorance" points to something more broadly significant. When Spud first arrives at the idea of prematurely attacking Clive, he does so in response to a note scribbled in pencil on the typed order from HQ: "make it like the real thing." When one of his men asks, "What do they mean by 'like the real thing,' Spud?" Spud replies, "Well, obviously our losses divided by ten and the enemy's multiplied by twenty!"[37] In an earlier draft of the script, Spud says more about what he understands as "the real thing": "Well, obviously prisoners must be bayoneted to death, women must be raped, our losses divided by ten and the enemy's multiplied by twenty!"[38]

Spud takes the brutalization of soldiers and civilians not as an unintended if inevitable consequence of conflict but rather as a realistic aspect of modern military strategy; rape, murder, and torture are acceptable—they are *the real thing*—because they work, because they hasten war toward a favorable conclusion. This understanding of war and its tactics is disturbing not least because the film ultimately means for us to accept Spud and what he represents; it recognizes Spud—and, thus, "brute force and ruddy ignorance"—as right for or at least tactically appropriate to the war at hand. This, we should understand, is at least partly what Powell and Pressburger had in mind when they advocated "a realistic acceptance of things as they are, in modern Europe and in Total War." To accept total war is to accept a different and less restrained relation to the use of violence.

Spud's sense of what's appropriate, what's really *real* about "the real thing" thus reflects the tactical dissolution of the difference between

"The real thing!"

civilian and soldier that defined the conduct of almost all parties during World War II: "The preponderance of [civilian deaths] was no accidental or peripheral feature of [World War II]; it reflected the central significance of civilians in the conflict, the indispensable roles that they played in the war's outcome, as well as the vulnerabilities that they shared, as a direct consequence, with the soldiers."[39] In addition to reflecting technological advances and, in particular, the exponentially expanded reach of aerial warfare, the broad militarization of the home front had far-reaching effects on the very idea of what war was and what it meant to imagine an end or an outside to war. As I suggest in the introduction, total war was as much a concept as a situation during World War II; it was how people thought about themselves and each other during war time.

Paul Saint-Amour states that the "expression 'total war' appears to have been coined by the right-wing French editor Léon Daudet in March 1916, during the early weeks of the Battle of Verdun."[40] Daudet's early sense of the potential totality of war was already a matter of imaginative scale: "For Daudet, with his blood-and-soil organicist view of the nation, modern warfare had become total partly in intensity, demanding that one extinguish rather than merely defeat the enemy. But it was the metaphorics of extent—the claim that war must encompass every space, every civil system, every aspect of national life—that was uppermost in his definition of total war, and would preoccupy military theorists for most of the interwar period."[41]

A war thought of in these terms threatened to erase real and theoretical differences between combatants and noncombatants: according to J. F. C. Fuller in *The First of the League Wars* (1936), total war "means that when war begins all private life comes to an end, and the nation has only one concern—war."[42] In addition to its dramatic physical and institutional effects, total war thus affected the meaning of things both large and small. Going to work, saving money, spending money, caring for family, eating, not eating, turning lights off or on: in total war, these behaviors are understood merely—if perversely—as diverse means to a single military end. Faced in 1929 with the prospect of aerial warfare's indefinite expansion of the front, Paul Whitcomb Williams anticipated later conditions when he wrote: "Who can say what are 'distinctively military supplies' in wartime when so much of the output of almost every factory producing anything from jam to steel goes to assist the conduct of military operations? No doubt this provision was designed to exclude jam factories and include woolen mills making army clothing, for example, but who shall say that meat is less important to an army in the field than raiment, and why should aircraft be permitted to bomb one and not the other?"[43] As opposed to an earlier idea of war in which the use of violence was limited to professional armies operating as representatives of a state's interests, a total war is not fought by proxy; if everyone and everything is mobilized, everyone and everything—both the makers and the consumers of jam—are necessarily acceptable targets.

As Spud seems implicitly to understand, what's real about total war is precisely how it affects what it is possible to think: "When I joined the Army," he says, "the only agreement I entered into was to defend my country by any means at my disposal, not only by National Sporting Club Rules but by every means that has existed since Cain slugged Abel!"[44] Cain and Abel are figures of an original, fratricidal violence; and, insofar as their legacy implies that every human being is at least potentially both a victim and a killer, Spud's reach back toward their example is proof not only of his modern commitment to any and all means but also of his innate understanding of the quasi-theological—the total—nature of total war: once begun, such a war denies as a matter of principle the difference between the innocent and the guilty, the civilian and the soldier. Put differently, insofar as Cain and Abel represent the two sides of an exchange (like the producers and consumers of Whitcomb Williams's jam), Spud's rhetorical synthesis of the two positions into a single object of identification works to give expression not only to extreme violence but also to a fantasy of perfect and enclosed totality. They represent a perverse because suicidal answer to alienation: if not a snake with its tail in its mouth, then maybe a man punching himself in the face.

War Is Nothing but a Duel

To return to the film's tracking shot: why would Powell and Pressburger bring together Clive's life, the more or less motivated stylistic choice to track and not to cut, and the open-ended violence that underwrites modern warfare? Let's look at another tracking shot—another no-cut—that appears at the culmination of a later, equally important scene: a duel fought between the young Clive and Theo Kretschmar-Schuldorff, a German officer who becomes both Clive's lifelong friend and something like the film's conscience. Clive visits Berlin in 1902 in response to a letter from Edith Hunter, an English governess working in Germany and the first of his three nearly identical loves. The letter describes rumors that are circulating about British misconduct during the Boer War. After arriving, Clive stages a showdown with Kaunitz, the apparent author of the rumors: "He's the most awful little skunk! He was spying for us, he was spying for the Boers, he made South Africa too hot for himself and skipped."[45] Clive and Kaunitz engage in a comic battle of wills in the Cafe Hohenzollern, each bribing the house orchestra with beer to play or not to play an aria from Ambroise Thomas's *Mignon* (1866). The tune, "I am Titania," was the only record they had at the blockhouse where Clive was an officer and Kaunitz a prisoner: "We had a phonograph and we broke every record but this one. We know it by heart."[46]

The centrality of "I am Titania" to this scene and, in fact, to the whole of the film's soundtrack is worth noting. Taking the place of Powell and Pressburger's initial choice—Wagner's "Brunhilde Aria"—Thomas's tune was not only recognizable and, as opposed to the Wagner aria, decidedly catchy but also a performance with a clear thematic and aesthetic significance for *Colonel Blimp*. First, because it was a French composer's (Thomas's) rendition of a German author's (Goethe's) use of an English playwright (Shakespeare), the song embodies nostalgia for a fragile, passing, and maybe only imaginary moment of European political and cultural comity; second, its association with Goethe's *Wilhelm Meister's Apprenticeship* (1795) calls to the surface the film's fraught and maybe stalled-out generic relation to the *Bildungsroman*, a form that follows the development of an individual from adolescence to maturity ("forty years ago!"); finally, Thomas's coloratura aria would have been well-known in 1902 as a technically demanding showstopper, a song that called specific attention to ways in which style can sometimes overwhelm substance. It is not only a famous melismatic

I am Titania.

challenge, one that forces singers to show off and swoop gratuitously up and down the scale (it was, said one critic with distaste, an "obvious concession to the virtuosity of the soprano"), but also a canny musical representation of its character's essential and, one might say, natural artifice.[47] Goethe's seductive, artlessly artful Philine is a consummate actor, a figure who thrives precisely because she treats identity as a protean form of play; it is no coincidence that she loves the role of Titania, Shakespeare's wonder-working queen of the fairies. The several associations embedded in the tune—its cosmopolitanism, its culture, its relation to play and to style—come together to stand in for a European milieu that the film sets implicitly against the present of realpolitik and twentieth-century modern war. Indeed, this, the film suggests, might be one reason why the opportunistic proto-fascist Kaunitz can't stand it; "I am Titania" represents not only a moment in the history of operatic style but also a system of values on the verge of extinction.

Finally confronting Kaunitz directly, Clive inadvertently insults the whole of the German army: because some of them are acquainted with Kaunitz, he shouts for all the café to hear, "the officers of the Imperial German Army ought to be ashamed of themselves!"[48] In response to this blanket insult, two exquisite German officers (Oberleutnants von Ritter and von Reuman) appear the following day at the British embassy to "demand satisfaction" and to arrange the details of a duel to be fought between Clive and Theo Kretschmar-Schuldorff, then also a young and rising officer.

At the embassy a diplomat, the military attaché, and two German officers sit down to hash out the details of the coming duel with the help of the Brown Codex: "This is our famous 'Brown Codex,' Major Goodhead, the 'Code of Honour' observed by all duelists."[49] They continue:

> VON RITTER: Do you prefer to strip the upper part of the body of the combatants or do you prefer them in shirtsleeves?
>
> GOODHEAD: Shirtsleeves. I see here [referring to the Brown Codex] that Paragraph 133 says: "It is advisable a few hours previous to the duel, to take a bath!"
>
> VON RITTER: Only the principals. Not the seconds. (*He laughs.*)
>
> 2ND SECRETARY: It is a very strange sensation to be preparing a duel between two people who have never even seen each other.
>
> VON RITTER: (*Carelessly*) It happens sometimes. Marriages also! (*He laughs again.*)[50]

Seen from one perspective, this attention to the details and apparently absurd rules that govern social life is broadly representative of an ethnographic delight in custom that characterizes many of Powell and Pressburger's films. This is as much the case with their attention to the structured and close-knit kinship rules that govern a traveling ballet company in *The Red Shoes* (1948) as it is in their interest in regional particulars in *I Know Where I'm Going!* (1945), *A Canterbury Tale* (1944), and even Powell's early *The Edge of the World* (1937).

Von Ritter's careless joke—"Marriages also!"—reveals yet another social aspect of the duel and the film as a whole. This, the first encounter between Clive and Theo, forms the basis of a lifelong friendship between men, a friendship that provides a larger frame for the film's thinking about war, for the unfolding of its plots, and for the complex ways in which desire is figured, directed, and redirected from one war and from one person to the next. In other words, the scene is, as Andrew Moor points out, charged with an erotic excess that neither the film nor the duel can easily discharge: "Shot-reverse-shot close-ups, when Clive first meets Theo for the duel in *Blimp*, intend to record the men carefully inspecting their opponent's mettle, and they certainly register mutual recognition and respect. Could this admiration of martial skill, military rank and athletic physique spill over into something more erotic though? The camera cranes away to the heavens almost before this thought can register. The answer, it seems, is a decisive 'no,' but the question still hovers."[51] The shot/reverse shot sequence that

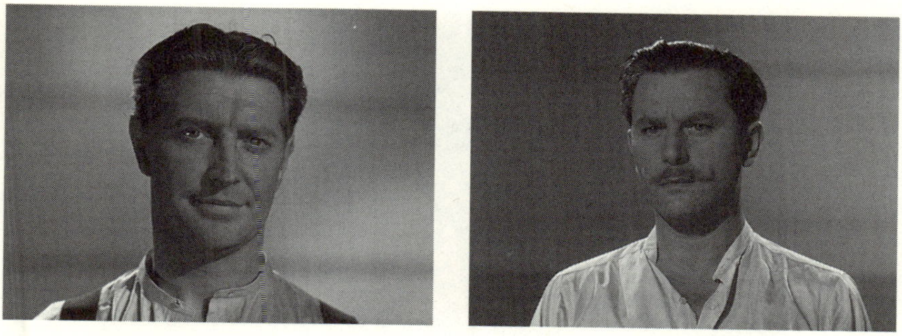

"Marriages also!"

initiates the duel is indeed punctuated with a charged moment that the film seems promptly to forget. First we see Theo's face: cold, ready, prepared. Then, when we cut to Clive, a faint but unmistakably friendly smile, oddly candid, plays across his face. Cutting back to Theo, we see his confusion: what can such a look mean? The smile might be part of Clive's strategy; it throws Theo slightly off guard as proof of Clive's ample confidence. It also makes clear Clive's understanding of the duel as game. Although deadly serious, a duel is nonetheless a form of play and Clive, the good sport, smiles at play. It might, though, also mean something more. It adds in other words a flirty charge to the scene, a first hint that there might be something more to Clive's affection for Theo than either the rules of the game or the terms of total war could contain.[52]

That said, we must see the Brown Codex not only as a book, not only about living life socially or erotically with others, but also about a strange and highly formalized way of managing and, indeed, producing death. According to Kevin McAleer, by the end of the nineteenth century, several books like the Brown Codex had appeared in Germany, setting the terms of how duels were to be fought: "a series of authoritative handbooks had been published which dispelled confusion and, in tandem with fate, stage-managed the whole drama from insult to post-mortem."[53] As McAleer suggests, what was most striking about dueling in the *fin-de-siecle* was the fact that it seemed to capture a more general and, as we will see in what follows, essentially fragile historical relation between social order, aesthetics, and an apparently basic human tendency toward aggression and violence; because the duel, he suggests, was not only violent but also an act of an apparently archaic and ritual violence, it stood as a point where contradictions necessary to social life at a given moment in time were revealed: "As the point of interaction between primordial destructive drives and civilizing impulses,

The Brown codex.

ritual violence in the modern age . . . provides historians with a prime example of humankind's perennially ambivalent nature."[54] The duel was, in that case, an especially concentrated and late expression of what Norbert Elias refers to as the "civilizing process," the particular ways in which particular societies both acknowledge and manage their aggression; for Elias, aggression is "bound . . . by the advanced state of the division of functions, and by the resulting greater dependence of individuals on each other and on the technical apparatus. It is confined and tamed by innumerable rules and prohibitions that have become self-constraints. It is as much transformed, 'refined,' 'civilized,' as all the other forms of pleasure, and it is only in dreams or in isolated outbursts that we account for as pathological that something of its immediate and unregulated force appears."[55]

In these terms, the duel needs to be understood as a form of both violence and violence-control. Although apparently gratuitous, the duel as ritual violence would represent a courtly and residual alternative to "immediate and unregulated" shows of force. It is, as it were, a secondary response to these primary processes. As I have suggested, it is exactly this specific and thus fragile compromise between the rules of the game and the barely repressed violence of the game that interests Powell and Pressburger. As terrible and wasteful as a duel is, it nonetheless represents a tentative, limited, and historically specific rapprochement between civilization and violence that seemed on the verge of being lost to the homogenizing and unrestrained pressure of total war.

However broken, the duel thus remains an expression of a civilizational ethos that Clive and Theo share and that both Elias and Huizinga associate with a particular phase of European life: "Being essentially a play-form, the duel is symbolical; it is the shedding of blood and not the killing that matters. We can call it a late form of ritual blood-play, the orderly regulation of the death-blow struck unawares in anger. The spot where the duel is fought bears all the marks of a play-ground; the weapons have to be exactly alike as in certain games; there is a signal for the start and the finish, and the number of shots is prescribed. When blood flows, honour is vindicated and restored."[56] Powell and Pressburger's tacit opinion of the duel as a highly ritualized and entirely serious form of play more or less follows Huizinga's; the seconds discuss the rules that govern the duel's duration ("You will start only at the command 'Los!'"), what weapons can be used ("You know, of course, that the saber must not exceed the maximum weight of 60 Dekagrammes!"), and its location (of course, a gymnasium, which Powell and Pressburger represent as organized with the geometric detail of a backgammon board).[57] Although all parties are in agreement about the possible diplomatic consequence and thus the seriousness of the duel, they also agree to treat the conflict as an honest and honorable game played out between equals. For Powell and Pressburger, as well as for Huizinga, the duel as game is thus an expression of a particular and passing moment in high bourgeois European culture; and although this playful spirit characterizes the plot, the dialogue, and the visual style of the film's first act, it more or less fades with the onset of Clive's second and third wars as the cultural conditions that made such a display possible or even imaginable had also all but faded away. This is once again to mark a historical difference between war as a game and war as "the real thing" that Spud embraces by ignoring the rule, "war starts at midnight." Unlike Clive and Theo, Spud not only betrays the rules of the game but also denies that war has any rules at all.

Clive, on the contrary, is associated with a variety of games throughout *Colonel Blimp*, with cards, polo, rugby, hunting, and so on. Indeed, his ready facility with the logic of the game and the terms and performance of the duel explicitly aligns him with the principal military theories of the late nineteenth and early twentieth centuries and, in particular, with those of Carl von Clausewitz, the great nineteenth-century philosopher of war. An early presentation "of the idea behind the story of Blimp" (probably prepared in the spring of 1942) describes Clive's military education in this way: "In his youth Clive Candy was full of enterprise and impatience with his elders. His opinions about war were no better and no worse than the principal military figures of his time. He was anxious to succeed in his

"War is nothing but a duel."

chosen profession, he saw active service early in his career and was lucky in obtaining promotion and distinction. He kept his eyes open during the South African campaign, he studied Clausewitz and the other military theorists. He was a promising young officer. There were hundreds like him."[58] It makes sense, then, that Clive's greatest moment of represented heroism takes the form of a duel, the type of combat that Clausewitz took as the purest form of war: "I shall not begin by expounding a pedantic, literary definition of war, but go straight to the heart of the matter, to the duel. War is nothing but a duel on a larger scale."[59] In placing a duel at the heart of their film's first act, Powell and Pressburger imply a historical connection between Clive, a theory of war that privileged the duel as a form, and a culture that made the man, the duel, and the theory possible.

The duel is Clausewitz's ideal form of combat for a few reasons. First, it stands, in its radical simplicity, as a necessary heuristic; because of its conceptual purity, the idea of the duel allows Clausewitz to draw an implied line between the theory and practice of war, between war as it would behave if left in a vacuum and war as it in fact occurs in a world defined by a whole range of difficult and conflicting causes and effects. Clausewitz thus focuses on what he calls "absolute war," a pure but only theoretical or idealized image of war against which the incalculably particular fog of real wars might begin to be measured and differentiated: "Once the antagonists have ceased to be mere figments of a theory and become actual states and governments, when war is no longer a theoretical affair but a series of actions obeying its own peculiar laws, reality supplies the data from which we can deduce the unknown that lies ahead."[60] For Clausewitz, absolute war cannot be achieved because limits specific to particular conflicts will always get in war's way; although war seems in and of itself *to want* to drive toward its extreme form, reality intervenes, setting limits to what any particular war can in fact achieve. These limits take the form of what he calls "friction," material conditions that the world throws up in the way of war's immanent drive toward its essence (bad weather, poor roads, the vagaries of human desire and ability); as Gary Wills puts it, "time and space militate against the abstract unity of war considered in itself."[61]

In addition to these material sources of friction, Clausewitz understood war as held back also by the political limits of any given conflict: "war cannot be divorced from political life; and whenever this occurs in our thinking about war, the many links that connect the two elements are destroyed and we are left with something pointless and devoid of sense."[62] Real wars are fought for worldly interests and ends, reasons antithetical to the idea of absolute war as an end in itself. As a result, states will always pull back from absolute war's pure and general end—that is, the wholesale destruction of the enemy—either once a particular political end has been achieved or once the military cost of a war threatens to outweigh its possible political gain. Wills writes, "Victory must never exist for its own sake at the strategic (as opposed to the tactical) level."[63] Although it is in the essential character of war *qua* war to seek out its absolute limit, material conditions and political ends that are both external and necessary to particular wars keep them in check and from reaching their immanent and absolute—their total—form. For Clausewitz, war works dialectically, driving itself relentlessly and abstractly forward toward the material and political limits that in turn hold it back. Jan Mieszkowski observes: "As a duel, war follows specific rules and has a precise beginning and end. A ritual or performance, it is a staged spectacle that obeys its own rhetorical logic irrespective of the uses to which it is put by its performers or audience members."[64]

The elaborate system of customs, conventions, and rules embodied in the Brown Codex thus produce the duel as an autonomous military event situated within and subordinated to a wider and more complex political context. Insofar as diplomats with political reasons of their own arrange the details of a duel that soldiers must fight, it is an embodiment of a war as both different from and a continuation of politics by other means. It serves specific political ends—Clive, without knowing or caring much about it, helps the embassy avoid an embarrassing international situation—and polices a difference that defines the Clausewitzian view: the ultimate difference between soldiers and civil servants, between combat and diplomacy, between war and politics.

"Then, without a Break . . ."

Given its centrality to the film's plot as well as its place in a larger historical discourse around the changing culture of European war, it is odd that we do not in fact see the duel. Instead of seeing the fight, we see drawn-out preparations for the duel and its very beginning before being swept away from it in a gesture that recalls the earlier no-cut, the tracking shot of Clive falling into a pool old and emerging from it a much younger man. As the swordsmen begin to fight, the camera tracks up and away from their combat, toward and then right through the gymnasium's high ceiling. Indeed, the gym's visual field is high, wide, and notably deep, a fact that allows Powell and Pressburger to track bodies and things as they move side to side, forward and back, and ultimately up *and even through the ceiling*. Powell and Pressburger's script describes their trick shot this way: "Then—without a break—the camera slips through the huge windows and we are out in the street."[65] The camera then hovers for a moment up in the lightly falling snow before tracking back down and in toward a carriage in which Edith awaits news of the duel's outcome. As in the earlier example, the shot is marked by its oddly fluid quality; where we might expect some kind of pronounced cut to announce the passage from inside to outside, Powell and Pressburger use an effect—a soft, self-effacing dissolve—that blurs the physical barrier between those different spaces.[66] Because they more or less obscure the cut, the inside seems in this sequence simply to become the outside.

The shot looks like and is, I believe, partly a deliberate reference to another, more famous shot: the look inside Kane's snow globe at the beginning of *Citizen Kane* (1941), a similarly retrospective film about how a past produces the present. In the case of Welles's film, the fluid, suspended space of the globe's interior conveys an almost amniotic sense of security and nostalgia. As, however, the globe rolls out of the dying man's hand and shatters, we trade the floating and oceanic feeling of its homely interior for the sharp reality of the world beyond. The move from one to the other is, in other words, proof of the hard difference between Kane's world-making narcissism and the friction of things as, after all, they really are. However whereas *Kane* shows us that where there is an inside there is also an outside and that the difference between them must matter, in *Colonel Blimp*, the ostentatiously unbroken movement away from the duel into the larger world beyond points to an interest in erasing not only the cinematic apparatus

Then without a break . . .

as presence but also the difference between inside and outside. Just as the camera's long, limpid tracking motion across the pool seemed to undermine the difference between present and past, so does the subtle move toward and through the roof seem to undermine the difference between inside and out, between the interior, organized play-space of the gymnasium and the inchoate world beyond. The break or cut that shatters the effect of fluid singularity in *Kane* never arrives in *Colonel Blimp*. As a result, the scene encourages us once again to feel the absence of the cut, the break, the difference both in its own terms and in relation to cinema.

Why, in a scene otherwise apparently invested in rules that allow for the constitutive, Clausewitzian difference between things (politics and war, friend and enemy, the beginning and end of combat) does the camera turn away from the differential logic of the duel in order to execute a shot that, at least the level of form, undermines what the scene had seemed to support? Why turn to the fluid space of the no-cut when something solid seems more appropriate? On the one hand, the drift away from the duel is, as Moor points out, a way of containing erotic possibilities that had been raised by the buildup to and the stripping down for the duel; just when we want most to watch, the film lowers a veil, preventing us from seeing Clive and Theo's bodies. (Some of this cinematically repressed erotic excess, I maintain, makes its return later in the film.) On the other hand, it is, I think, at this point that the film makes at the level of style its clearest argument about the nature of the move away from earlier ways of thinking about war toward Spud's rough prescription: "brute force and ruddy ignorance!" Insofar as the shot blurs the difference between inside and outside, its style seems to run against the grain of its content and implicitly to question the idea that war picks up where politics leaves off. Where limited, Clausewitzian war depends on rules that maintain the difference between politics and war, total war—the war that Spud endorses—refuses to see politics or private life as safe in or different from war: "when war begins all private life comes to an end."[67]

Whereas, at the level of its content, the film makes a case for the historical separation of military and diplomatic imperatives, at the level of film style, the dissolution of the difference between inside and outside—between the bound, rule-based world of the duel and the fluid chaos of everyday life, between the restricted economy of the game and the general economy of everything else—anticipates the collapse of a social and cultural order that allowed wars to be imagined in limited terms and that was already on the verge of slipping away in 1902. Philipp von Hilgers writes:

> The duel—which had been the principle to which, when in doubt, all complexities of war were still reduced up to the First World War—had thereby served its time. The Thirty Years' War might have produced the monopoly of violence, but the world war realized it in its totality. The threat of the death penalty in Prussian law did not put an end to the duel. Nor did Kant's appeal to reason, which argued that duelers by no means demonstrated the courage of the warrior, which was instrumental to states. No state power was able to fight an institution that allowed the suffering and the exercise of violence for the restoration of honor. The duel is finally abandoned with the First World War, due to the intrinsic killing mechanisms of the war, which revoke the equivalence with the duel.[68]

The years between Clive's first, second, and third wars thus coincide with a broad European repudiation or revision of Clausewitz's sense of the necessary structuring difference between real limited war and the ideal, heuristic form of absolute war, a revision that, as we've begun to see, affects aspects of living and thinking that go beyond the technical abstractions of military strategy. Powell and Pressburger's representation of Clive Candy as a follower and embodiment of Clausewitzian principles takes place against these changes. They take care to portray Clive as a late and residual survival of the same bourgeois culture that produced Clausewitz and that had been all but undone by the events of World War I.[69] More, though, than simply tracking a passage from one idea to another about war, the film asks what difference that passage makes. Was the violence of World War II different in kind from what had come before, or was it simply a more direct, a more honest expression of what has always been at stake in war? Should we understand the doctrine and the tactics of total war as a tragic and insane exception, a lapse from a continuous logic of European civilization, or instead as a particularly virulent expression of a violence necessary to and always at work at the heart of that civilization? What makes *Colonel Blimp* capable of arguing for war and of saying something significantly *more* than that is the fact that it can, however incoherently, hold on to two ideas at once, seeing total war and its violence as both exception and rule.

The Rules of the Game

Colonel Blimp casts the elaborate structure of games, duels, hunts, codes of behavior, and good sportsmanship that characterize the lives of educated Europeans in 1902 as an important part of a shared social, political, and military life. As David Bell puts it in relation to the long history of eighteenth and nineteenth-century European war, "This state of virtually permanent but restrained warfare seemed entirely natural and proper to the noblemen who led Europe's armies under the Old Regime, for it allowed the aristocratic values of honor and service to find full expression without serious threats to social stability and prosperity."[70] War, because it was understood as an important but distinct (because professional) part of life, could exist alongside a coherent and stable social world; because it was both continuous with and different from the rest of life, it could exist as a natural and ordered—if violent—aspect of European existence. That said, although his manners owe a self-conscious debt to that earlier moment of war as serious play, Clive is not himself exactly of that old order; he is rather a representative of what Franco Moretti has taken as the bourgeois *déjà-la,* one of those "already existing things," to which a class and culture turn when their survival is under threat.[71] Clive's old-fashioned sense of war and his commitment to antiquated codes of chivalry thus draw on residual cultural forms in a manner that both gives his way of life its last historical chance (it borrows, as it were, a stability from that past that it can't muster in the present) and stands as sure evidence of the decline and demise of that way of life.

Spud is, on the other hand, a resolutely modern and historically dominant example of what Huizinga refers to as the spoil-sport: "The player who trespasses against the rules or ignores them is a 'spoil-sport.' The spoil-sport is not the same as the false player, the cheat; for the latter pretends to be playing the game and, on the face of it, still acknowledges the magic circle. It is curious to note how much more lenient society is to the cheat than to the spoil-sport. This is because the spoil-sport shatters the play-world itself. By withdrawing from the game he reveals the relativity and fragility of the play-world in which he had temporarily shut himself with others."[72] Because he rejects not only the war game ("war starts at midnight!") but also the idea that war could itself be understood as a kind of chivalric contest with rules of its own, Spud represents the end of an already attenuated civilizational project, a fading bourgeois way of life that the film encourages us to understand both in terms of a larger compromise between politics and society and in terms of the way that project allowed for and was reflected in the individual's psychic management of aggression and desire.

I have argued elsewhere that a similar tension between residual and emergent attitudes toward violence is at work in Jean Renoir's *The Rules of the Game* (1939).[73] That film's careful representation of the formalized chaos of an antic week in the country and the hunt that is its thematic and aesthetic highlight is threatened at every turn with a violence that would undo a narrow-bandwidth symbolic order that continues—if only barely—to organize the desires and aspirations of its bourgeois participants. Clive inhabits much the same civilizational twilight as La Colinere's partygoers. His behavior seems at once to represent the successful logic of a certain moment in time, a moment when ritualized performances of violence kept another "immediate and unregulated" violence at bay, and to anticipate the moment when those performances could no longer manage or bind that other violence. We might consider Clive's dozens of animal heads, trophies he collects between wars when he is forced to play at the hunt instead of at war. Powell and Pressburger handle the appearance of these heads with considerable cinematic wit. In order to mark the passage of years between the film's three acts, the heads "pop" onto the wall in one jump cut after another, a style that anticipates the swinging-sixties cinematography of Richard Lester or even lighter moments in Godard.

That said, the scenes' lightness doesn't entirely dampen the raw intensity of Clive's taste for the kill. The sheer number of heads is something shocking, evidence of a kind of biocidal compulsion. His globetrotting is cast in terms of a Blimpish indifference to the broad violence of a waning British Empire that, as we have seen, Orwell took as the war's big lie; when asked about the pain of losing his wife in a foreign country, he responds, "It

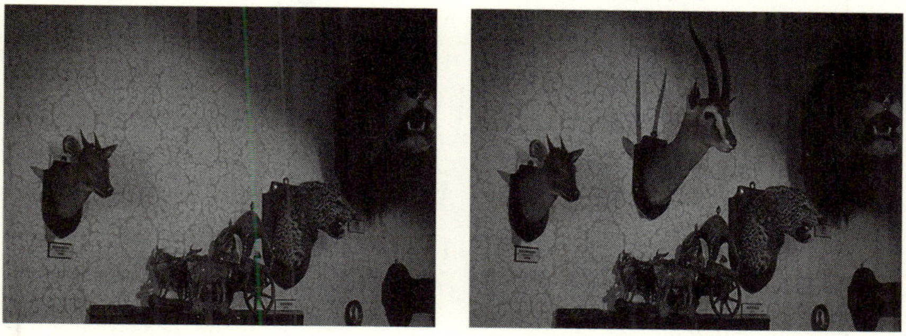

Candy's collection.

wasn't a foreign country. It was Jamaica."[74] The film also introduces Clive's role in World War I with a last cut to an image of a German spiked helmet accompanied by a plate that says, "Hun. Flanders, 1918." The inclusion of this helmet in his collection is, of course, tasteless, suggesting limits internal to Clive's residual system for managing what pleasure he takes in organized violence. Whereas the game was meant to stand as a *cordon sanitaire* separating play violence from real violence, the trophy helmet points to an affective contradiction that was always at work in Clive's gentlemanly type of impulse control. The gesture thus remains a late representative of a residual cultural logic while it shows the degree to which that logic was always already on the verge of fraying into obsolescence both because of external historical pressures and because of the disarraying force of a necessary contradiction.

Clive's growing collection of animal heads points also in two other related directions that, once again, undermine differences between past and present wars, between the imagined chivalry or legality of Clive's early military experience and the indiscriminate brutality of total war. In the first case, the imperial cast of Clive's collection reaches explicitly back to his unrepresented experience in the Boer War, the film's off-screen conflict that, I maintain, stands in *Colonel Blimp* as a more or less explicit contrast to the enormity and violence of World Wars I and II. Of course, it makes sense that, seen from the perspective of those later wars, the Boer War might be dimly remembered as an aristocratic game or, indeed, a boy's adventure tale. In his 1937 memoir of the conflict, J. F. C. Fuller called it "the last of the gentlemen's wars": "It belonged to the days when kings fought kings, and not to a democratic age when demented, newspaper-fed masses of men vilify and tear each other to pieces. It belonged to the days of the sword and the lance and not to those of the magazine rifle and machine gun."[75]

Fuller's halcyon memory of the Boer War says much about the revisionary force of World War I, an experience that not only shaped Fuller's career as an increasingly critical (and, indeed, increasingly Clausewitzian) military historian but also made him into an early advocate of a fast, mobile, and limited type of warfare also associated with Basil Liddell Hart.

However, as Fuller himself later admitted, there was little that was gentlemanly about the Boer War, a conflict in which the British indeed earned some of the vitriol that brings Clive to Berlin in 1902: "They hate us in Germany. They are spreading propaganda all over Europe that we are killing women and children in South Africa, that we are starving them in concentration camps, shooting mothers, burning babies—you wouldn't believe the things they have invented!"[76] Whatever else, the Boer War was a brutal, modern war. Once the Boers—outgunned and outnumbered—transitioned into guerrilla tactics after the battle of Paardeberg in February of 1900, the viciousness of the fighting and the cruelty of the fighters became more pronounced. This was partly a consequence of technological developments that would be perfected later in the century: with, for instance, the invention of smokeless gunpowder, "the old terror of a visible foe had given way to the paralyzing sensation of advancing on an invisible one, which fostered the suspicion that the enemy was everywhere. A universal terror, rather than a localized danger, now enveloped the attacker."[77] The British move to counterinsurgency tactics led to even more disturbing kinds of excess: "Thousands of Boer homesteads were burned as part of a British 'scorched earth' policy designed to deprive Afrikaner guerrillas of their primary sources of support in the countryside."[78] In addition to the destruction of Boer homes, the British also established a network of concentration camps, a fact made all the more uncomfortable given the phrase's later association with the Nazis (the words had already become a grim punchline in Ernst Lubitsch's 1942 comedy, *To Be, or Not to Be*). By October 1901, "the concentration camps had acquired a terrible notoriety. Overcrowding, insanitary conditions, an insufficiently balanced diet, and inadequate planning caused a tragic loss of life. Women and children, swept into the camps from isolated farms, were easy prey to a variety of diseases, and measles, typhoid, jaundice, malaria, bronchitis and pneumonia all took their toll."[79]

Although Powell and Pressburger's film seems largely to support—or at least not explicitly to contradict—Clive's idea of the Boer War as different in kind from what came after, that war's equivocal reputation—the violence of the conflict, the controversy that surrounded the camps in Germany and England, and the real severity of British methods—puts destabilizing and immanent pressure on a difference between wars to which the film seems

"A simple South African."

otherwise committed.[80] Indeed, the appearance of the brutally effective South African officer, Major Van Zijl, in the film's middle section suggests as much: "Now listen! I am in command here now and I know how to deal with you scum. I am not a simple English gentleman but a simple South African and I assure you that I have means to get what I want."[81] While the film draws a clear and immediate distinction between his apparent willingness to torture World War I German prisoners and Clive's more humane and less successful approach, the scene and Van Zijl's scarred face seem tacitly to suggest that his expertise might have been hard won at English hands a decade and a half before, a possibility that hints at something darkly tenacious within Powell and Pressburger's history of British violence.

This brings us to an even more suggestive and immediate second aspect of Clive's hunting trophies. If the appearance of animal's heads one after the other would suggest a general sense of British sportsmanship, the same strain of aristocratic play that the young Fuller fantasized as at work in the Boer War, it would also have invoked one sportsman and politician in particular: Lord Halifax, the former foreign secretary who, along with Chamberlain, had emerged by 1943 as nearly synonymous with the policy of appeasement. Halifax was a highly visible hunter, having been made master of the Middleton Hunt in 1932. As a result, he was invited in late 1937 to attend the International Sporting Exhibition in Berlin. Members of Chamberlain's government, particularly Sir Neville Henderson, ambassador to Germany, were eager to take the invitation as an opportunity for Halifax to meet

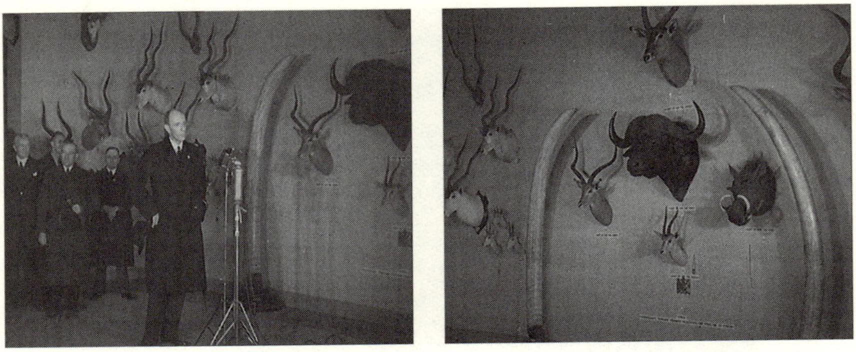

Halifax in Berlin.

informally with Hitler and to feel out his intentions in Europe. Halifax's meeting with Hitler at the Berghof, his Bavarian mountain retreat, had been well-publicized in the British press and amounted in hindsight to the first disastrous step in the process that would culminate with Chamberlain's concessions to Hitler in Munich. Going against the counsel of Anthony Eden, the foreign secretary he would soon replace, Halifax suggested to Hitler that, under the right circumstances, Britain would not resist an expansion of Germany's borders: "I said that there were no doubt other questions arising out of the Versailles settlement which seemed to us capable of causing trouble if they were mishandled, e.g. Danzig, Austria, Czechoslovakia. On all these matters we were not necessarily concerned to stand for the status quo as today, but we were concerned to avoid such treatment of them as would be likely to cause trouble. If reasonable settlements could be reached with the free assent and goodwill of those primarily concerned we certainly had no desire to block."[82] This, of course, was exactly what Hitler wanted to hear, and it helped to set in motion events that would lead to war.

Although there's much to say about Halifax's visit and its consequences, of interest here is its visual association with the 1937 hunting exhibition. Newsreel footage of Halifax's visit has him in front of a wall of mounted heads that made up the British corner of the exhibit; we see an antelope "shot by H. M. the Queen" alongside other grisly examples. What's more, the voiceover makes explicit links between the exhibition and Halifax's not-so-secret mission, calling the trip a show of "friendship for Germany" and pausing significantly to describe Halifax's passing look at a map of "Germany's lost colonies," a clear reference to the Sudetenland Crisis. The oddity of the footage and its clumsy yoking together of Halifax's taste for hunting and what would come to be seen as Britain's shame is striking and would likely have made an impression on Powell and Pressburger, who decorate Clive's study in a similarly sanguinary style; looking back from the film to the footage, it seems as if Halifax could have delivered his remarks from Clive's room, an association that invokes a connection between Clive's apparently harmless sense of sportsmanship and the misguided values that allowed Hitler to rise so quickly to power.

Such a connection between these images in 1937 and Powell and Pressburger's 1943 film might seem strained if it weren't for the fact that David Low, creator of the original Colonel Blimp character, had himself used the image of Halifax surrounded by mounted heads as the basis of a pointed caricature printed in the *Evening Standard* on November 19, 1937. Entitled "Nazi Hunting Exhibition," it shows a doddering Halifax arm-in-arm with Hitler in front of mounted heads labeled "Weimar," "Versailles," and "Locarno," suggesting that Hitler's choice of game included the governments and treaties that had stood and might continue to stand in his way. Next to those heads are three or more empty plaques, each about ominously to be filled with another treaty, another government, or, indeed, another country. Mussolini giggles in secret beneath a nearby chair while the British lion looks with appropriate anxiety at the wall's waiting vacancies. Powell and Pressburger gesture toward and add to Low's list in their second hunting sequence when the montage of appearing heads culminates in an otherwise inexplicable shot of a map of Munich, using a series of juxtapositions to suggest that the conference turned out indeed to be another of Hitler's

Nazi hunting exhibition.

trophies and that an English commitment to the logic of the hunt led in some inevitable and occult way to the disaster of appeasement and all that followed.

Taken together, the newsreel footage of Halifax in 1937, Low's caricature, and Clive's trophy room make a tacit case for a relation between a set of values—sportsmanship, fair play, and so on—and the folly of appeasement. They also suggest something important about the cultural limits of those values when they were brought face to face with Hitler and the threat of total war. One of the most awkward moments in Halifax's visit came when he tried to engage the dictator in a conversation about the hunting exhibition. The vegetarian Hitler, it turned out, hated hunting: "I can't see what there is in shooting; you go out armed with a highly perfected modern weapon and without risk to yourself kill a defenseless animal. Of course Göring tells me that the pleasure lies not in the killing, but in the comradely expedition in the open air. Very well. I merely reply: 'If that's the case, let's spare ourselves all bother and make a comradely expedition to a slaughter-house where in the greatest comradeship we can together kill a cow in the open air.'"[83] The moment was awkward because Hitler was a spoil-sport. Whereas Halifax was the consummate sportsman, seeking comradeship "in the open air," Hitler took the trouble to call the whole thing stupid, to reveal as foolish the rules that had organized the hunt and a whole way of life. Taken by itself, Hitler's distaste for hunting is a morbidly ironic bit of trivia; understood, as Low seems already to have done in 1937, as part of the failure of a larger civilizational project, it is rather indicative of a rejection of the rules of the game that Hitler represents. Having turned the defunct treaties of the past—Versailles and Locarno—into trophies, Hitler reveals himself as unbound by the traditional rules of the game, which in this case were embodied in the form of treaties that had ostensibly underwritten European political life. Dan Reiter writes: "In the 1930s, appeasers like Chamberlain put faith in the hope that a true settlement granting sufficient concessions to dissuade Hitler from going to war might be possible. Churchill vehemently disagreed. After Germany remilitarized the Rhineland in March 1936, in violation of the Versailles Treaty, Churchill remarked that 'Herr Hitler has torn up all the Treaties.'"[84] This is the difference that Low tried to capture in 1937 and that Powell and Pressburger sought to represent in 1943: the fragile, maybe false, but no less consequential difference between those who order life according to the rules of the game and those who deny the existence of rules altogether; as Lord Winster put it in "Stop Playing the Game!," a 1942 piece for the *Evening Standard*: "Hitler does not play bowls, he plays bombs."[85]

Colonel Blimp thus casts a paradox internal to the British experience of World War II as a historical opposition between two different kinds of war, the war that fully exhausted its violence when its self-consciously limited strategic and political goals were achieved and the war that found its strategic ends subordinate to violence as an end in itself, a war that could, however misguidedly, be thought of as some kind of game or gentlemanly adventure and a war that self-consciously suspended not only the rules of the game but also rules that had seemed to give a bourgeois European culture its coherence. Put differently, in working to represent a moment on the cusp of two opposed cultural responses to the idea and the practice of organized warfare, the film begins to make a complex case both for the difference between those two types of war and for the continuous violence that links them. The film both really acknowledges what circumstances made the Boer War and World Wars I and II different from one another and makes a quietly disturbing case that those differences might not survive scrutiny. In other words, where we might see the violence of total war as different in kind from other types of violence, Powell and Pressburger ask us to consider the possibility that violence—historical violence, original violence, human violence—does not change but instead finds different expressions in different wars; this is violence as a stable and recalcitrant content that is variously inflected by the different forms of war.

Sic Transit Candy

Colonel Blimp opens with a shot of an ersatz early modern tapestry, one Powell and Pressburger commissioned from the Royal College of Needlework; the image's details activate a number of broadly familiar, chivalric codes: a central courtly figure, a pastoral landscape, and a coat of arms. Instead, though, of an anonymous knight, the image features a tricked-out version of Low's familiar cartoon Blimp, sitting big-bellied and barefoot on a horse and lifting his lance proudly and ridiculously into the air. His coat of arms, buttressed on either side by Michael Powell's Irish Setters, features the paraphernalia of his class: mustaches, a cricket bat, a glass of port. The insertion of these wry and trivial modern touches into the chivalric context of the tapestry does a number of things. It anticipates the quixotic nature of Clive's commitment to the past as well as his doomed pursuit of his "feminine ideal," the Dulcinea who drifts through his life as Edith, Barbara, and then, at last, Angela or, as she calls herself, "Johnny." Its untimely mix of objects and styles is a compressed instance of the film's larger effort to represent both life and history as a series of distinct, overlapping, related, and sometimes discordant layers. And, as it suggests inevitable conflicts between past and present values, it also imagines the possibility that the

Et in arcadia ego.

history of European culture might best be understood as a continuous if serpentine line. Insofar as the film is, as I have suggested, concerned with the relation between the British past and a logic of total war that threatens to undo that past, the tapestry works both to suggest the long lifespan of courtly values in British and European life and another, darker story that calls those very values contrapuntally into question.

In evoking a specifically chivalric style, the tapestry suggests a set of more particular ideological connections between past and present; the image's mix of ritualized play and real violence—war planes fly over cricket and rugby fields, tanks roll on toward foxglove—suggests a complicated set of relations between violence and civilization. The tapestry's mix of natural imagery and modern violence offers in part a concentrated expression of a relation between war and pastoral that Kate McLoughlin takes as essential to some representations of war: "Intrusion and interaction, then, characterise the relationship between the bucolic and the bellicose. War is immanent in the rural, insofar as its sounds may penetrate the quietude at any moment, converting ready-made agricultural implements into weaponry. (The lurking land-mine is a perverted sort of immanence in the earth.) Erwin Panofsky, referring to Virgil, suggests that suffering creates a 'dissonance' in Arcady that must be 'resolved,' and yet it seems that such resolution is indefinitely deferred. Dissonance—the warlike—is ineradicable from Arcadia."[86] And just as William Empson famously cast the pastoral as a matter "of putting the complex into the simple," so can we see Powell and

Pressburger's tapestry as an effort to manage contradictions immanent to the experience of modern war, tensions that exist between the present and the past, play and violence, art and war.[87] Leo Mellor sees something similar at work in accounts of the wartime "greening" of bomb sites, in various efforts to capture the pastoral ambiguities of "implausibly lush zones in the midst of London . . . that resulted from incendiary and high-explosive bomb attacks."[88] One might look for yet another version of pastoral in the propaganda films of Empson's friend and sometimes collaborator, Humphrey Jennings. In more but mostly less motivated ways, his films *Words for Battle* (1941), *Listen to Britain* (1942), and *Fires Were Started* (1943) feature nearly identical shots of wind blowing through a tree's leaves—Jennings's related effort to capture the pagan and, perhaps, antinarrative energy of Empson's pastoral on film.

The tapestry thus embodies the difficult and dialectical cultural logic that Empson had sought to capture in *Some Versions of Pastoral* and that Elias describes in *The Civilizing Process,* where the "sociogenesis" of courtly life was tied to the long, slow rise of modern capitalism, the increasing economic integration of an increasingly diverse Europe, and thus the greater and greater need for individuals to control their apparently native impulses toward aggression and violence. For Elias, an innate human need for violence was both the root cause of and the single greatest threat to the civilizing process. As he later wrote in "The Breakdown of Civilization," what was maybe most disturbing about the violence unleashed by World War II was the fact that it stood as a practical repudiation of the idea of European culture as essentially progressive: "And in fact, people who as children had been brought up in the idea that their own, higher civilization was a part of their 'nature' or their 'race,' might very well have fallen into despair and been driven to the opposite extreme when, as adults, they noticed that this flattering belief was contradicted by events."[89]

The tapestry, in other words, presents us with a condensed version of a bind in *Colonel Blimp*: on the one hand, the image offers a neat emblem for the aesthetic repression of violence that Elias takes as essential to the civilizational development of a particular segment of European society; on the other hand, the image suggests that the civilizing process might contain within itself an immanent trace of its own destruction. Placing tanks and bombers in the midst of a pastoral representation of nature, chivalry, and play is to recall the terms of Panofsky's great 1936 essay, "'*Et in Arcadia Ego*': Poussin and the Elegic Tradition." However, whereas earlier versions of the phrase and its pictorial representation had pointed to the inevitability of death—"Even in Arcady I, Death, hold sway"—in *Colonel Blimp* the ineluctable presence of war's violence within the weave of the pastoral reveals rather the anxiety that, as opposed to an interruption in or an exception to a longer and progressive European history, war and violence are rather essential to human life at even its most civilized moments: even there, the tapestry seems to say, violence holds sway.

As opposed to presenting total war as something different in kind from an earlier type of combat, Powell and Pressburger's tapestry and film seem rather to suggest that the violence of total war was in fact always already there and that a return of a violence that had been repressed but neither mastered nor destroyed was more or less inevitable within European culture. Instead of a new violence, total war was a deferred but apparently inevitable expression of an "original violence" that Huizinga and Elias saw as the motive force for the development of European civilization in the first place.

> Things have now come to such a pass that the system of international law is no longer acknowledged, or observed, as the very basis of culture and civilized living. As soon as one member or more of a community of States virtually denies the binding character of international law and, either in practice or in theory, proclaims the interests and power of its own group—be it nation, party, class, church or whatsoever else—as the sole norm of its political behavior, not only does the last vestige of the immemorial play-spirit vanish but with it any claim to civilization at all. Society then sinks down to the level of the barbaric, and original violence retakes its ancient rights.[90]

That this encounter with the civilizational tenacity of violence is managed within an ersatz courtly tapestry is all the more important given the film's commitment to presenting its history of the twentieth century as a history of style. As the film moves through each of its three wars, it also shifts its use of cinematic technique, its soundtrack, its palate of colors, and its presentation of character. Moving from one act and one war to the next, the film's colors become more muted, its spaces deeper and more complex, and its performances increasingly naturalistic. The overall arc of the film from the beginning to the middle of the twentieth century is, in that case, cast in distinctly stylistic terms. After the film's opening in the future-present, its plot begins with the sharp contrasts and bright colors of 1902, moves through "the Khaki period" of World War I, to end back with a more or less recognizably realistic representation of 1942. In other words, the film seems to gesture from within toward a whole history of cinema, embedding in its own internal development a logic that moves us toward its lived present of cinematic style and total war.

There are a few ways to understand this. First, the film refers self-consciously to cinematic history (the technological difference between black-and-white and color) and, more specifically, to *The Wizard of Oz*'s (1939) shift from black-and-white to color in order to mark a passage from one to another world (they of course both return to and reverse this logic in *A Matter of Life and Death* [1946], where ordinary life on earth is presented in color and heaven appears in a silvery black and white); there are a number of direct references to *Oz* in *Colonel Blimp* (prior to his early attack, Spud jokes that he is off to see "the Wizard"—Candy's code name—"because of the wonderful things he's done").[91] Second, there's an effort here to specify a more determinate relationship between cinema, memory, and history. Powell and Pressburger write in the notes to their script that they rely on these stylistic shifts because, "Sights, sounds, but above all, colours, make up the memories of a generation: more so in the case of the period with which we have dealt. 1902 was the commencement of the Edwardian era, full of charm, prosperity, spaciousness and leisure, to which it seemed there could never be an end."[92] The past is represented differently both because it really looked different and because the film tries to register the feeling of that difference between past and present as something in itself.

Powell and Pressburger were pioneers in the use of Technicolor, and, as we can see from *Colonel Blimp*, their use of color extended well beyond its capacity for spectacle; rather, because they believed that memory was itself a play between vision, sound, and color, a Technicolor film would be able to reproduce the force of memory and thus living history in a way few other mediums could. Neil Rattigan writes that in *Colonel Blimp* color literally makes "the past glow."[93] We can see this at work in the film's middle "Khaki" section. After wandering through the wasteland of the front line, Clive enters a convent where he will once again encounter his romantic ideal, this time in the form of Barbara Wynne, a war nurse. The scene is striking because of how the red of the nurse's uniforms, particularly the red of their red crosses, leaps from the screen and threads a hint of ecstatic possibility through the drab weave of World War I; red seems in fact to have leapt from the film's first section into its second and to stage a hopeful confrontation between the stylized simplicity of 1902 and the horror of 1918. Color in this case is not simply a means of getting at the past; it is rather a way to hop ecstatically from one moment in time to another. It is, as Wordsworth says of his poetic "spots of time," "a renovating virtue," an untimely leap that brings the past into the present as something other than a memory. Indeed, the Technicolor prominence of those red crosses suggests another link between the film and a longer tradition of chivalry upon which it depends; Clive appears here as a weary Redcrosse Knight in search of his lady and just emerged from a scene of despair where "old stockes and stubs of trees,/Whereon nor fruit nor leafe was ever seene,/Did hang upon the ragged rocky knees."[94] An electric splash of red thus connects the past and present of Clive's life—it is a "renovating" short-circuit—while revealing a deeper connection between apparently incommensurate moments within English cultural history.

What's most important here is what Powell and Pressburger have to say about the stylistic, the cultural, and the political force of the past. *Colonel Blimp*'s version of 1902 is brightly colored and marked with high contrasts, brilliant golds, and deep reds; its sound is the sound of a waltz that seems never to end; and its characters sound exaggerated single notes, including the braying soldier, the crusty career diplomat, the university wag, the brassy old aunt, and the German stiff-neck. While 1902 was, of course, different from what came later, Powell and Pressburger present its differences strategically. Like the tapestry, the style of the film's first act seems to come not from "forty years ago" but rather from an entirely other age, an age described by Huizinga in *The Waning of the Middle Ages*: "To the world when it was half a thousand years younger, the outlines of all things seemed more clearly marked than to us. The contrast between suffering and joy, between adversity and happiness, appeared more striking."[95] The at once reduced and exaggerated palate of the film's first act—particularly when read in relation to the tapestry and the film's broad commitment to the residual virtues of chivalry, fair play, and cultural continuity—seems to evoke a set of values and images associated with an idea of the late Middle Ages that took on a special urgency between the wars and in the work of Huizinga, Elias, Marc Bloch, and others. In each of these cases, what was striking about the idea of the late Middle Ages was the fact that it seemed to have found a way not to avoid violence and aggression but rather to find managed forms—chivalry, games, more or less ordered forms of combat—in which to indulge or to express aggression while also minimizing its social consequence. Although undoubtedly a fantasy, the idea was that the late Middle Ages had found restricted, ritualized, and fragile social forms that let an earlier time have its violence without being completely consumed by its violence.

Colonel Blimp thus represents a more general interest in placing the present of total war in some kind of relation to a longer British and more broadly European history of war, violence, and society. As I will show in the next chapter, this is also an important aspect of Olivier's *Henry V* (1944), a film that offers a modern cinematic representation of an early modern theatrical performance of an earlier modern battle. Looking both at that film and at *Colonel Blimp*, we can see in the British cinema an effort to understand the violence of modern warfare in terms of a longer social history. We might, in other words, understand both films as part of a larger effort to represent the relations between past and present in terms both historical and ethical, an effort that Orson Welles associated with his own Vietnam-era take on the Henriad: "Even if the good old days never existed, the fact that we can conceive of such a world is, in fact, an affirmation of the human spirit. That the imagination of man is capable of creating the myth of a more open, more generous time is not a sign of our folly. Every country has its 'Merrie England,' a season of innocence, a dew-bright morning of the world. Shakespeare sings of that lost time in many of his plays, and Falstaff—that pot-ridden old rogue—is its perfect embodiment."[96] A turn back to an idealized late medieval or early modern past was common in the interwar and war years: "The unprecedented horrors of the Great War may have stimulated a reaction against romanticism among some interwar modernists, but it also imparted a renewed life to the moribund arts and crafts tradition: the war was critical to the transformation of nineteenth-century romantic medievalism into twentieth-century medieval modernism."[97] One can point to several important figures who saw a look back to the imagined *medievalism* of the later Middle Ages as necessary to understanding the violence of the twentieth century. To take just two figures I discuss in what follows, both Huizinga and Marc Bloch drew knowingly on an idea about the past in order to imagine a better future in the midst of the Nazi occupation: Huizinga died a prisoner after speaking out against the Nazis in 1942, and Bloch was tortured and shot as a member of the French Resistance in 1944.

Medievalism—not medieval—is the right word here: as opposed to a "real" Middle Ages, the figures I follow look back more or less self-consciously to the fantasy of a past (a "Merrie England") that might, in its symbolic difference from the present, suggest a better or at least more manageable future. Contrary to expectations, however, the difference they try to capture is not (or at least not entirely) the result of a conservative or nostalgic wish to get back to a time prior to the related depredations of capitalist rationality, social dislocation, and total war. It is rather an effort to imagine a time that might have differently managed its relation to its own beliefs, and as a result, somehow managed both to have and to contain its ineluctable aggression.[98] The fantasy of a late medieval or early modern past thus represents a historiographical as opposed to a historical ideal. Steven Justice writes, "The conceptual power of 'the middle ages' as a historiographical category, which originated in the contexts of philological and literary as well as religious polemic, derived from its success installing in the historiographical scheme a period of different, darker, historical subjectivity."[99] What characterizes the imaginary other subjectivity of the past for some of the figures I look at is its imaginative capacity to fit what it takes as a natural human proclivity for violence into a barely but nonetheless still adequate framework of forms, ritual, and play, a capacity that was, perhaps, possible in the cinema where it was no longer possible in present life.

We might in that case understand the resonant work of Huizinga, Elias, Olivier, Welles, *and* Powell and Pressburger as part a larger effort to represent the relations between past and present in terms both historical and ethical. Several of Powell and Pressburger's other films also fall within this tradition. *The Edge of the World* (1937), *I Know Where I'm Going!* (1945), and *A Canterbury Tale* (1944) each evoke an idealized past understood through forms of regional particularity in order both to identify what might be lost in war and to imagine what British culture could or should be like after the war.[100] A turn back to an idealized medievalism was indeed common in the interwar and war years. We might think of T. S. Eliot's *The Four Quartets* (1942), where he briefly adopts a cod Chaucerian style in order to contemplate the relation between past and present in the midst of total war, seeing in the image of "man and woman / In daunsinge, signifying matrimonie" a rough pastoral figure for a cyclical time shot through with a pedal tone of death and decay: "Feet rising and falling. / Eating and drinking. Dung and death."[101] We might think, too, of Virginia Woolf's *Between the Acts* (1941), which offers a long, fragmentary, and gently ironic verse history of "Merry England" presented as part of an amateur village pageant staged in the midst of war: "This is a pageant, all may see / Drawn from our island history / England am I."[102] In each of these cases, a renewed relation to an imaginary English past offered an alternative or contrapuntal history based—however naively—in what was pictured as the energetic, playful, childlike, and direct experience of the late Middle Ages.[103] Accounting for the interwar and wartime resurgence of the early modern pageant, Jed Esty writes, "The recovery of such forms marks an important departure from modernist primitivism; rather than model art (or life) on ethnographic data collected from the colonies, these English intellectuals increasingly sought inspiration in the island's own imagined past."[104] If the games, rituals, and beliefs attributed to the late Middle Ages could be imagined as the source for what was good about European culture—namely, that it had found a way to manage its innate taste for violence—then a return to those values might provide a way back from the more recent experience of culture's wane in the face of war.[105]

A Very Common Type of Girl

I have argued that we need to see the achievement of *Colonel Blimp* in a few related ways. First, we need to take seriously the idea that Powell and Pressburger saw their film as a contribution not only to the war effort in general but also as a specific argument about the necessity and the costs of total war. While the confrontation between Clive and Spud is indeed a choice between an outmoded, "Blimpish" type of English sportsmanship and Spud's new, effective, and necessary form of warfare, it also works to make us aware of what we risk as a result of that choice: a residual civilizational logic that Clive and Theo represent and that Elias, Huizinga, and others imagined as capable of managing or binding an essential human violence within the structure of ritual, chivalry, and play. In this way, Powell and Pressburger work to represent the paradox or dilemma that stood at the heart of the British experience of total war, the fact that English values would need to be suspended in order to protect and to preserve those same values, that "it takes a fascist to fight a fascist." Second, and in a way that connects *Colonel Blimp* with Powell and Pressburger's other films, it uses the presentation of historical difference in order both to reflect nostalgically on the passing of an age and to understand the nature of an original violence that underwrites all wars. Rather than seeing violence as an effect of this or that war, *Colonel Blimp* confronts a tendency toward violence that would seem to exist both before and beyond any particular war. What seems, in that case, to characterize total war is its especially unbound relation to a violence that earlier wars seemed somehow to manage within the twin contexts of international law and the ritualized violence of chivalric play. The film makes these arguments more at the level of form than of content; because reflections on the real and inevitable nature of violence would be difficult if not impossible to make in the midst of war, Powell and Pressburger use elements of film style—color, cinematography, different kinds of cut—to embody arguments that would be hard to make otherwise. Taken together, this is to propose that Powell and Pressburger use their film to develop a mode of immanent cinematic history suitable to the compressed and difficult experience of total war as well as to structural paradoxes that resulted from the idea of World War II as a war for national survival and an encounter with a national culpability that followed from Munich 1938. I want to turn now to another aspect of the film that both advances and complicates these related arguments, the strange love story that shadows and inflects Clive's lifelong experience of war.

As already mentioned, Clive's experience of his three wars trails three lost-and-found encounters with his romantic ideal, a woman (*the* woman) who appears first in the form of Edith Hunter, a governess he meets in Berlin who goes on to marry his friend Theo. Realizing only too late that he is also in love with Edith, Clive goes on in subsequent wars to meet women who are uncannily like Edith (the suffragette): first, the nurse Barbara, whom he marries, and, then, after Barbara's death, his young Auxiliary Territorial Service (ATS) driver, Angela. In order to underscore this effect of romantic repetition within historical difference, Powell and Pressburger cast Deborah Kerr in the role of each of the three women. As a result, her face, her voice, and her considerable charisma run under the film and its wars like a pessimistic and inexplicably held note; an updated version of Goethe's *Ewig-weibliche,* Kerr's women represent the degree to which Candy's life and personality are structured by the twinned reality and impossibility of desire. The romantic oddity of the device—Ian Christie calls it "aberrant"—is increased as a result of the frank notice that other characters take of it; Clive, after seeing Barbara for the first time, tells his man Murdoch about it:

> CANDY: Last night, Murdoch, I saw a girl—a nurse straight from England . . . I've never seen a more striking resemblance . . .
>
> MURDOCH: She must have been a very common type of girl, sir—the young lady in Berlin, I mean.
>
> CANDY: She was a most *un*common—what the devil d'you mean, Murdoch?
>
> MURDOCH: There was that girl in the film, sir. You remember, you went nine times. And there was that girl in the group out of the Bystander! We lost it in the Big Push. And there's . . .[106]

In a way that runs against his apparent simplicity of character, Clive's life has been organized not only by war but also around a series of encounters with representatives of an ideal that always finally escapes his grasp; as he puts it to Theo, "That's just it, I never did get over [losing Edith]. Theo, this may sound a damn silly thing to say to you but I never got over it. You may say she was my ideal—if you were some sort of sickening long-haired poet—all my life I've been looking for a girl like her—so now you know."[107]

Clive's doomed search after his ideal is, among other things, evidence of something surprisingly neurotic at the core of his otherwise blustery character, a "modern problem" that would appear to distance him from the stoic poise of the war hero or the one-dimensionality of Low's cartoon. Instead, like Freud's bourgeois patients or Matthew Arnold's modern portrait of

"I never got over it."

the antique Empedocles, Clive is sick with desire; as Arnold puts it, "What those who are familiar only with the great monuments of early Greek genius suppose to be its exclusive characteristics, have disappeared; the calm, the cheerfulness, the disinterested objectivity have disappeared: the dialogue of the mind with itself has commenced; modern problems have presented themselves; we hear already the doubts, we witness the discouragement, of Hamlet and of Faust."[108] This type of character was a preoccupation with Powell and Pressburger, one that begins with *Colonel Blimp*: after Clive there is Thomas Colpepper, the darkly obsessive "Glue Man" of *A Canterbury Tale* (1944); Peter Carter, the brain-damaged, hallucinating poet-hero of *A Matter of Life and Death* (1947); Sammy Rice, the brilliant, alcoholic, amputee scientist of *The Small Back Room* (1952); and even Mark Lewis, the murdering man-child of Powell's *Peeping Tom* (1960).

Clive's strongest connection is, perhaps, to the titular hero of *The Tales of Hoffman* (1951). The repeated appearance of Hoffman's ideal in one inaccessible form after the other—Olympia, Giulietta, and then Antonia—is at the opera's and the film's mysterious and tragic core. Although Powell and Pressburger chose to cast different actors in each of the three roles, Offenbach's opera comes, in fact, closer to *Colonel Blimp*, typically casting a single soprano in the roles of all three women. Like Clive, Hoffman is doomed to repeat, to meet and lose the same woman, to come close to his ideal only to lose it to death, destruction, and the equally real and thus insulting desires of others. In Offenbach this repeated encounter between the realized ideal and its final impossibility is tragic because it reveals a destructive tension between the human capacity to imagine an ideal and the human incapacity to realize that ideal: "Hoffmann, a benevolent, optimistic pilgrim of desire, endlessly searching for a self through love, through fulfilling relationships with women, is at every step held back by the disorientations of socially constructed images of femininity. Olympia, Giulietta, Antonia are at once the film's brilliant representations of his distorted fantasies and a vivid dramatization of its bleak conclusion about the impossibility of desire's ultimate fulfillment."[109] In each case, Powell and Pressbuger's characters are both motivated and undone by a phantasmic encounter with, desire for, and loss of an impossible ideal. They are all, in other words, neurotics in a precise psychoanalytic sense. Instead of seeing Clive as exceptional or pathological, though we should understand how this quality situates him exactly within the culture that raised him, a culture that Freud understood as essentially neurotic and that was in danger of passing away with the onset of total war: "If the development of civilization has such a far-reaching similarity to the development of the individual and if it employs the same methods, may we not be justified in reaching the diagnosis that, under the influence of cultural urges, some civilizations, or some epochs of civilization—possibly the whole of mankind—have become 'neurotic'?"[110] As I have argued, the games, rules, and rituals that Clive holds dear are all aspects of a civilizational imperative that Freud, Huizinga, and Elias associate with a particular moment in European culture, with a long civilizing process that has been rendered obsolete by the onrush of later modernity and total war. What is at stake in *Colonel Blimp* is not only the quality of that neurotic character but also the possibility that with the onset and experience of total war something even more modern and more terrifying has come into being, an unbound and untroubled relation to desire and aggression that, insofar as it bypasses the civilizing force of repression, can qualify only as psychotic.

It Is Definitely Better

Clive's unexpected emergence as a obsessional neurotic or, better, as what Friedrich Schiller would call a *sentimental* as opposed to *naive* hero in Faust or Hamlet's modern mold is, in fact, where the film's two levels come together, where his status both as an increasingly out-of-touch old warrior and as a courtly lover searching, forever searching after his ideal inform one another.[111] In other words, Clive's neurotic search after his ideal is a part of the larger cultural imperative that he represents. His chivalric bearing, his Quixotic yearning, his broken faith that the rules of the game can limit the damage of war—all are aspects of the same bourgeois (or, one might say, the same neurotic) culture that produced Clive in the first place. The neurotic, we know, depends on repression. It is because the individual represses antisocial (but not immoral) desires—both sexual desire and the desire for violence—that the unconscious is formed and the psyche needs to manage itself via the meaningful production of symptoms. To be neurotic, in that case, is to be part of a culture that accepts limits on personal happiness in the service of a stable society. Put differently, seemingly incommensurate aspects of Clive's character—his gentleman's aggression, his sportsmanship, his romanticism, his bullheadedness, his tenderness—are all, in fact, characteristics that make sense within the terms of a culture structured around a sense of play as a more or less incomplete form of repression. *The Life and Death of Colonel Blimp* might be said to be tragic because it brings its main character into contact both with the civilizational ideal he represents and the limits of that ideal. Put differently, the "aberrance" of Clive's doomed relation to his desire is a critical aberrance. Powell and Pressburger insert a neurotic excess or difference or eccentricity into the flatly epic figure of

David Low's Blimp; flatly epic is, indeed, a good way to characterize one bathetic aspect of the tapestry I discussed earlier. As a result, they point to the ideological impoverishment of a view of history and life that would flatten its particularity, or eccentricity, into mere ideology or formalism. Another way to see Clive's romantic longing is as an effect of his own sharp sense of the present's relation to the past.

Clive's attempt and indeed his need to connect 1942 to 1902 as linked "spots of time" is reflected in the museum-like quality of the room where he keeps both his animal heads and the picture of his dead wife Barbara. When asked by Theo why he has the picture next to his trophies, he says: "She wanted it. I call this my Den, you know. She knew I always used to come back here, we had a joke about it—all my stuff is here. It would be an awful gap without her."[112] In addition to its place as a figure for the related kinds of violence I described above, Clive's Den is also a kind of memory palace, a space that links the past materially to the present via a network of more and less related objects. In this way it both stands in for the film's larger historiographical project, its effort to link the past and present, and offers proof of the critical nature of a residually neurotic relation to war. Like some of Freud's most famous patients, Clive "suffers mainly from reminiscences," and it is his relation to the past that, in spite of the real necessity of total war, holds out some hope for civilization's future. This is the main difference between Spud and Clive. Spud has repudiated the past and future in the service of winning a war in the present. That, I think, is what "brute force and ruddy ignorance" means: that in a war like World War II, in a war for national survival, one needs to bracket the past, to forget both how we got into war and the sources of ambivalence that might dissuade us from fighting. This is why the film recognizes the real and pressing need for Spud and his way of war. That said, if the film knows that we *need* men like Spud, it *loves* Clive Candy because of the courtly, civilized, and obsolete values he represents; what's more, it *wants* him for what he and his searching, romantic, and neurotic desire represent: a future, the promise of which keeps us going in spite of all that is terrible and pressing about the present.

What Spud and his New Model Army represent isn't in that case just another phase in the story of culture, but rather the bad negation of both culture and history. Insofar as Spud embraces violence and rejects the structuring order of the war game, he represents a denial of the limits that allowed people like Clive to channel their aggression—however incompletely—into forms of prosocial (or at least mostly non-antisocial) behavior. The film makes the case that Spud can embrace this attitude precisely because he doesn't care about the past, because he has no idea what

Clive's den.

things were like "forty years ago." His methods are, as he says, "Nazi methods" because he denies—as Hitler denied before him—the past as well as the limiting, structuring force of its treaties, games, and rules. Without the game, which is to say without repression, Spud frees himself to have his full pleasure, to indulge his aggression, and to live out the asocial *jouissance* of the psychopath. William Plomer, writing with greater menace, made this side of Powell and Pressburger's case even more directly: "Blimps who persist in being Blimps will perish, if they have not done so already; they are simply not built to compete, as we must, with Nazi energy, cunning and power of organization."[113] And, because his unproblematic embrace of his own aggression is a structural condition that he shares with his war—a total war that denies the difference between things—he *fits* into this war culture in a way that the neurotic Clive could never fit in with his world; not fitting is, after all, what it means to be neurotic. In other words, the shared structural conditions of the psychopath and psychopathic war lead back—although in the style of a nightmare—to the full promise of epic as imagined by Lukács at the outset of *The Theory of the Novel*, a social world in which there is no dissonance or difference between world and self; Paul Saint-Amour paraphrases this view of modern epic as "the genre of organic national holism galvanized by war."[114] Clive's aberrant, neurotic, and tragic, obsession stands as a critical and residual response to the psychopathic monoculture of total war.

Neil Rattigan argues that Spud's disregard for the rules is evidence of an underlying and maybe unconscious argument about class resentment in *Colonel Blimp*: "[I]t is his lower-class background that provides him with the perception that rules do not count in total war. A disrespect or simply ignorance of the need to observe the decencies—the rules of war, of social behavior—delineates Wilson as lower class."[115] Read in this way, Spud's aggression is more a structural effect of an antiquated socioeconomic system than a response to the particular conditions of total war. Spud's rise is, however, not simply the story of a single delinquent, the "angry young men" of postwar films such as *The Loneliness of the Long Distance Runner* (1962) or *This Sporting Life* (1963). Spud's rejection of a game, of a repression, of a civilization that relied, however unhappily, on the neurotic's ability to translate desire into obsession is rather a version in miniature of the logical consequences internal to the concept of total war. In other words, *Colonel Blimp* is interested in how a seemingly necessary and total military strategy could also become a total way of life, a way of life that, because it denies and forgets that the historical and ontological differences on which European society had depended (past and present, war and politics, soldier and civilian, front and home front) demands the destruction of that other society and maybe society as such.

One can see this effort to capture an old and endangered particularity in the film's representation of a gentlemen's dinner party Clive throws immediately after World War I. Having invited Theo, just released from a POW camp and on his way back to Germany, Clive goes around the table introducing each of his other guests: "Colonel Hopwell, aide to the Governor of Gibraltar—Sir William Rendall, on the Viceroy's staff—George Metcalf of Uganda—Sir John Bembridge, just back from Jamaica—Colonel Mannering, known to the press as the uncrowned king of Southern Arabia—Mr. Christopher Wynne, of Bradford, England, my father-in-law. Embodiment of all the solid virtues."[116] As Clive makes his introductions, overwhelming both Theo and his audience with names and titles, the camera lingers closely on each aged figure, working and waiting in every case to capture the specificity and, more, the hardening, expressive eccentricity of the individual face; some have mustaches, some are clean-shaven, some have small beards; two sport monocles and one has a small bandage on his forehead; another, a slightly shaggy dandy, wears a red rose on his lapel. The care with which the film registers the look and, more to the point, the character of each of these faces seems gratuitous because, although we have met two or three of them before, these are men we will never meet again; they are, despite this careful level of visual scrutiny, mostly the most minor of characters.

The dinner party.

That, however, is the point; held at the end of an epoch, Clive's dinner party represents the last gasp of a culture of particularity on the verge of being overrun by the totalizing logic of total war. Of course, the colonial pedigree of so many of these men points, as I also suggested in the introduction, in another direction as well, toward the role that eccentricity and particularity played in and against the fact of empire. Casting "the uncrowned king of Southern Arabia" as a more or less lovable because embodied individual, Powell and Pressburger call canny attention to the play between what I refer to in the introduction as official and unofficial modes of eccentricity; at the same time that these faces assert the specificity of the British character as a value worth defending, they also reveal the degree to which eccentricity had also to be seen as an ideological answer to a larger and, as Orwell and others saw, damaging proximity between totalitarianism and empire. The dinner party is thus another example of wartime cinema's late style, as a form of aesthetic eccentricity or stylistic excess that reveals contradictions structurally immanent to the British experience of total war. The loving care with which Powell and Pressburger attend to these aging faces alerts us to the fact that they represent both a set of values that the film holds dear and a political impasse that needs to be overcome in order to fight and to win the war. Cinematic eccentricity and particularity are thus posed paradoxically as values that need to be suspended in order to be preserved.

This all brings us back to the beginning, to the cut that is not a cut. As I argued earlier, key moments in *Colonel Blimp* use tracking shots to suggest movement in time or space where we might otherwise expect cuts. This use of a single, fluid shot where we might look for montage is important because it suggests two related but different arguments about the film's relation to war. On the one hand, that one of these moments occurs at the climax of a duel, and because the film tacitly but consciously associates the duel with ideas and values connected with Clausewitzian, limited war, they would seem to seek to embody the logic of total war, a war that looks strategically to erase differences (cuts) between categories that older forms of war worked to maintain (differences between war and politics, soldier and civilian, front and home front, etc.). On the other hand, the fact that cuts are at both moments so obviously, so spectacularly absent suggests an attempt to make us feel, mourn, and, perhaps, reverse the drift away from an earlier model of war's limited as opposed to total relation to life. We are now in a position to expand on this difference. The difference between the cut and the no-cut is not only the difference between limited and total war; it is also the difference between a society built on games, on the belief that a magic circle could be drawn around violence so as both to release and to manage it, and a society that would reject the game and the compromise it offers as decadent, silly or weak.

Insofar as the cut is also a figure for the production of a lack that helps to organize the psychic life of the neurotic—it is the Oedipalizing cut of castration that makes one unhappy, social, and analyzable all at once—its absence would suggest something like the antisocial complacency of the psychopath. That is to say, finally, that the film's two key representatives, Clive and Spud, are also figures for the larger social difference between the cut and the not-cut.[117] Clive takes on the obsessional neurotic's impossible and courtly responsibility to lay hold of the object of desire, a quest that takes the happily unhappy form of good sportsmanship, fair play, and true love; when asked by the exquisite Colonel Borg, referee of the duel and Swedish military attaché in Berlin, whether he would like to roll up his sword arm's sleeve or to cut it, Clive opts to cut: "It is definitely better," replies the Colonel. Spud, however, embraces torture, murder, and rape without self-consciousness—without conscience—in the service of a war that is psychotic because it must reshape the world in its image.

This, at last, is what *The Life and Death of Colonel Blimp* is about. It is about the confrontation between an ideal—both an ideal woman and an ideal if flawed or only imaginary European civilization—and that ideal's real and inevitable ethical limits. At the same time that Powell and Pressburger work in good faith to support a war that they understood as necessary, so do they encode in their film a set of thematic and formal moments that stand not as a criticism of the British effort against the Nazis, but rather as a tacit meditation on the nature and the violence of war. This is what makes *Colonel Blimp* an authentic example of a really and oxymoronically democratic propaganda, a propaganda that could both persuade an audience to face hard truths about modern war and to reflect critically and intelligently on the violence, the waste, and the shame of war. The life, the culture, the play, and the repression that Clive Candy represents worked because they were fragile, tenuous, ultimately insufficient, and maybe only imaginary ways of managing a more "original violence." Because, however, *Colonel Blimp* shows us that violence, shows us the systems that seemed once to hold that violence in check, and, finally, shows us what the world could look like when those systems are simply abandoned, it demands that we both confront that violence directly and at least imagine what other system, what other world could or should take their place.

2 Pistol's Two Bodies

Henry V at War

I have without good help danced myself out of the world.
—Will Kemp, *Kemp's Nine Days' Wonder* (1600)

Falstaff: Banish plump Jack, and banish all the world!
Prince: I do. I will.
—William Shakespeare, *The First Part of King Henry the Fourth* (1598)

No one needs to ask what Laurence Olivier's *Henry V* (1944) is all about. Whereas *The Life and Death of Colonel Blimp* seemed to have too much to say about its war, *Henry V* was immediately taken as successful and straightforward wartime entertainment. One of the most celebrated British films of the forties, *Henry V* satisfied audiences, critics, and even the prime minister because it appeared to suspend elegantly the difference between art and propaganda, between Britain's long cultural history and its present experience of total war. Whereas *Colonel Blimp* seemed self-conscious, eccentric, or odd, *Henry V* just worked, giving the home front exactly what it seemed to want. That said, *Henry V* and *Colonel Blimp* continue to invite comparison and not simply because Olivier was Powell and Pressburger's first choice to play Clive Candy. The films are both Technicolor spectacles, big productions that draw on early modern styles in order to evoke a simpler and more unified Britain; *Colonel Blimp*'s initial reliance on the look and style of a medieval tapestry returns in the self-consciously flat middle sections of *Henry V*, which Olivier modeled after the early fifteenth-century miniatures of the Limbourg brothers. Both films track the development of a protagonist from youth to maturity; where Clive makes his way from hotheaded youth to Blimpish maturity, the wise and sober King Henry is, as everyone knows, what a young and wild Prince Hal looks like all grown up and oats sown. Both films employ three-tiered narrative structures in order to manage their respective representations of history; *Colonel Blimp* creates a fantastic and visually varied palimpsest out of 1942, 1918, and 1902, and *Henry V* offers a 1944 cinematic representation of a 1600 theatrical representation of a 1415 battle in three stylistically distinct and nested acts.

However, whereas *Colonel Blimp* faltered under the weight of its outsized complexity, Olivier's *Henry V* was a critical because gently ideological triumph. James Agee wrote at the time:

> Poem and film link the great past to the great present. It is unlikely that anything on the subject has been written to excel Shakespeare's short study, in *Henry V*, of men stranded on the verge of death and disaster. The man who made this movie made it midway in England's most terrible war, within the shadows of Dunkirk. In appearance and in most of what they say, the three soldiers with whom Henry talks on the eve of Agincourt might just as well be soldiers of World War II. No film of that war has yet said what they say so honestly or so well.[1]

The past and the present, old wars and new wars, soldiers on the fields of Agincourt and in "the shadows of Dunkirk": whereas *Colonel Blimp* widened the gulf between an imagined British past and the real present of modern war, *Henry V* seemed—at least to the American Agee—to bring past and present fully and evocatively together. Whereas Powell and Pressburger's film revealed fissures and contradictions within both modern British identity and the concept of total war, Olivier's film seemed rather to clarify things, to know the difference between heroes and villains, and to cut through ethical fog of modern war. *Henry V* also did much—however obliquely—to imagine life after wartime. Whereas films like *The Lion Has Wings* (1939), *Contraband* (1940), *49th Parallel* (1941), and *Colonel Blimp* thought from within the thick of things about why and how we fight, *Henry V* appeared when victory seemed more or less certain; it was indeed a film less of Dunkirk than of D-Day. What, it thus asked, should life be like after the violence, the social dislocations, and the real social *promise* of the war? What would happen when the warriors returned home?

Henry V approaches these ideas in different ways: it tries to see war as a sane experience that, after and against the hardened and maybe psychotic realpolitik of *Colonel Blimp*'s New Model Army, could work alongside traditional English virtues; its light handling of relations between different British ethnicities—Scottish, Welsh, and, to a lesser degree, Irish—supported other attempts both to contain and to transcend regional and socioeconomic particularity; and its awkward comic coda, featuring the light but forced banter between Henry and his French fiancé, Princess Katherine, both raised key questions about the wartime and postwar experience of sex and gender and proleptically embodied a generic transition from the violent and uncertain middle space of history to the closural and thus conservative compensations of comedy.[2] The critic Vincent Canby put matters simply: "Olivier's *Henry V* is a splendid film that is also splendid propaganda."[3]

That said, the film has had its detractors. While Agee saw the film as an honest and stirring confirmation of values that underwrote Britain's conduct during the war, as truly good, which is to say ethical, propaganda, some later viewers have had a harder time accepting Olivier's implicit view of the war, his apparently conservative hopes for British society, and what can seem like a baldly patriotic reading of Shakespeare's play. For Martin Buzacott, Oliver is "the theatrical (and more successful) General Alexander Haig," working in "a political and theatrical environment where truth is a casualty of credibility and rhetoric overcomes the limitations and contradictions of reality."[4] Graham Holderness argues that the film can't sustain its initially critical analysis of war and at last accepts the ideological romance of the good fight: "The illusions of naturalism and of conventional theatre have succeeded in dominating the imagination: and through those illusions the film's ideological integrity is reasserted."[5] Norman Rabkin writes that Olivier's film "prettied up" Shakespeare's ethically opaque play, reducing its essential ambivalence about war to a single, jingoistic slogan: "God for Harry, England, and Saint George!"[6] Alan Stone argues that "Olivier's *Henry V* shows us a children's make-believe war." For Stone, writing in 2005, the example of Kenneth Branagh's grittier, post-Falklands version coupled with the then fresh disaster of the Iraq War made it hard to take Olivier's bucolic vision of war seriously; whereas Branagh and Shakespeare showed war as it was, Olivier offered disingenuous fairy tales.[7] For viewers like Buzacott, Stone, Rabkin, and Holderness, the film fails because its need to make a particular case about and for a particular war overpowers its ability to do justice to the larger ethical and historical complexities of Shakespeare's play. Whereas Agee and Canby saw the film as an inspired instance of what the Ministry of Information wanted from its strained and, as I have argued, avowedly oxymoronic ideal of a "democratic propaganda," these writers see it as ideologically reductive: it was propaganda pure and simple.

Depending on whom you ask, Olivier's *Henry V* is thus either a great and honest film about war or the worst kind of cinematic warmongering. As it turns out, versions of this disagreement have characterized the reception of Shakespeare's play since it first appeared. Based on the historical events that surround them, interpretations of the play drift back and forth between celebrations of its patriotism, condemnations of its bellicosity, and appreciations of its ironic ambivalence. To begin at the beginning, Shakespeare's first audiences would have been reminded—perhaps favorably—of the Earl of Essex, Robert Devereux's doomed campaign to suppress Irish rebellion: "The period of the play's composition must have coincided almost exactly with a period of great national enthusiasm for an expansionist military adventure, led by a young, flamboyant, and popular general."[8] Seen in that light, *Henry V* looks like war propaganda *ab ovo*; seen, however, in relation either to a public ambivalence about the Irish campaign that Joel Altman has described or, more obviously, to the 1601 execution of the then disgraced hero Essex, the play looks quite different.[9] Later, in 1817 and the wake of Waterloo, William Hazlitt saw Shakespeare's young king in terms of his abuse of the throne: "Because he did not know how to exercise the enormous power, which had just dropped into his hands, to any good purpose, he immediately undertook (a cheap and obvious resource of sovereignty) to do all the mischief he could."[10] In 1859, however, Charles Kean staged *Henry V* as a patriotic spectacle designed to mitigate the psychological effects of the Crimean War; while "the general feeling of the present day may be opposed to the evils of war," Kean wrote in his production notes, "there are few amongst us who can be reminded of the military renown achieved by our ancestors on the fields of Crecy, Poitiers, and Agincourt, without a glow of patriotic enthusiasm."[11] In 1919 and the immediate wake of another war, Gerald Gould wrote: "None of Shakespeare's plays is so persistently misunderstood as *Henry V*, and one is tempted to think that there is no play which is more important to understand. . . . The play is ironic: that is, I venture to think, a fact susceptible to detailed proof."[12] Gould's proof of the play's essential irony was, of course, to be found as much on the fields of Ypres, Verdun, and the Somme as in the play itself, a fact that anticipates Paul Fussell's great argument about war and the invention of modernist irony in *The Great War and Modern Memory*. These are only a few examples of responses that can't help but tack between the play's two apparent and apparently immanent and inevitable extremes in order to meet the specific needs of their own times. It seems that every war will look for and find its own *Henry V*.

In the face of this vacillation, recent critics have sought to read the play as essentially doubled, as stretched between the poles of irony and sincerity, patriotism and critique, subversion and containment. In his 1977 essay, "Rabbits, Ducks, and *Henry V*," Norman Rabkin argues that, like Wittgenstein's famous gestalt figure that can look like either a rabbit or a duck but not both at once, *Henry V* is defined by two available but incommensurate interpretations, the "rabbit" of heroism, leadership, and the proper consolidation of kingly authority and the "duck" of jingoism, political opportunism, and unjust war: "I want to show that *Henry V* is brilliantly capable of being read, fully and subtly, as each of the two parts of *Henry IV* has respectively anticipated. Leaving the theatre at the end of the first performance, some members of the audience knew that they had seen a rabbit, others a duck. Still others, and I would suggest that they were Shakespeare's best audience, knew terrifyingly that they did not know what to think."[13] Building explicitly on Rabkin's analysis, C. L. Barber states, "We are either with him or against him, depending on whether or not *we* supply the dissenting or qualifying perspective."[14] Claire McEachern writes: "These two sides—the inspiring and the calculating—constitute the double face of Henry, but it is a duality that does not so much discredit his rulership as render it all the more compelling. He is both righteous and ruthless, glorious and repellent, and the combination serves to make him both difficult to grasp and a king for every moment."[15] For these critics, the play functions as a sort of inkblot, a test that allows different periods to see their own implicit assumptions about, hopes for, and fears of war reflected back at them.

Within this context, Rabkin takes Olivier's film as a more or less crass attempt to steer an exhausted wartime audience toward a possibly therapeutic but nonetheless limited reading of the play: "To be sure, Olivier's camera and Walton's music prettied up the atmosphere, transporting their war-weary audience to the fairy tale world of the Duc de Berry."[16] Instead of showing audiences an irony that they needed to see, Olivier gave them what they wanted to see, a piece of make-believe that reduced war to something that could, in the end, make ethical sense. Olivier's film, I maintain, is also less straightforward than either its critics or its admirers have suggested; in fact, it uses resources specific to cinematic style to confront both the rabbit and the duck of British political feeling during World War II. More to the point, Olivier's cinematic management of Shakespeare's play and, in particular, a structural relation between the heroic protagonist, Henry, and the minor comic grotesque, Ancient Pistol, helps to foreground a characterological ambivalence about war that shadows but does not at last undo Olivier's commitment to the war as he found it. This complex and searching play of light and shadow makes *Henry V* an instance of "democratic propaganda," which is to say a film that can imagine the real necessity of a war while nonetheless confronting the intractability of its political, aesthetic, and ethical contradictions. Put differently, rather than seeing Shakespeare's play as a sterile or merely formal opposition between terms, Olivier uses, I maintain, its fundamental ambivalence to capture a necessary, practical, and strategic suspension that conditioned the British experience of war;

this is the larger ambivalence or contradiction embodied by the phrase, "it takes a fascist to fight a fascist." Olivier's film thus manages to capture a felt ambivalence, a strategic contradiction that helped however tenuously to give shape to the British experience of total mobilization and total war. Looking to the real historical force of that enabling contradiction, we will be able to say of Olivier's film what Rabkin says of Shakespeare's play: "The inscrutability of *Henry V* is the inscrutability of history."[17]

Mobilizing Shakespeare

Olivier's film was of course just one part of a large and unsystematic wartime effort to use Shakespeare to connect the violence of the present with the experience of the past. Churchill made frequent reference to Shakespeare and to *Henry V* throughout the war and "was moved to ecstasies by a screening of Laurence Olivier's [film] not least because he was in no doubt about who was playing the king's part in England's comparable mid-twentieth-century epic."[18] In Powell and Pressburger's *The Volunteer* (1944), Ralph Richardson—playing himself—begins his story of the war reminiscing about how an announcement of the 1939 Nazi invasion of Poland abruptly ended his production of *Othello*, a turn of events that puts Shakespeare at the start and center of Britain's war (Ernst Lubitsch's *To Be or Not to Be* [1942] begins similarly, as the Nazi invasion of Poland brings a Warsaw production of *Hamlet* to a sudden halt). David Lean's *This Happy Breed* (1944), a film about a salt-of-the-earth family making its way between the wars, takes its title from *Richard II*:

> This royal throne of kings, this sceptred isle,
> This earth of majesty, this seat of Mars,
> This other Eden, demi-paradise,
> This fortress built by Nature for herself
> Against infection and the hand of war,
> This happy breed of men, this little world,
> This precious stone set in the silver sea,
> Which serves it in the office of a wall
> Or as a moat defensive to a house,
> Against the envy of less happier lands,—
> This blessed plot, this earth, this realm, this England.[19]

The critic G. Wilson Knight took the title of his strange Shakespearean pageant, *This Sceptred Isle: Shakespeare's Message for England at War* (1940), from the same speech; mixing dramatic recitation and ideologically driven analysis, Knight stitched together bits and pieces of Shakespeare's text into a proleptic and patriotic response to the pressures of modern total war. Harder to pin down but no less suggestive was "Operation HK," a secret plan to move the British government to Stratford-upon-Avon in case of an invasion. Simon Barker speculates that someone in some office might have hoped that Hitler's well-known love for Shakespeare would prevent the city from being bombed; and, indeed, unlike London, Coventry, or Canterbury, Stratford made it through the war unscathed.[20] Olivier himself wrote: "Looking back, I don't think we could have won the war without 'Once more unto the breach . . .' somewhere in our soldiers' hearts."[21]

Scholarly readings of the Henriad also became more prominent and pointed during the war. After the spectacle of *This Sceptered Isle*, Knight published a short book, *The Olive and the Sword* (1944), in which he argued that Shakespeare's plays both embodied English values under threat and somehow predicted England's ultimate preservation of those values: "We need no Messiah, but we might, at this hour, turn to Shakespeare, a national prophet if ever there was one, concerned deeply with the royal soul of England."[22] Knight's reading of *Henry V* is straightforwardly appreciative: "You can see how carefully Shakespeare is laboring to create in Henry a blend of Christian faith and martial heroism."[23] The book takes pains to account for and to motivate one of the most uncomfortable aspects of the Henriad: Henry's brutal rejection of his friend and mentor Falstaff at the end of the second part of *Henry IV*. Henry needed Falstaff, Knight suggests, because Falstaff helped him to understand something natural and true about the English character; he also needed ultimately to reject Falstaff because what he represented had no place in war:

> It is, I think a supreme stroke of Shakespeare to have apprenticed his hero-to-be, Henry V, to such a tutor as Falstaff: because within the very essence of the national temperament exists not only a sense of humor but a closely allied and deeply satiric sense of the futility of military ambition, as an end in itself: "There's honor for you." The more continental and Fascist Hotspur . . . seems trivial by comparison; though of course Hal must eventually prove himself the better soldier. This, too, has before now happened with Great Britain, as a nation.[24]

Knight is explicit here: just as Henry somehow saves Falstaff and the values he represents in the very act of rejecting Falstaff, so does Britain need to suspend certain of its characteristic values (broad-mindedness, irony, fair play) so that those values might ultimately be saved. This, as we saw in the case of *Colonel Blimp*, is the paradox of total war: faced with its possible destruction, a culture must be suspended so that a culture might be saved.

The tension felt in Knight between national security understood as a non-negotiable value and Falstaff's wonderful freedom of expression, his willingness to speak difficult and unpatriotic truths about war in the midst of war, indeed recalled in more specific terms debates about propaganda, censorship, free expression and freedom of the press, and totalitarianism that had occupied British thinking since the passage of the Emergency Powers (Defence) Acts of 1939 and 1940. According to Mark Donnelly: "[The act of 1940] gave the state sweeping powers to do whatever it believed was necessary for the war effort. Internal security requirements and the material demand of war obviously meant an enhanced role for the state, but it should be acknowledged none the less that an immediate corollary of this was an erosion of civil liberties."[25] Cutting to the chase, Marina MacKay writes that the act of 1940 "turned Britain into a totalitarian state."[26] Donnelly continues: "There was no question that the government had a duty to prevent the leakage of information to the enemy which might be of military value. The problem lay in interpreting this duty and defining the circumstances in which censorship could be justified, not least because of the way in which Britain's war effort came to be portrayed as a defense of democratic values against totalitarianism."[27] This tension between the liberty and censorship or democracy and totalitarianism was thus a pressing and obvious political problem from the war's beginning. For instance, I've already quoted Churchill as he acknowledged on September 3, 1939, that it might "seem a paradox that a war undertaken in the name of liberty and right should require, as a necessary part of its processes, the surrender for some time of so many of the dearly valued liberties and rights."[28] And on September 31, 1940, another member of the House wondered aloud if the Emergency Powers Act wouldn't put the government in a "position by no means inferior, as regards the scope of powers over newspapers, to that occupied by the distinguished Dr. Goebbels in Germany."[29]

When, in that case, Knight and others returned to the conflict between Henry—a surrogate for martial law, moral hygiene, and national security—and "Plump Jack" Falstaff, a character best defined by his willingness ironically and excessively to utter and embody truths that went against the grain of those official values, they managed to find in Shakespeare the terms of a fraught and current debate about the practical demands of total war. It is indeed in just these terms that J. Dover Wilson's *The Fortunes of Falstaff* (1943) worked to deflate the romantic myth of Falstaff embraced by earlier critics like William Hazlitt, Maurice Morgann, and A. C. Bradley: "It is they, and not Shakespeare, who have been swept off their feet by Falstaff. Bewitched by the old rascal, they have contracted the disease of not listening to the play, even the malady of not marking all the actions he himself performs. No modern critic, as far as I know, has ever been to the trouble of furnishing a straightforward account either of the main features of Falstaff's character or of what actually takes place in the comic under-plot; they have been too busy expressing their own sense of enjoyment and emancipation."[30] Wilson celebrates the young king as "English Harry, in whose person Shakespeare crowns noblesse oblige, generosity and magnanimity, respect for law, and the selfless devotion to duty which comprise the traditional ideals of our public service."[31] Although there must remain a place for the "bliss of freedom" that Falstaff represents, the plays also reveal the need sometimes to limit that bliss in the name of security, a need once again revealed by contemporary "scenes on the battlefield before [the eyes] of the modern soldier, or bombs in the streets of London."[32] For both Knight and Wilson, the war helped to uncover what Hazlitt and Bradley had selfishly overlooked: the fact of an essentially Shakespearean, which is to say essentially English, commitment to security at the possible expense of liberty.

The World Picture at War

This focus on security and liberty is also an aspect of a pair of more considerable and influential wartime works, E. M. W. Tillyard's *The Elizabethan World Picture* and his *Shakespeare's History Plays* (first published in 1942 and 1944, respectively), books that offer an account of a highly structured belief system—a "world picture"—that Tillyard takes as characteristic of the Elizabethan frame of mind and that critics sometimes link directly to the look and themes of Olivier's film. Graham Holderness is most explicit about Olivier's at least ambient debt to Tillyard. He argues that, in identifying order and security as central Elizabethan and thus preeminently English values, Tillyard made possible a "remarkable logical slide from a description of Renaissance ideology to the celebration of an apparently immutable social and cultural entity called 'England.' . . . Without making any explicit acknowledgement of the fact that England of the Second World War is as much an object of address as that of the sixteenth century, Tillyard invokes and affirms values which were being assiduously—and much more openly—cultivated in the culture as a whole."[33] Although he admits that Olivier's film is initially more complex, Holderness nonetheless sees Olivier as part of this larger ideological project: "The critical exigencies of the contemporary situation pull the film . . . into complicity with the ideologies of patriotism, war enthusiasm, and national unity."[34]

While Holderness's sense that Tillyard and Olivier share points of reference is certainly right, it is not the case that Tillyard makes no "explicit acknowledgment" of his work's dual historical address. Indeed, Tillyard makes the link between the distant political contexts of Elizabethan England and twentieth-century Britain as explicit as can be:

> There is . . . no need to be ashamed of having an affection for Falstaff, as long as we acknowledge that we must also cast him out. The school of criticism that furnished him with a tender heart and condemned the Prince for brutality in turning him away was deluded. Its delusions will probably be accounted for, in later years, through the facts of history. The sense of security created in nineteenth-century England by the predominance of the British navy induced men to rate that very security too cheaply and to exalt the instinct of rebellion above its legitimate station. They forgot the threat of disorder which was ever present with the Elizabethans. Schooled by recent events we should have no difficulty now in taking Falstaff as the Elizabethans took him.[35]

What connects 1944 to 1600 and separates both from the false and decaying overconfidence of an equally imperial and romantic nineteenth century is, in other words, their shared insecurity, their related if historically distinct experiences of foreign wars as threats to national survival. I've already written about the degree to which Churchill and Powell and Pressburger cast World War II in terms of the "supreme emergency" and the possible death both of the state and of a civilizational project that the state represented. Tillyard's implicit suggestion is that, just as the Spanish Armada threatened the existence of Elizabeth and Elizabeth's England, so did the Nazis pose an existential threat to Britain, to Europe, and to all that for which they stood. As a result, while Britain in 1944 was closer in time to Victorian England, it was closer in both situation, character, and precarity to its more fragile Elizabethan counterpart. This comparison had, of course, already been given cinematic treatment in Alexander Korda's 1937 propaganda feature, *Fire Over England*. Intended partly as a reaction to tepid British responses to Germany's rearmament and Hitler's rise to power, the film, which also starred Olivier, "made a fairly obvious equation between 16th century Spain and Nazi Germany, Philip II and Hitler and the Inquisition and the Gestapo."[36] Like Korda's film, Tillyard's argument depends on the idea that both periods inhabited states of emergency, times when, as we saw with *Colonel Blimp*, the old rules had to be suspended in order to paradoxically safeguard and preserve those same old rules.

We can see elements of Tillyard's larger account of the Elizabethan compromise between disorder and order in Olivier's cinematography, his handling of character, and his casting. In the film's second act, the world is rendered in the aesthetically compact style of a fifteenth-century miniature: its colors are exaggerated and sharply delineated; its presentation of architectural space is flat; its actors and objects are arranged vertically as if forced into a shallow, shared, and hierarchically significant two-dimensional space: "I decided to base the costumes and scenery very meticulously on medieval illustrations in storybooks, especially those of the Limbourg brothers, with their bright and pastel colors, prettiness, odd perspectives and, sometimes, no perspectives at all."[37] The first shot in this section of the film seems governed by ideas that might have underwritten both Henry's thoughts about kingly right and Shakespeare's own ideas about power and history. As opposed to the bare look of the French court or the hurly-burly of the Globe Theater, the port of Southampton and fifteenth-century England as a whole are imagined as a vital, risky, but ultimately stable play of differences managed within the frame of a coherent and externalized conceptual scheme. The crowded, chaotic, but finally arranged look of the shot is an economical visual presentation of Tillyard's world picture: "Here is a picture of immense and varied activity, constantly threatened with dissolution, and yet preserved from it by a superior unifying power."[38]

Tillyard, Our Contemporary

Of course, neither Tillyard nor Olivier is as straightforward as that. Although readings of Tillyard as conservative, reductive, and ideological are common enough, they tend to miss what's most suggestive and difficult about his wartime analysis of English culture and history. While there is undoubtedly a conservative aspect to his thinking, his apparent nostalgia for the order of the Elizabethan age is in fact partial at best; instead of a panacea, his is indeed an anxious world picture of impending collapse in the face of a "bursting and pullulating world": "the world they lived in was becoming ever more difficult to fit tidily into a rigid order: the mathematical detail of the correspondence became less and less apt; you could not base your faith on the endless accumulation of minutiae. At the same time the desire for order was there."[39] For Tillyard's Elizabethans, order is what one wants but cannot have. As opposed to seeing order as an organic and safely Elizabethan value, Tillyard makes the case that whatever order governed the age was a fragile holdover from an earlier, less self-conscious time, a residual comfort almost wholly unsuited to the complexity of early modern life; "it was," he says, "a simplified version of a much more complicated medieval picture."[40]

World Pictures.

That earlier, "more complicated" culture was characterized by its dependence on the same elaborated residual system of rules and games at work in Powell and Pressburger's *Colonel Blimp*: "One is tempted to call the medieval habit of life mathematical or to compare it with a gigantic game where everything is included and every act is conducted under the most complicated system of rules."[41] The Elizabethan age thus differs from what came before in both its relative simplicity and, paradoxically, its extreme fragility: "But though the general medieval picture of the world survived in outline into the Elizabethan age, its existence was by then precarious. There had been Machiavelli, to whom the idea of a universe divinely ordered throughout was repugnant, and in the seventeenth century men began to understand and heed and not merely to travesty and abuse him."[42] In other words, while the late medieval game somehow managed to keep life's disorder in check, it had begun by Shakespeare's time to run out of steam. In other words, although critics sometimes dismiss Tillyard because he seems motivated by an anachronistic and war-weary longing for an old order, his Elizabethan age was in fact not at all an age of unproblematic regularity and routine; it was rather an age of anxiety, self-consciousness, and paranoia.

The Elizabethan world picture was not something Tillyard wanted for modern England; it was, rather, an early and telling anticipation of a darker contemporary logic:

> Finally it must be confessed that to us the Elizabethan age is a very queer age. . . . Yet we shall err grievously if we do not take [its seriousness] into account or if we imagine that the Elizabethan habit of mind is done with once and for all. If we are sincere with ourselves we must know that we have that habit in our own bosoms somewhere, queer as it may seem. And, if we reflect on that habit, we may see that (in queerness though not in viciousness) it resembles certain trends of thought in central Europe, the ignoring of which by our scientifically minded intellectuals has helped not a little to bring the world into its present conflicts and distresses.[43]

The Elizabethan "habit of mind" is not, in that case, something that Tillyard hopes either to preserve or to resuscitate. Rather, he identifies the Elizabethans' fraught preoccupation with structures, systems, and designs, on the one hand, with what Huizinga called "original violence" ("we have that habit in our own bosoms") and, on the other, with the specific rise of central European totalitarianism. As opposed to a medieval condition in which layers of order emerge organically as an effect of an elaborate and ridiculous but nonetheless productive game, a game designed to do its best with what it saw as an inevitable and natural *disorder*, the less ingenuous Elizabethan embraces order as what he or she knew to be a false consolation, seeking disastrously to remake the world in its ersatz image. If, in other words, the tension between Falstaff and Henry can be understood in terms of a shifting tension between freedom and security, Tillyard's account reveals a problem or, rather, a familiar paradox. On the one hand, he sees that a romantic over-investment in rebellion for its own sake has no place in wartime. Just as Henry had to leave Falstaff and the Boar's Head behind in order to rule, Britain needed now to grow up and face facts in order to fight a war that needed to be won. On the other hand, a world without Falstaff (or, for that matter, a world without Clive Candy) is exactly what England was fighting against. Whereas Knight proposed that Henry's rejection of Falstaff amounted to a neat sublation of rebellion into a more capacious kingly authority, Tillyard writes himself self-consciously into a corner; that is not to say that he is in bad faith. Rather—as with Powell and Pressburger and, I maintain, Olivier—Tillyard ends up articulating a contradiction necessary to the democratic commitment to total mobilization. In order to save Falstaff, we have to kill Falstaff. In order to be free, we must renounce freedom. In order to defeat totalitarianism, we must become totalitarian. It takes a fascist to fight a fascist.[44]

The Paradox of the Actor

When we first encounter Olivier, he is an actor playing an actor who is, in turn, preparing to play Henry amidst genial disorder backstage. A quiet cough calls our attention to the nervous, all-too-human presence of the performer moments before he moves on stage to become a king. In this first section of the film, Olivier's actor is heavily and sort of cheaply made up, a fact brought into relief by the presence of boy actors shaving and adjusting their wigs, rouge, and prosthetics in order to play Mistress Quickly and Princess Katherine. When, however, Olivier's actor crosses the threshold between backstage and stage, the transformation is complete: his Henry is handsome, upright, and supremely confident. The crowd responds accordingly, applauding him as he makes his way center stage to utter his first line: "Where is my gracious Lord of Canterbury?"[45] The camera remains backstage for a few moments to foreground the threshold between actor and character, person and king. Olivier was later explicit about the transformative significance of this sequence: "Henry, historically and in Shakespeare's eyes, had an unheroic beginning, so I would start with me, the Elizabethan actor playing Henry, waiting in the wings, while the audience got to know the other characters."[46]

“Where is my gracious Lord of Canterbury?”

Olivier understood this effort both to transform actor and character and to dramatize the moment of that transformation as essential to his direction of *Henry V*: "If Shakespeare has a flourish and a big speech, bring the camera back; if he has moments of humor and poignancy, bring it forward. I first tested this out in *Henry V*. [When] I wanted a big climax . . . I crept the camera back and back until [I delivered a line] in a full theatrical climax which, to my utmost delight, I saw the camera could take."[47] In order to fashion a synthesis between stage and screen acting, Olivier developed a hybrid method that would allow him to drift between states of interiority and exteriority, a mobile style he saw as his signature contribution to the cinematic adaptation of Shakespeare. This tracking style is at work in Henry's first big speech of the film, his reaction to the Dauphin's mocking gift of tennis balls. The sequence begins with a close-up shot of Henry's face; he smiles barely, subtly in a way that could only be captured in a close-up. As the smile fades, several things become clear: the king, for a moment, considers the joke from the perspective of his old, antic self and has at least grudgingly to smile; at the same time, the quick suppression of the smile is evidence of an effort not to reveal too much to the Dauphin's emissary; then, the turn of smile to frown suggests that he feels at least some of the insult's sting; and, last but not least, the self-possession that stands behind both smile and frown is proof of some colder strategic satisfaction. The feckless Dauphin has given Henry just what he wanted: a political excuse to go to war.

Because these several overlapping registers of the look would not have been available on stage, the cinematic close-up allows Olivier to pack these different registers into a single, restrained gesture. As, however, he speaks, his volume increases and the camera tracks back, giving him room to become more and more theatrical, to inhabit and to fill the stage; it does not stop until the details of Henry's face can no longer be made out clearly. As Olivier's shooting script puts it, "track back to show all the stage."[48] This shift from a close-up of a face to a long-distance shot of a whole stage is not only a move from one mode to another, from the specificity of the cinematic close-up to an effect more appropriate to the stage; it is also a shift from the suggested interiority of that almost imperceptible smile to the broad public exteriority of the stage speech. Olivier thus creates a continuum between styles that would otherwise seem opposed.[49]

Olivier uses this same trick twice more, first with Henry's "Once more unto the breach" speech and later with the "Band of brothers" speech. In each case, the camera pulls not only back but also back and up, tracking above Olivier and the other actors in a way that both allows us to see Henry emerge as structural focus of a much larger group and lends the camera

"I crept the camera back and back . . ."

a conspicuous objectivity, a god's-eye or sovereign point of view that also seamlessly links the biographical and emotional particularity of Henry's adventure with the larger stakes of world history. What Olivier's cinematic and Henry's political achievements represent is thus a sovereign synthesis of both public and private political spectacle and realpolitik, biography and history, real man and state symbol.

This synthesis is brought to a finer point with Henry's famous nighttime soliloquy; making his way through the camp incognito, Henry speaks with a few ordinary soldiers, an experience that gives him insight into the local and personal effects of war and encourages him to mediate on the inevitable loneliness of a king. In a manner more or less impossible in the theater but entirely natural to the cinema, Olivier converts the stagiest of dramatic conceits—the soliloquy—into an utterly convincing display of almost novelistic psychological realism. For three full minutes, the camera tracks slowly in toward Henry's almost still face as we listen to him ruminate in voiceover on the uneasiness of the head that wears the crown: "What infinite heartsease/Must kings forgo that private men enjoy!"[50] The nuances of the speech are accented with tiny shifts in Olivier's eyes as they appear both half shadowed and sparkling by the light of the campfire.

Olivier thus uses specifically cinematic effects in order to offer the transformation of actor into character, exterior into interior, public into private as an allegory for what Ernst Kantorowicz famously referred to as the king's two bodies, the idea that the king brought together in one person

"What must kings forgo?"

the mortal and fallible body of the natural man and a sacred and eternal body politic. Eric Santner summarizes the argument: "Kantorowicz shows that this complex set of linkages was largely, if often unstably, secured by the peculiar doctrine that the royal personage had two bodies, one natural and subject to the fate of all mortal flesh and one supernatural, whose representational or official corporeality gave quasi-divine legitimacy, presence, and enduring substance to governmental authority across the succession of generations."[51] The film thus aligns a few versions of this same logic: the passage from actor to character, the synthesis of the sacred and profane bodies of the sovereign, the biographical passage from dissolute youth to disciplined maturity, and the ideological and developmental resolution of the narrative tension between two of the Henriad's other representative bodies: the grossly present body of Falstaff and the ascetic, fading body of Henry IV. Henry's more or less successful synthesis of these alternatives offered Shakespeare a way to solve a structural problem that dogged the whole of the Henriad, beginning with *Richard II*: for Richard, "the Universal called 'Kingship' begins to disintegrate; its transcendental 'Reality,' its objective truth and god-like existence, so brilliant shortly before, pales into a nothing, a *nomen*. And the remaining half-reality resembles a state of amnesia or sleep," a state that Henry prophylactically invokes and dispels in his own nocturnal meditation on sovereignty and war: "O hard condition,/ Twin-born with greatness."[52]

However, we also need to see Olivier's film as something more than an essay on early modern political theology; it was, as Olivier and others have understood, a rigorously contemporary propaganda film, an effort to imagine and to embody the stakes of modern world war and the possibility of political and cultural consensus in the wake of total mobilization. Although the film pursues this in a number of ways (its late turn to the marriage plot, its tacit rejection of Falstaff and the lively disorder he represents, its management of different regional identities with Captains Jamy, Fluellen, MacMorris, and Gower), its most persuasive argument comes with Henry himself, or rather with the figure that emerges from the formal and historical synthesis of the early modern actor, the earlier modern king, and the modern movie star. Although he would become more and more of a character actor, Olivier was a bona fide star in 1944. The *Los Angeles Times* loved him; the *New York Times* called him "one of those once in a lifetime things"; and Hedda Hopper wrote, "When Laurence Olivier says, 'Come here, you're mine,' how gladly you'd go."[53] By 1944 he had appeared as Maxim de Winter in Hitchcock's *Rebecca*, as Mr. Darcy in Robert Leonard's *Pride and Prejudice*, and Lord Nelson in Alexander Korda's *That Hamilton Woman*, and, most famously, as Heathcliff in William Wyler's *Wuthering Heights*, roles that made him into "a Hollywood star of the first rank."[54]

In Britain, Olivier was even more recognizable, making uncredited and cameo appearances in several important wartime films. He appears as himself pulling faces through a window in Powell and Pressburger's *The Volunteer* (1944); he provides the introductory voiceover for David Lean's *This Happy Breed* (1944); and, wonderfully and weirdly against type, he plays Johnny, the heroic French Canadian trapper in *49th Parallel* (1941). While serving as a pilot for the Fleet Air Arm of the British Navy, he starred in propaganda shorts, gave patriotic speeches to the troops, and delivered hours of patriotic radio broadcasts that self-consciously blurred the already thin line between Shakespearean and Churchillian rhetoric: "We will attack; we will smite our foes; we will conquer; and in all our deeds, in this land and in other lands, from this hour on, our watchwords will be: urgency, speed, courage."[55] As Holderness puts it, "Olivier's role in *Henry V* was indistinguishable (apart from the uniform) from his real-life role as a patriotic orator, a Churchillian inspiration to the Home front."[56] The film's larger achievement as propaganda appears, as it were, fully formed in Henry's first appearance onstage and onscreen; it pursues, in other words, the idea that Olivier, the actor Olivier played, and the king that actor played while Olivier played him could come together as a Tillyardian microcosm for the state, a state that in turn stands as an ordered and aspirational surrogate for both the requirements of total mobilization and the promise of postwar consensus.

The Game Is Up!

Olivier signals his interest in the Tillyardian tension between rules and rule-breaking, order and disorder with games that others play and that Henry more or less rejects. (This is another way in which *Henry V* recalls moves made in *Colonel Blimp*.) For instance, our first view of the court of the French King, Charles VI, is presented as a static tableau. Overall, the shot conveys a feeling of dreamy listlessness which again adopts the style of the Linbourg brothers but without the compressed vitality that animated the earlier image of the English embarking at Southampton. Olivier orders the space within a pronounced but subtly crazy visual field: at first glance, the court seems organized into a series of parallel visual planes, each divided from the others by a row of delicately ornate columns; a closer look reveals, however, lines and angles that don't quite add up, an effect that turns architectural perspective against itself in the style of Escher or Piranesi. With this, Olivier both exploits a tension between "mathematical exactitude" and "human contingency" that Erwin Panofsky takes as essential to "perspective as a symbolic form" and reveals the French court as a structure on the verge of collapse, as a visual and, as it were, ethical system caught on the edge of its fall into the involutions of the Baroque.[57]

The mad king sits on the floor—lost, abject, terrified—while his advisers stand about the room, loitering, looking out windows, waiting for something to happen. At the shot's center, the Duke of Orleans stands, idly playing a solitary game of cup-and-ball or *bilboquet*. The Duke's game does a few things for *Henry V.* It adds to the languor that Olivier wants generally to convey; in addition to the game—it is a boring way to combat boredom—and the squatting king, we see guards lying prone around the edge of the frame, symbols of France's unwitting unpreparedness in the face of Henry's mobile English threat. The game's status as a pastime also suggests that the French inhabit a different and stalled temporality, a time that has more or less fallen out of the shared flow of European and world history. Indeed, bilboquet had long been associated with the failure of kings, appearing both in accounts of the sixteenth-century court of Henry III ("He took a fancy to bilboquet, or cup-and-ball, and never went anywhere without one.") and in *War and Peace*, where Tolstoy draws attention to its unmotivated presence in a portrait of Napoleon's infant son: "A quiet handsome curly-headed boy with a gaze resembling the gaze of Christ in the Sistine Madonna was depicted playing bilboquet. . . . It was not entirely clear precisely what the painter meant to express by presenting the so-called king of Rome skewering the terrestrial globe with a stick, but the allegory, to all those who had seen the picture in Paris, and to Napoleon himself, obviously seemed clear and quite pleasing."[58] The stylized look, the languorous pace, and the general oddity of the scene in the French court suggests that the whole of fifteenth-century France is also a game, a self-contained and merely coherent hobby on the verge of being rendered obsolete by the onward rush of Henry's tactical modernity.

The Duke's game of cup-and-ball also recalls the mocking tennis balls that the Dauphin sends to Henry at the beginning of the film. For the Dauphin, the joke was meant to end an argument, to acknowledge, with a certain biting but nonetheless managed wit, the young king's lack of gravitas and capacity and thus to cow him into submission. Henry, however, refuses the joke as joke:

> And tell the pleasant Prince, this mock of his
> Hath turned these balls to gun-stones, and his soul
> Shall stand sore-charged for the wasteful vengeance
> That shall fly from them: for many a thousand widows

Cup-and-ball.

Shall this mock mock out of they dear husbands,
Mock mothers from their sons, mock castles down:
Ay, some are yet ungotten and unborn
that shall have cause to curse the Dauphin's scorn.[59]

The Dauphin's teasing gag indeed recalls Clive's playful effort to irritate Kaunitz with music at the Cafe Hohenzollern; and, like Henry, Kaunitz refuses to play and instead mocks the game itself: "You should have thought of that before you started your little joke!"[60] Henry thus pulls back the veil from the Dauphin's civilized figural aggression to reveal and, indeed, to revel in aggression in and of itself. Whereas the Dauphin meant for his tennis balls to imply or to figure some other insulting thing, Henry chooses a vulgar if eloquent candor: a cannon ball is a cannon ball is a cannon ball. Holinshed's 1587 account of the gift (on which Shakespeare drew for his play) accentuates Henry's refusal of diplomacy as a form of play:

Whilest in the Lente season the Kyng laye at Kenilworth, there came to him from Charles, Dolphin of Fraunce, the Frenche King's eldest sonne, certayne Ambassadours, that broughte with them a barrell of Paris balles, which they presented to hym for a token from their maister, whiche presente was taken in verie ill parte, as sent in scorne, to signifie that it was more mete for the King to passe the tyme with suche childish exercise, than to attempte anye worthy exployte: wherefore the Kyng wrote to hym, that ere ought long, hee

> woulde sende to hym some London balles, that should breake and batter downe the roofes of his houses about hys eares.[61]

Instead of responding to the Dauphin's code with another code (the art of diplomacy), Henry mocks mockery itself, suggesting that the diplomatic and social rules that underwrite the Dauphin's playful attack no longer obtain; a knowing inversion of the child's claim that "sticks and stones will break my bones," Henry promises to meet the Dauphin's "Paris balls" with the literal destructive force of cannon shot. War and its implements will "mock mock" out of him.

This denial of war as game is reinforced when, during the siege of Harfleur, Captains Fluellen, Jamy, Gower, and MacMorris meet to discuss the war. While Fluellen, "the fussy Welsh pedant," wants to assess matters in terms of "the true, Roman disciplines of war," in terms, that is, of war understood as a theoretical pursuit, an exasperated MacMorris cries out that "this is no time to discourse, so God save me!"[62] On the one hand, Fluellen appears in both the play and the film as especially capable; on the other hand, MacMorris has a point: under this king, war isn't a matter of theory or discourse. Indeed, as the captains sit "discoursing," the king delivers his all-too-real ultimatum to the governor of Harfleur: "How yet resolves the Governor of the town? This is the latest parley we'll admit." If that seems benign as ultimatums go, that is because it is one of several scenes that Olivier cut back to avoid confusing or disturbing his audience. In Shakespeare, the king warns that without surrender, Harfleur will see:

> The blind and bloody soldier with foul hand
> Defile the locks of your shrill-shrieking daughters;
> Your fathers taken by the silver beards,
> And their most reverend heads dashed to the walls;
> Your naked infants spitted upon pikes,
> Whiles the mad mothers with their howls confused
> Do break the clouds.[63]

In a way that both recalls and prefigures the effective and amoral intensity of Colonel Blimp's Spud, Henry threatens to lay waste to the city, to brain the elderly, to rape the women, and to murder and defile the children; he threatens, in other words, to make his war like what Spud understood as "the real thing." Showing that he is willing to push war to and past the limits of the accepted "disciplines of war," Henry lets Harfleur know he isn't playing around.

Kriegsspiel!

It is in that case telling that, as Henry threatens Harfleur, his captains sit over a tabletop war game, a simulation made up of blue and red pieces standing in for troops and fortifications. Seen against the barely suppressed image of women raped, old men beaten, and infants staked, the anodyne and fussy abstraction of Fluellen's game seems hopelessly naive, as much an artifact from another age as the Duke of Orleans's lazy game of cup-and-ball. Seen in relation to 1415, 1600, or 1944, Fluellen's game is an anachronism. Although war games are as old as war itself, the tabletop simulation that occupies Fluellen was a more recent invention, appearing well after the play's early modern setting and context. The most famous of these table war games was the *Kriegsspiel* (war game) cabinet that Georg Leopold von Reisswitz designed for Kaiser Wilhelm in 1812: "the *Kriegsspiel* established conventions of war gaming, such as identifying opponents as red and blue, the use of maps and umpires, and fundamental rules for movement and combat resolution."[64] If, however, Fluellen's game would have seemed impossibly avant-garde in either 1415 or 1600, such simulations had come to seem old-fashioned by 1944. Although strategic models were in fact used in the lead-up to and during World War II (particularly by the Germans prior to the successful invasion of France in 1940), they had begun to seem at least symbolically inadequate to the political and operational realities of war:

> It seems probable that both tactical and strategic ideas flourished in Britain in the 1920s for two main reasons: there was considerable public impetus

> behind the writers' concern to analyze and profit from the painful experience of 1914–1918; and the absence of an immediate obvious enemy provided a comparatively relaxed atmosphere in which theories could be developed in a quasiscientific way. A marked contrast existed between the unspecific "Redland versus Blueland" exercises of the 1920s and the practical realities that became all too apparent when likely enemies appeared after 1933.[65]

Although strategically useful, the war game had—like the duel—lost its ability to represent war over the course of the twentieth century. In his *Little Wars* (1913), H. G. Wells had already imagined a war game (his is played with toy soldiers and miniature cannons) not as practice for but rather as an ironic and critical alternative to war: "How much better is this amiable miniature than the Real Thing! Here is a homeopathic remedy for the imaginative strategist. Here is the premeditation, the thrill, the strain of accumulating victory or disaster—and no smashed nor sanguinary bodies, no shattered fine buildings nor devastated country sides, no petty cruelties, none of that awful universal boredom and embitterment, that tiresome delay or stoppage or embarrassment of every gracious, bold, sweet, and charming thing, that we who are old enough to remember a real modern war know to be the reality of belligerence."[66] Fluellen's abstract interest in "fighting wars out of books" thus puts him at odds both with the martial realism of Henry's French campaign and with the unruly facts of war in 1944, facts that had revealed war games as either an inadequate representation of or a naive alternative to the real violence of modern warfare.[67]

Olivier indeed takes care to present Henry's army as especially and presciently modern: as opposed to the heavily encumbered French, his army of lightly clad bowmen is quick, mobile, and ruthless. This depiction of the English at Agincourt has some basis in fact. As John Keegan writes, "The bowmen of Henry's army were not only tough professional soldiers. There is also evidence that many had enlisted in the first place to avoid punishment for civil acts of violence, including murder."[68] Keegan goes on to argue that the weight of the French armor combined with muddy conditions allowed the English archers to corral the French, producing a series of highly efficient "killing zones": "If the archers were now able to reproduce along the flanks of the French mass the same 'tumbling effect' which had encumbered its front, its destruction must have been imminent. For most death in battle takes place within well-defined and fairly narrow 'killing zones,' of which the 'no-man's-land' of trench warfare is the best known and most comprehensible example."[69] More to the point, the improvisatory lightness and mobility of Olivier's archers was meant to conjure the very modern warriors to whom

Olivier explicitly dedicated his film, the "Commandos and Airborne Troops of Great Britain." As I pointed out in the introduction, the commando was a figure of considerable ambivalence during and after World War II, provoking "apprehension as well as respect. He was brave and skilled, but his style of fighting was unsportsmanlike, 'dirty,' suspiciously un-English. The name connoted a flirtation with illegality, an impatience with mere rules, a willingness to mete out justice with direct action regardless of the methods employed. The commando was a bit of a brute. He brought gangster values to the battlefield."[70] (Once again, we're reminded of *Colonel Blimp*: "Get out of here, sir, you and your gang of awful militia gangsters!") The commando represented a relation to warfare that worked because it refused to recognize the rules of the game. As a result, Olivier's conscious invocation of the commando would cut in two directions or, rather, would once again help to reveal a difficult tension at the heart of thinking about war.

Banish Plump Jack

The Henriad's most important figure of games, play, and their disputed ability to manage life is of course Falstaff. As David Wiles and many others have pointed out, "Falstaff is like a Lord of Misrule, a personification of Shrovetide or summer, who has the power temporarily to halt the normal progress of the calendar."[71] After more or less starring in both parts of *Henry IV* and having become one of Shakespeare's most popular creations, Falstaff did not appear in *Henry V*, having died, we're told, of a broken heart between the end of *2 Henry IV* and the beginning of *Henry V*. This unexpected absence would have been all the more noticeable and upsetting to early modern audiences given Shakespeare's promise at the end of *2 Henry IV* that Plump Jack would in fact return: "If you be not too much cloyed with fat meat, our humble author will continue the story, with Sir John in it, and make you merry with fair Katherine of France."[72] Why, then, doesn't Falstaff return? Why does Shakespeare kill him off in the nonspace between plays?

Some critics answer the question in practical terms: perhaps Falstaff was left out because Shakespeare had said all he could with the character; or because Will Kemp, the actor who played Falstaff, had left the Chamberlain's Men; or because Shakespeare was inching in 1599 toward a more naturalistic style that had less room for the traditional figure of the Vice or the clown.[73] Other accounts of the play turn rather on the meaning of Falstaff's disappearance. "What," A. C. Bradley asks in his great essay on Falstaff, "do we feel, and what are we meant to feel, as we witness this rejection? And what does our feeling imply as to the characters of Falstaff and the new

King?"[74] Does Hal truly regret the loss of his old mentor or was rejection always part of his plan? Is Falstaff's eleventh-hour declaration of love—"my Jove!"—proof of his sincerity or is it rather evidence of his innate, do-or-die duplicity?

Wartime readers of the Henriad took, as we have seen, this aspect of the plays as especially significant and made a special point of disparaging Falstaff, his origin, and his motives. Knight remarks that Falstaff "grows out of his setting of noble rivalries and military prowess like a vast green cabbage."[75] Near the end of *The Fortunes of Falstaff,* Wilson writes, "If my readers have followed me to this point they will, I think, be prepared to agree that the rejection has become inevitable."[76] And Tillyard admits, "There is thus no need to be ashamed of having affection for Falstaff, as long as we acknowledge that we must also cast him out."[77] As opposed to what they understand as the falsely romantic nostalgia of Hazlitt, Morgann, and Bradley, these wartime critics accentuate the venal aspects of Falstaff's character to account for what emerges as the only apparent brutality of Hal's rejection; and each casts his own critical rejection of Falstaff explicitly in terms of the immediate context of the war and total mobilization. Wilson calls efforts to imagine a more glorious military career for a younger Falstaff wishful thinking: an "'old soldier' is not the same as [a] 'good soldier'; and the attempt of Morgann and others to make out Falstaff to be a warrior who had for years enjoyed a considerable military reputation rests upon a number of mistaken notions."[78]

We can see what's at stake here: if one good soldier can turn bad, can repudiate "all heroisms," what's to stop any or every soldier from doing so, particularly when reeling under the pressure of combat, the threat of invasion, aerial bombing, and systematic deprivation? In these terms, a complex Falstaff, a Falstaff both a little good and a little bad, could reveal dangerous limits within the logic of total mobilization. What would happen to the war—to any war—if soldiers were allowed to ask Falstaff's great and ironic question from the first part of *Henry IV,* "What is that word honor?"[79] It is, we know, essential to the nature of irony to refuse totalization, to stand against the idea that either any concept or state could be autonomously true or good; it is for this reason that the presence and the example of Falstaff posed a threat both to Henry's status as sovereign and to a war effort dependent on accepting totality as a lived condition.

Banish All the World

It is striking, in that case, that Olivier chooses—whereas Shakespeare didn't—to feature Falstaff in his film, filming a death scene that the play alludes to but does not in fact show. Falstaff's death is shot in a naturalistic, immersive style that anticipates the film's third act and the Battle of Agincourt itself. Indeed, the way in which this section of the film plays with chiaroscuro effects, groups its figures within a compressed but no less natural space, and highlights individual and *almost* exaggerated details of wardrobe and face seems to move from the lightly architectural perspective of the Limbourg brothers to tactile, foregrounded, and luminous obscurity of Rembrandt's late style. The camera tracks in past an iconic Boar's Head Inn sign into a window at the top of the house, where an old man lies prone, attended by Mistress Quickly and a single candle (the tracking shot in toward dim light emanating from the lone upper-story window is another possible nod to the opening of *Citizen Kane*, a connection that will come full circle with Welles's 1965 version of the whole Henriad, *Chimes at Midnight*). When she leaves him, he sits up in bed and stares as if confused and then shouts out to no one: "God save thy grace, King Hal, my royal Hal." Then, as his mind silently wanders, we hear but do not see Olivier in an echoey voiceover (itself an echo of Blimp's Falstaffian "Forty years ago!"), delivering the speech with which Henry finally rejects Falstaff at the end of *2 Henry IV*:

> I know thee not, old man, fall to thy prayers.
> How ill white hairs become a fool and jester!
> I have long dreamed of such a kind of man,
> So surfeit swelled, so old and so profane,
> But being awaked I do despise my dream.
> Reply not to me with a foolish jest,
> Presume not that I am the thing I was;
> For God doth know, so shall the world perceive
> That I have turned away my former self
> So shall I those that kept me company.[80]

During the recitation, the camera tracks in slowly toward a close-up of Falstaff's face as he registers real hurt at the relived memory of Hal's rejection. With this mix of close-up and voiceover, Olivier gives Falstaff the same cinematic interiority that we saw at work in Henry's nighttime vigil. Just as the camera tracks in toward Olivier's face as we listen to his rumination on the burdens of the great, so does it track in toward George Robey's face as his Falstaff winces and finally crumbles at the remembered violence of Henry's words. That Olivier films Falstaff in the same style as Henry lends the old, dying knight a representational dignity otherwise reserved for the king: only Henry and Falstaff are filmed in this way. As the speech comes to an end, Falstaff lies down and dies; and because he had stood for the possibility of play and managed misrule within a world otherwise organized by the demands of domestic and foreign war, his death represents an especially poignant version of the passage away from the logic of the game that I described in the previous section. As opposed to some of the dismissive wartime readings that I've described, Olivier takes care to register Falstaff's death as a real and significant loss, as something as fully momentous as the death of a king; and although the film seems almost to forget this moment in the rush of Henry's war on France, the aesthetic and affective pressure it puts on the film's whole style, on what other close-ups or tracking shots can mean, allows a melancholic, critical, and unexpectedly Falstaffian countermelody to play out under *Henry V*'s otherwise martial tone: "What is honour? A word. What is in that word honour? What is that honour? Air."[81]

In other words, whereas the wartime critics sought to denigrate the knight in order to celebrate the king, Olivier seems genuinely to mourn the loss of Falstaff and what he represents. The tone of Henry's remembered or hallucinated rejection speech is anything but heroic; Olivier's performance is, within the larger context of the film, uncharacteristically nasty. His voice is thin and hectoring, a marked contrast to the confident warmth and wry self-consciousness that informs the rest of his performance, and it is impossible to take the pain that passes across Falstaff's face as anything but sincere. Compared with other iconic representations of a plump and smiling Jack (and, indeed, with George Robey's own earlier portrayal in 1935), this Falstaff is hollowed out, his gaunt face proof that the king's rejection had indeed left him, as Pistol says later in the scene, "fracted and corroborate." This Falstaff, a wreck of a once-formidable man, demands at least our pity, maybe our respect, and almost certainly our love. The palpable melancholy of the scene makes his death, and thus Hal's rejection, register not as an inevitability but rather as a real and regrettable loss. Olivier's implicit account of the scene comes in some ways close to Bradley's early and more openly generous account: Falstaff's death proves "beyond doubt that his rejection was meant by Shakespeare to be taken as a catastrophe."[82] To lose Falstaff is, however necessary, to lose a whole way of life: "Banish Plump Jack and banish all the world."

What Falstaff brought to the world of *Henry IV* and what must die with him is a sense of relief, freedom, and the possibility of even temporary release from the seriousness of life at court and on the battlefield. "The achievement was Falstaff himself, and the conception of that freedom of soul, a freedom illusory only in part, and attainable only by a mind which

Fracted and corroborate.

had received from Shakespeare's own the inexplicable touch of infinity which he bestowed on Hamlet and Macbeth and Cleopatra, but denied to Henry the Fifth."[83] Bradley looks to that "touch of infinity" both to see something like an outside or an alternative to Henry's fully managed world and to find a figure for a living irony that Schlegel associated with the related figure of the opera's comic *buffo* ("the mood that surveys everything and rises infinitely above all limitations, even above its own art, virtue or genius").[84] For William Empson, writing between the wars, Falstaff embodied the tense, critical, political potential of pastoral itself: "But to stretch one's mind round the whole character (as is generally admitted) one must take him, though as the supreme expression of the cult of mockery as strength and the comic idealization of freedom, yet as both villainous and tragically ill-used."[85] In 1945, Orson Welles returned to Bradley's romantic sense of the relation between the excessive and critical vitality of Hamlet and Falstaff in "Orson Welles' Almanac," his regular column in the *New York Post*: "Not long before he was killed, the Prince of Denmark visited England. Suppose he'd stayed there and avoided the ghosts and graveyards (he didn't like them, anyway), and lived to be old and fat. . . . Did he change his name? . . . I think Falstaff is Hamlet—an old and wicked Hamlet—having that drink."[86]

Chimes at Midnight

Welles's extended reading of Falstaff in *Chimes at Midnight* (1965) is, I think, a late and useful thematic expansion of the character's brief appearance in

Olivier's film. For Welles, the rejection and death of Falstaff stood for a sense of cultural decline that was his main theme in *The Magnificent Ambersons* (1942): "You see, the basic intention was to portray a golden world—almost one of memory—and then show what it turns into."[87] Just as the invention of the automobile signaled the end of an older way of experiencing time, community, and thus storytelling, so does the story of Falstaff's fall offer an account of disenchantment and decline. As Peter Bogdanovich points out, the style of the framing shot of Falstaff and Shallow in *Chimes*, their faces caught in the glow of a fire, recalls a similar close-up of the elderly Major Amberson in *The Magnificent Ambersons* as he reflects in the reflected light of a fire on his life's imminent end: "he realized that everything which had worried him or delighted him during this lifetime, all his buying and building and trading and banking, that it was all trifling and waste beside what concerned him now." In both cases, reflection in the present—a reflection compared implicitly both to the flickering lights of a fire and the similar flicker of the projected cinematic image—is an act that both recalls and remakes the past. In Welles's words: "Even if the good old days never existed, the fact that we can *conceive* of such a world is, in fact, an affirmation of the human spirit. That the imagination of man is capable of creating the myth of a more open, more generous time is not a sign of our folly. Every country has its 'Merrie England,' a season of innocence, a dew-bright morning of the world. Shakespeare sings of that lost time in many of his plays, and Falstaff—that pot-ridden old rogue—is its perfect embodiment."[88] Welles thus gets at a logic that runs throughout this book. The look back to an innocent past that I've been tracking through and around these films is not simply a misplaced nostalgia for what never really existed; rather what's at stake is the very ability to imagine a position from which to see either past or future in the midst of an otherwise totalized present. What is under threat for Powell and Pressburger, Welles, and, as we will see, Olivier isn't one or another past (although that's part of it). It is "the imagination of man" as such that has been put at risk by the logic of total war.

The loss of this at once real and imagined "Merrie England" runs throughout *Chimes*, from a silhouetted opening shot of Falstaff and Shallow making their way across an evacuated and wintry landscape (a shot that recalls the end of Bergman's *The Seventh Seal*) to his enervated confrontation with physical limit and mortality in the arms of Doll Tearsheet: "I am old, I am old." This anxiety about modernity's onset is maybe most visible in Welles's treatment of the battle of Shrewsbury, where he pushes the modern logic of guerrilla warfare already present in Olivier's film toward a violent but logical extreme. Just as Welles collapses and rearranges elements from across the Henriad, so does he seem to import details from Agincourt—particularly Henry's reliance on quick, lightly armored commando fighters—into the earlier encounter with Hotspur on the fields of Shrewsbury. He approaches the battle with a mix of Brueghelian gusto and real horror that anticipates other stylized Vietnam-era representations of violence such as *Bonnie and Clyde* (1967) and *The Wild Bunch* (1969). Soldiers kill each other with swords, arrows, and spiked clubs; bodies pile up in a muddy tangle of limbs; horses rear up wild-eyed with terror. In one brief and inexplicable shot, a man appears to sit, hacking away at a dead horse while battle rages all around. Almost as soon as the sequence begins, it becomes impossible to differentiate one army from the other, a fact underlined both by increasingly muddy conditions on the field and by shots that are largely unframed, asymmetrical, and thus resistant to a shot/reverse shot logic that organizes many conventional fight scenes. Welles uses handheld cameras and rapid cuts not only to capture the intensity of battle but also its essential confusion. As the fight proceeds, the musical soundtrack seems to recede further and further into the scene's acoustic mix as diegetic shouts, groans, and the clang of metal against metal begins to overwhelm everything else. Welles cuts several times to individual, bloodied faces; in each case, the camera holds onto a face just long enough to register the bare fact that a face is individual before once again cutting away, a rhythm that just introduces the dimmest idea of a person before reducing that person to matter.

Welles punctuates the sequence with shots of a fully, ridiculously, and massively armored Falstaff running for cover from tree to tree. Like the shots that represent him, Falstaff is isolated and uncharacteristically mute during most of the battle of Shrewsbury. Welles sometimes seems to shoot him running around the battle's outskirts at a higher speed, an effect that hearkens back to the harried, frenetic look of silent-age comedy. These shots, however, are not funny; they, along with similarly brief, terrified reaction shots from Bardolph and Pistol, seem rather to stand as a kind of structural witness to the battle as well as an essential failure of comedy in the face of violence. Like Henry's effort to mock mockery itself, the battle seems to have revalued Falstaff's otherwise splendid superfluity. While his eccentric excessiveness of person and personality once had been an opportunity for irony, play, and critique, he is suddenly reduced to something merely extraneous, something simply without a role to play; this dissolution of comic potential provides a point of structural commentary on the scene's gratuitous loss of life. This bad superfluity—a comic excess that fails all at once to be funny—is also an aspect of the larger generic structure of Welles's film

The fog of war.

and of Welles's interpretation of the Henriad. Whereas another version of the scene might have played Falstaff's appearances for comic relief, Welles takes pains to present Falstaff's failure as the failure of comedy itself. In other contexts, the tension between comedy and tragedy has been understood as an essentially Shakespearean understanding of what's meaningful about both. For Coleridge, "Shakespeare's comic are continually reacting upon his tragic characters."[89] More recently and more pointedly, Lawrence Danson writes: "[T]he *Henry IV* plays are a virtual dialogue between tragedy and comedy. The biggest sign of this . . . is Falstaff."[90] Insofar as *Chimes at Midnight* is an attempt to register the loss of Falstaff and his world, it is also an analysis of genre's dialectical failure, a failure that finds its way also, I maintain, into Olivier's *Henry V.*

A Little Song, a Little Dance

Of course, both Shakespeare and Olivier do end with a turn to comedy, the play's turn to canned marriage comedy at its end: "The generic slide from history to comedy in act five of the play celebrates the procreative and dynastic convergence that war has brought about in the course of events. It also extends the happy ending from realms of politics and love to those aesthetics and epistemology."[91] This entirely instrumental comedy couldn't be further from the critical spirit of misrule that characterizes Falstaff's humor. Indeed, whereas the presence of Falstaff and the world of the Boar's Head seems to activate, clarify, and augment other plots, the turn to Henry and

Katherine's frankly awkward love talk at the end of *Henry V* stands instead as the final rejection of Falstaff and the comic potential he represents. As opposed to Falstaff, who seemed often to open things up, Henry's grossly sexual aggression ("in loving me you should love the friend of France, for I love France so well that I will not part with a village of it—I will have it all mine") brings things to a depressing close. The ideologically leaden shift from history to comedy at the end of *Henry V* is thus different in kind from the complex comic dialectic explored in the earlier parts of the Henriad. Whereas *Henry V* ends with the promise of a wedding, *2 Henry IV* ends with a jig, which would have been danced by Will Kemp, the actor who had most likely played Falstaff: "As the fifth act comes to a close, Sir John Falstaff—played by Kemp—is hauled off to the Fleet prison, and it looks for once as if Falstaff, that great escape artist, will not be able to wriggle out of trouble. But Kemp suddenly dashes back onstage. A moment or two passes before playgoers realize that the play really is over and that Kemp is delivering an epilogue not as Falstaff but more or less as himself."[92] Kemp would then deliver the play's epilogue, which announced both that Falstaff would return in *Henry V* and that a jig was immediately to follow: "My tongue is weary. When my legs are too, I will bid you good night."[93] Unlike other players, Kemp never let you forget he was Kemp, no matter what the role: "In the long-established manner of the Clown or Vice, Kemp/Falstaff repeatedly ruptured aesthetic codes which other players sustained."[94] Clowns like Kemp "weren't intended to be believable characters, that is to say, like real people, not even when playing fully fleshed-out roles like Falstaff. This was because leading clowns were also always playing themselves, or rather, the stage identity they so carefully crafted."[95]

Both Welles and Olivier refer implicitly to the influence of Kemp with their casting decisions for Falstaff. As Welles understood, he wasn't the sort of actor who could disappear into a role even if he wanted to: "There are personalities who seem to be overstatements *in themselves*. Unhappily, I'm one of those. The camera doesn't just enlarge—it blows me up."[96] (One can see how fully Welles had internalized Falstaff: "A plague of sighing and grief! It blows a man up like a bladder.")[97] Joss Ackland, who played the role in 1982, claimed Welles as an influence on his own Falstaff; but rather than look to Welles's portrayal of Falstaff, he looked instead to "the real Orson Welles": "As a man Welles exploded brilliantly, and then didn't know where to go. Like Falstaff, I believe he could have achieved so much, but it was frittered away. He gives everyone a lot to laugh about and can laugh at it too. But inside he is crying. He can see the waste, because he is not a stupid man."[98] Welles is in this way a perfect Falstaff. Not only does he mange to capture the outsized vitality of Shakespeare's character, but he also manages—by virtue of his very inability to disappear into the role—to capture an essential element of Shakespearean dramaturgy.

Olivier's choice of George Robey for the role was similarly inspired. Like both Kemp and Welles, Robey was a famous song-and-dance man whose style of music hall comedy had more or less disappeared by the middle of the 1940s. Robey's presence in *Henry V* reveals a complex and highly impacted set of allusive layers: Robey had played Falstaff before and so brought—like Olivier—some trace of the stage into the cinematic world of *Henry V,* a fact that adds to Olivier's effort to create a productive hybrid of film and theater. Robey's immense success as a stage clown (he called himself the prime minister of Mirth) reminds us of Kemp in relation both to his humor and to the fact that Kemp had left the Lord Chamberlain's Men prior to the composition of *Henry V*; like Kemp and Falstaff, events had rendered Robey and his particular set of skills more or less obsolete. Robey thus reminds us of a certain type of historically specific comedy as well as of the occasion for that comedy's disappearance. The waning of Robey's particular brand of music hall comedy had been widely registered as a significant cultural loss; in a 1922 "London Letter," T. S. Eliot wrote, "I thought of Marie Lloyd again; and wondered again why that directness, frankness, and ferocious humor which survive in her, and in Nellie Wallace and George Robey and a few others, should be extinct, should be odious to the British public, in precisely those forms of art in which they are most needed, and in which, in fact, they used to flourish."[99] For Eliot, the waning of the music hall signaled the end of a larger cultural project that had all but disappeared: "The poet's dark apprehension [about the death of the music hall] stems from the deeper realization that a certain kind of critical project has passed."[100]

Aligning Kemp, Robey, and the fate of the music hall with the figure of his dying Falstaff, Olivier raises the idea of a loss that transcends the terms of one old man's love for a young prince. The casting of Robey allows us to see in Falstaff a loss specific to the period of modern warfare that Olivier is working to manage. Left there, we could say that Olivier's bracketed introduction of Falstaff into his film registers a loss that was necessary to the wars that Henry and Churchill needed respectively to fight. Writing about the progressive and eccentric tenor of J. B. Priestley's BBC "Postscripts," Angus Calder writes: "If Churchill evoked Henry V and Thomas Babbington Macaulay, Priestly's heroes were Falstaff and Sam Weller. He depicted the 'little man,' who preserved the spirit of English comedy within himself, embattled against Nazis whom he variously described as 'robot men,' 'warrior ants,' and 'overgrown tormenting, cruel schoolboys—middle-aged 'dead end kids.'"[101] This is, in other words, another expression of the paradox of total war that I've been tracking: that we need to suspend the values—of play, irony, eccentricity, and good cheer—that Falstaff represents in order to save those values. Falstaff was sacrificed to save Falstaff.

Lambkins, We Will Live!

This, though, would be to miss the more central and more unruly way in which the spirit of Falstaff lingers on in *Henry V*. Although he doesn't appear in Shakespeare's play and appears only briefly (although, as we have seen, suggestively) in Olivier's film, Falstaff is remembered in both by his more resilient if less lovable followers from the Boar's Head. Immediately after Falstaff's death, Pistol, Bardolf, and Nym pack up and follow Henry to war. Upon hearing of Falstaff's imminent demise, Pistol shouts out, "Let us condole the knight. For, lambkins, we will live!" And live Pistol does: although he plays only a small role in *2 Henry IV* and does not appear at all in *1 Henry IV*, Pistol is certainly the most important of Falstaff's survivors in *Henry V*. He appears more often than either Bardolph or Nym and is in fact the only character from Falstaff's world allowed to outlive the events of the second teratology; he is thus "a constant reminder that the price of Harry's greatness is the rejection of Falstaff."[102] Although he is, as Samuel Johnson puts it, at least "beaten into obscurity," Pistol is not dead at the play's end and promises in a late soliloquy to return home: "To England will I steal, and there I'll steal."[103]

It makes a kind of sense that Shakespeare would promote the perfectly minor Pistol to a major role in *Henry V*. For one, he provides an important foil for the young king, offering, with his mix of ersatz military aggression, impotent bluster ("Pish for thee, Iceland dog, thou prick-eared cur of Iceland!"), and essential cowardice, a neat figure against which the king can shine; he thus offers another "contagious cloud" for the king to blow away in order performatively to secure his greatness.[104] Pistol's presence thus weakly doubles the king and is thus a knowingly compromised gesture back to the more robustly dialectal structure of both parts of *Henry IV*, where the oppositions between Hal and Hotspur, Henry IV and Falstaff, the court and the Boar's Head, comedy and tragedy provided a ready set of semiotic squares out of which *Henry V*'s sovereign values could eventually emerge. Pistol, more shadow than double, both connects and distances the conceptual structure of *Henry V* from the rigorous conceptual design of the earlier plays, offering a last hint of a historical logic that comes to a close with the end of the Henriad. Pistol's dim and sardonic reflection of Henry's military bearing thus functions both as an appropriate reminder of the history that brought Henry to Agincourt and as final proof that the problems that motivated that history have all but come to an end.

Pistol, however, is not simply minor; he is aggressively minor. According to Coleridge, "Pistol, Nym and *id genus omne*, do not please us as characters but are endured as fantastic creations, foils to the native wit of Falstaff."[105] Hazlitt, referring to the overall weakness of the comedy in *Henry V*, writes, "Falstaff is dead, and without him, Pistol, Nym, and Bardolph are satellites without a sun."[106] Pistol's special minorness is in part an effect of a style that seems out of sync with his context. He is a walking anachronism. Whereas Falstaff and Henry are both characterized by their differently but resolutely modern speech, Pistol talks as if he has wandered in from another play, namely from Christopher Marlowe's *Tamburlaine*; his bluster and ornate verse diction are self-conscious parodies of Marlowe's style, a fact underlined by Pistol's habit of incoherently misquoting his model: "Shall pack-horses / And hollow pampered jades of Asia, / Which cannot go but thirty mile a day, / Compare with Caesars, and with Cannibals, / And Trojan Greeks!"[107] The implicit comparison between Shakespeare's ideal king and Marlowe's earlier hero is meant to assert the measure and prosy modernity of Henry's style. And, if Marlowe is meant to be read as old-fashioned within the context of *Henry V*, Pistol's proximity to Marlowe marks him as simply out of touch: "if Pistol is a Tamburlaine-figure, he is a Tamburlaine who is frozen in time, who cannot escape the cadences, affect, and consciousness of 1588."[108] Pistol thus represents both the incomplete incorporation of another style within the otherwise homogenous context of *Henry V* (especially homogenous when compared with the dialectical work of both parts of *Henry IV*) and the parodic presence of another, older kind of violence working alongside the modern military and political tactics that Henry embraces and represents.

There is another, more formal aspect to Pistol's minorness. Whereas Falstaff relies on a delicate compromise between cerebral self-possession and bodily absurdity for his comic effect, Pistol seems almost entirely to lack self-consciousness. Whereas Bradley could imagine Falstaff as possessing a "touch of infinity" because he is a character in a play who seems to know that he is a character in a play, Pistol represents a raw and unknowing excess of energy that falls specifically short of Falstaff's critical irony. His anachronism, his excessive style, his tendency to fly off the handle and to take up too much space all suggest that, instead of somehow rising above the limits of his form, he embodies something like that form's failure. Pistol thus offers a good example of what in another context Alex Woloch refers to as the more exaggerated of the "two pervasive extremes of minorness."[109] As opposed to *the worker*, Pistol is *the eccentric*, "the minor character [who] grates against his or her position and is usually, as a consequence, wounded, exiled, expelled, ejected, imprisoned, or killed."[110] When Pistol first appears in the Henriad, he appears mostly as an opportunity for Falstaff to chase him out, a scene that anticipates his final disgrace and exile: "No more, Pistol; I would not have you go off here. Discharge yourself of our company, Pistol."[111] Like the men Falstaff drafts as "food for powder"—Mouldy, Feeble, Wart, and others—Pistol's very name seems to mark (or, in the language of the Elizabethan draft, to "prick") him as a necessary and inevitable sacrifice to his own excessively particular literary function.

Put in related terms, Pistol is a bearer of what Scott Bukatman, following Sianne Ngai and using Daffy Duck as an example, calls "animatedness": like Daffy, Pistol "is animated: as in, mobile and kinetic. He is animated: as in, energetic and vital. He is animated: as in, 'exaggeratedly emotional.' He is animated: as in, *over*animated, annoying, irritating (other ugly feelings)."[112] This might be one reason that the part of Pistol has the reputation of being nearly impossible to carry off: "Pistol's marvelous tight-rope balancing of grandeur and incongruity too easily degenerates into unfunny and unbelievable shouting and posturing."[113] Pistol is thus what Falstaff and Henry are not; he has neither Falstaff's self-conscious and ironic "touch of infinity" nor Henry's ability to force together oppositions—man and king, court and tavern, body and mind—in the service of the state. As opposed to the specific and critical force that Falstaff activated within the two previous plays, Pistol's minorness exists baldly and badly in opposition to just about everything, which is to say he exists in opposition to nothing at all.

Exit Stage Right

Soon after Henry's first appearance onstage, Olivier reveals Robert Newton's Pistol in a strikingly similar manner. I've already described Henry's entrance: Olivier, playing an actor preparing to play Henry, waits backstage for his cue. After a slight cough, he crosses the threshold and seems transformed from an actor into a king; or, rather, the body of the actor seems to have been absorbed into the represented person of the king. As I've suggested, Olivier manages this entrance to make another kind of argument about the authority that the king represents. He not only gestures toward the political theology of the king's two bodies but also embodies the promise of wartime and postwar consensus. Because World War II was a total war and depended on broad commitment to total mobilization, it became necessary to overcome old differences (socioeconomic, sexual, ethnic) that might prevent society from working efficiently toward its shared goal. As the war drew to its conclusion, it became increasingly important to imagine what society would look like after years of social, cultural, and economic disruption. Part of what makes *Henry V* "splendid propaganda" is, as I've mentioned, that its implied synthesis of actor and character, man and king, king and state could model that necessary unity.

It is striking that Henry and Pistol's first appearances are treated in so similar a manner. The actor playing Pistol (who is in turn played by Robert Newton) enters via the same door that Henry passed through a few scenes earlier. He is also met with a vigorous burst of applause. Once again, a modern actor playing an early modern actor playing an earlier modern character enters stage right to enthusiastic applause; both acknowledge the crowd's reaction and begin to play their respective parts; then, when their scenes are done, they exit the stage, bowing appreciatively to an appreciative audience. That, though, is where the similarities end. Whereas Olivier's performance collapsed actor and character, Newton's actor instead exaggerates the space between the two, playing the role more like a celebrity playing himself than an Elizabethan actor playing a Shakespearean character. Where we had watched Henry from across a threshold between backstage and stage, we see Pistol enter from an audience member's point of view. The audience is indeed more fully realized here; we get a reaction shot of delighted groundlings, giving us the sense that the performance is a sort of shot/reverse shot dialogue between performer and viewer. Pistol (or rather the actor playing Pistol who is in turn played by Newton) hams it up. "Pistol appears to elicit a show of accustomed pleasure from the groundlings who 'seem to be responding to a star comedian rather than to the role he is playing.'"[114] He moves to the front of the stage and plays to the crowd, doffing his cap, sticking out his tongue, and rolling his eyes. The actor playing Pistol appears to use his other actors more or less as an opportunity to address the audience directly. At the end of his scene, he lingers on stage, soaking up the crowd's applause for a few extra beats, and needs the Chorus to usher him off with a grateful but slightly exasperated wave before the play can continue.

Mr. Newton Tears His Cat

Newton's performance thus adds to the argument Olivier made when he cast George Robey as his dying Falstaff. Just as that decision forces us into a position of double exposure where we see both Robey and Falstaff, which is itself an echo of Kemp and Falstaff, so does the self-conscious staginess of Pistol's first entrance alert us to the doubled or rather trebled presence of an actor playing an actor playing a character. As I've already suggested, the

Enter ancient Pistol.

Elizabethan clown or Vice worked at an angle oblique to the rest of a play's cast. Whereas other actors would be expected to stick to their lines and subordinate their performances to the larger structure and intent of a play, part of a good clown's appeal came from his tendency to go off script, to improvise, to take up space. Olivier thus illustrates an older relation between the hero and the clown with the cinematic difference between the leading man and the character actor: "The character actors' acting surrounds that of the heroes like a baroque frame surrounds a renaissance painting. The fat uncle with a monkey and a traveling blanket, the skinny piano teacher with a bun and a pince-nez, the decrepit mayor, the hunchback inventor, the Galician profiteer, the bloated ship's cook—these are the character actors."[115] Pistol—with his leering eye, feathered cap, and broken sword—would fit nicely into Arnheim's list; he both stands as a sort of comic grotesque and, as we have seen, offers an indigestibly specific point against which the sovereign generality of the king might become visible. We might leave things there and say simply that Olivier and Newton work together in *Henry V* both to offer and interpretation of Shakespeare's play and to reveal historical aspects of the Elizabethan theater in terms that a modern audience would immediately understand; as with the rejection and death of Falstaff, the grotesque particularity of Pistol stands as a conceptual precondition for the king's less distinct but no less important generality.

However, leaving things there, we would miss a fundamental aspect of Newton's performance. Just as Welles, Robey, and Kemp seemed born to play Falstaff, Newton seems to have been born to play Pistol. If to play Pistol is almost necessarily to overplay him, this was a risk with which Newton would have been all too familiar. Simply put, Newton was a ham. "Newton not only chewed the scenery, but spat it out as well"; he was "a star character actor with a rolling eye and a voice to match; a ham, but a succulent one"; his were "rip-roaring characterizations"; in one part, he "rolled his eyes and leered and mouthed"; and his portrayals in general were "eye-popping, vein-bulging."[116] Although these aspects of Newton's acting style became exaggerated over time and reached a kind of culmination with his iconic take on Long John Silver, they were already aspects of his reputation when Olivier cast him in *Henry V*. Newton's considerable appeal as an actor thus stems precisely from his ability to push performances toward and sometimes past expressive limits without losing the thread of a performance or his considerable charisma. One critic writes of his Ferrovius in *Androcles and the Lion* (1952) that his performance "has a bizarre quality which—partly, one feels, by natural accident—is effective."[117] The question in that case is, what are we to make not only of the innate energy of Shakespeare's Pistol but also of how Olivier understood that energy when he cast Robert Newton? If Robey's gently autumnal Falstaff worked to signal the film's sense of a cultural loss that connected the waning of music hall with the experience of modern warfare, what is the doubly animated Pistol doing within the context of Olivier's otherwise "splendid" propaganda? Put differently, if much of Olivier's film seeks to marry the externalized artificiality of the stage with a more internal, naturalistic, and tasteful film style, what are we to do with the exaggerated and, perhaps, unexpected centrality of Newton's absurd and "eye-popping" Pistol?

With few exceptions, Newton's roles from the period follow a pattern: the characters he plays are outsized, violent, charismatic, and often drunk. In Lance Comfort's frankly florid *Hatter's Castle* (1942), he plays James Brodie, the cruel and increasingly unhinged hatter of the film's title; a creature of intense pride, Brodie builds a mansion he cannot afford in an effort to assert his importance. Brodie bullies everyone: he is monstrous to his terminally ill wife; he sends his pregnant daughter out of his home and into a rainstorm; he drives his young son to suicide. In the meantime, increasingly humbled by events, he becomes more and more unstable and rarely appears without a glass of whiskey in hand. The film ends with Brodie burning his castle down and dying with much bathetic sound and fury. Newton plays the role with a low Scottish burr and a feeling of barely restrained and enormous rage; one reviewer wrote that the film "provides a part to tear a cat in, and Mr. Newton tears his cat magnificently."[118] In 1947 he appeared in Carol Reed's *Odd Man Out*. The film follows Johnny, an Irish revolutionary wounded in a botched bank robbery, as he makes his weary way around a nightmare Belfast seeking and failing to find sanctuary. The film is striking for a number of reasons: filmed by Robert Krasker, the film anticipates the noir look of *The Third Man*, another of his collaborations with Reed. Krasker's Belfast is full of long shadows, streets luminously slick with rain, and rubble left behind from the Belfast Blitz. The film also anticipates *The Third Man* in its bleak postwar view of humanity; with each new meeting, Johnny learns that average people either want only to protect themselves or to exploit him to gain power, influence, and money. Like *The Third Man*, *Odd Man Out* offers a dark and barely displaced comment on both the aftereffects of war and of the experience of ethical compromise under occupation. Within this dismal context, Newton plays Lukey, a "wild-eyed and drunken painter," living in an abandoned house with a small-time grifter and a washed-up, alcoholic doctor.[119] Once the wounded Johnny ends up in their house, Lukey decides to paint his portrait, hoping to capture some ecstatic essence of the dying man as he passes from one world to the next. Once again, Newton's performance is broad, overstated, and utterly compelling, particularly when held against James Mason's portrayal of Johnny, the film's elegant martyr. Newton would go on to play a number of similarly broad and driven roles: the enormously violent Bill Sykes in *Oliver Twist* (1948), Long John Silver in *Treasure Island* (1950), and the monomaniacal Etienne Javert in *Les Miserables* (1952). His turn as solid middle-class paterfamilias, Frank Gibbons, in *This Happy Breed* (1944) is something of an exception; that said, Lean and Coward manage nonetheless to give him one scene in which to get rip-roaring drunk.

Like Kemp, Robey, or Welles, Newton often seems to run against the grain of the worlds in which he appears. In these terms, Newton's performances can recall Alexander Nemerov's account of Skelton Knaggs's brief and bizarre appearance as "the Finn" in Val Lewton's *The Ghost Ship*: "There the sense of being constrained, of being unimportant—of having to strum up a hyperbole of gargoylish effects all in an instant that somehow still comport with the idea of 'soul,' of having to lay down intimations of depth across the flat signatures of sudden triviality—makes it Knagg's most poignant and socially meaningful moment as a screen actor."[120] In Newton's case, the irrepressible eccentricity of the character actor stands as a similarly enigmatic answer to the film seen as an aesthetic whole; like Knaggs, Newton "stands out, obdurate and strange, instead of retiring into the background."[121] To cast the aggressively, irrepressibly minor Newton in a film was, as Olivier must have seen, to make argument in and of itself. Given this larger context, we should understand that when Olivier cast Newton as Pistol, he was both responding to and helping to solidify the actor's relationship to a particular type of character, a type that carried with it a set of significances that work not only to support ideas in and about *Henry V* but also to make the character and the film legible in relation to the film's status as propaganda. There are, in that case, a few questions. What did Olivier and his audience see when they saw Robert Newton? What does Newton's particular position as a recognizable type add to *Henry V*? And what did the presence of Robert Newton have to say about the war?

Pistol's Cock Is Up!

As mentioned previously, Olivier puts Pistol and Henry into a sort of competition via their similar but different entrances. Whereas Olivier's performance allows us to imagine a successful fusion of actors and characters, men and kings, individuals and states, Newton's performance accentuates the space between the character and the actor. Although Newton, the actor he plays, and the character that that actor plays are all animated by a similarly manic energy, that energy sets them all at odds with each other and with the scenes that would otherwise contain them. Newton thus evokes a counterfactual desire that, as David Thomson suggests, follows from other great and minor film performances: "Just by virtue of their color, eccentricity, vivacity, and fidelity, don't our most beloved character actors suggest a logic, or a passion, in which their characters are at least as important as any others on view?"[122] In this sense, Newton participates in a struggle that Nemerov, drawing on Alex Woloch's *The One vs. the Many*, takes as central to Lewton's wartime films: "The subversive potential of the bit player most often took the form of a contest between minor and major actors in the same scene, a competition visible now thanks to . . . Woloch's theory of the jostling between minor characters and protagonist in the space of the novel."[123] The eccentricity, the particularity, the vivacity, and the anarchic charm of the bit player can thus exceed his or her structural function and to stand as an implicit or explicit criticism of norms that a film might otherwise seem to support; Nemerov quotes the great Manny Farber: "The era's movies were 'never more savage and uninhibited than in those moments when a whirring energy is created in back of the static mannered acting of some Great Star.'"[124] This potential for structural violence in the encounter between major and minor is something that both Woloch and Nemerov illustrate with an example from *The Iliad*; and, if Pistol has an equivalent in Homer's epic, it is certainly Thersites, a figure whom Woloch calls "the first truly minor character in Western literature."[125] What set Thersites apart from his fellow Greeks was both his particularity (he is not just ugly but the *ugliest* man around) and his satiric aggression: "Thersites exceeds, and threatens, the hierarchical framework of the Greek army camp."[126] Nemerov adds that Thersites's "physical and verbal domination signals a disruption of established order, an absence of authority in which he attains a powerful realization."[127]

This description could just as easily apply to Pistol, who in the absence of Falstaff emerges as the Boar's Head's leading light. He has married Mistress Quickly and become the de facto leader of Falstaff's band of misfits and drunks, whom he in turn leads as camp followers to France. However, where Falstaff had real force and stood, at least for a time, as a potent ethical threat to Henry's authority, Pistol has, as played by Newton, only his exaggerated and weird vitality to carry him through. In addition to his convoluted, pseudoliterary jibes and insults, he is marked in Olivier's film by his sharply drawn physical characteristics: an unruly mop of hair, an often protruding tongue, rolling eyes, a feathered cap, and suggestively broken sword. Taken together, his verbal performance—crazy, profane, oddly compelling—and his physical appearance allow him to take up space that might seem otherwise to belong to the protagonist. And while Pistol is at last dispatched, he nonetheless seems, at least for a moment or two, to command as much attention and admiration as a king; this is the Pistol's threat, just as it was Thersites's threat. (Indeed, Shakespeare's own Thersites has more than a little Pistol in him: "The plague of Greece upon thee, thou mongrel beef-witted lord!"[128])

That said, neither Woloch nor Nemerov go on to say what happens next to Thersites. As part of his effort to rally the Greeks for war, Odysseus makes a spectacular example of Theristes, calling him a "cur" before striking him with Agamemnon's scepter:

> And he cracked the scepter across his back and shoulders.
> The rascal doubled over, tears streaking his face
> and a bloody welt bulged up between his blades,
> under a stroke of the golden scepter's studs.
> He squatted low, cringing, stunned with pain,
> blinking like some idiot rubbing his tears off dumbly with a fist.
> Their morale was low but the men laughed now,
> good hearty laughter breaking over Thersites' head.[129]

At one stroke, Thersites is wounded, humiliated, and silenced; and this is the last we hear of a character who seemed for a moment capable of bringing down a whole army. Pistol meets a similar fate at the end of *Henry V*. After the battle has been won, Captains Gower and Fluellen discuss Pistol's probable behavior upon his return to London; Gower says, "Why, 'tis a gull, a fool, a rogue, that now and then goes to the wars, to grace himself at his return to London, under the form of soldier, and what such of the camp can do among foaming bottles, and ale-washed wits, is wonderful to be thought on."[130] When Pistol inevitably appears, Fluellen accosts him and demands that he eat his leek, a token of Welsh identity that Pistol had mocked the day before: "I peseech you heartily, scurvy lousy knave, to eat, look you, this leek."[131] Pistol draws his sword with a "Base Trojan, thou shalt die." Fluellen then takes the sword away, bangs him on the head, at which point Pistol falls to his knees, just as Thersites had before him. Fluellen then forces him to eat the leek: "If you can mock a leek, you can eat a leek. Bite, I pray you." Like his king, Fluellen mocks the mock, removing the leek from its position as a metaphor and asserting its dumb and aggressive identity with itself: a leek is a leek is a leek—so eat it. Although Olivier tempers the violence of the scene (in Shakespeare Fluellen strikes Pistol several times, drawing

"Base Trojan, thou shalt die."

blood), it is nonetheless disturbing. Pistol has been a fool, of course, but does he deserve this?

Why does Pistol receive Thersites's treatment in Shakespeare and then later in Olivier? Why must he be punished? In part, this is a simple and diminished repetition of the earlier and more definitive rejection of Falstaff. As I have suggested, in order to secure his authority as a king and soldier, Hal had to reject Falstaff, to reduce the complexity both of his own personality and his world. This need to reject or disavow freedom in the name of security is, as we have seen, an element of the second teratology that wartime critics returned to again and again in order to find justifications for the culture of total mobilization. It is also an expression of the paradox at the heart of total war: in order to save culture, we must sacrifice culture; in order to save Falstaff, we must kill Falstaff. Beating, humiliating, and finally chasing Pistol away might, in that case, be taken as a late reminder of what has been lost (liberty, humor, play) and gained (military and political victory) with the banishment of Falstaff at the end of *2 Henry IV*.

We might also see the humiliation of Pistol as part of a larger argument about Henry and Olivier's respective hopes for a postwar Britain. This late scene brings the Welsh Fluellen and the English Gower together and sets them genially plotting about how to teach Pistol a lesson. And, while Pistol speaks in as distinctive a manner as Fluellen, the latter's speech is marked by regional particularity whereas Pistol's is marked by its archaic literariness and its almost pure eccentricity. In other words, the conflict between

Fluellen and Pistol should, in some sense, be understood as the conflict between an ethically capacious, postethnic future and an archaic and atavistic literary past or, alternatively, between the official and unofficial modes of eccentricity that I laid out in the introduction. Fluellen's attack on Pistol can be seen as part of a larger argument about postwar compromise that Olivier develops in terms of World War II as much as in the context of early modern conflict. Or we might say, again following Woloch, that Pistol's humiliation is something like a formal allegory for a political idea that the play and the film represent. Insofar as the second tetralogy is about how a young man emerges from a mix of companions and competitors to become a nation, a play, and history's protagonist, then Pistol's banishment—which would amount to something like the banishment of minorness itself—would stand as a neat emblem or memorial for a process that has stretched across four plays, years of writing and performance, and, indeed, the whole of British history.

King Lush

There is, though, another aspect to the humiliation of Pistol, one that Olivier brings quietly to the surface of the film through his decision to cast Robert Newton in the role. In addition to his reputation as a hammy if brilliant character actor, Newton was also infamous for his own bad behavior and, in particular, his binge drinking. Like his father Algernon before him, Newton had been invalided out of military service and was a committed and public drinker; in 1941 he had been rejected by a naval officer selection board "for a commission on the grounds of [his] general lack of sobriety."[132] His drinking was also often a threat to the films he acted in. Ronald Neame recalls bailing "him out of Bow Street police station" in the midst of one production. "The only remembrance Bob had was waking up in jail with a monumental hangover."[133] David Lean worried that he would fall off a roof during the filming of *Oliver Twist*: "we attached a rope to his belt and fed it through the tiles of the roof as a safety wire in case he stumbled."[134] The actor Kenneth Griffith remembers:

> He lived in a sort of fantasy world, which was very alarming; but when he had to do his acting, he was very remarkable. I remember him meeting me one morning at the studio and saying, "I'm having an affair with a lady wrestler!" I used to sit with him at lunchtime in the grand baronial hall at Pinewood, along with all the important producers and accountants with all that essential shit going on. One day they were all being very respectable and you could see Robert moving. He suddenly said, "I've got the twinges! I've

> got the twinges!!" and everyone got deeper into their soup. Then he took up a great bread basket and swished it around, and people were trying to pretend it wasn't happening![135]

During the war, Newton used air raids as an opportunity to sneak a few drinks while others sought safety underground: "When the alarm went and everyone raced to the shelters . . . Newton . . . would stay behind, retrieve [his] bottles and settle down on the property furniture for a solid period of self-indulgence until the company reemerged."[136] Richard Burton, a boozing protégé who referred to Newton as "King Lush," recalled his giving him a ride to the set of *Waterfront Women* (1950) in his battered, old Bentley: "It was winter and the car had a thin covering of frost and refused to start. Newton handed Burton his flask, went back into the house and returned with a horsewhip and began laying into the bonnet. When they tried the ignition again the Bentley revved up."[137] David Niven remembers Newton during the filming of *Around the World in 80 Days*: "Bobbie confessed to me that . . . his doctor had warned him that one more session with the bottle would almost certainly be fatal." One day "when he arrived for work, a roaring delivery of 'Once more unto the breach . . .' announced alarming news. 'Oh, Bobbie,' I said, 'what have you done to yourself?'" Newton's reply is heartbreaking. With tears in his eyes, he implored Niven, "Don't chide me, dear fellow, please don't chide me."[138]

Although Newton might seem like just another "hell-raiser" of the British cinema—like Burton, Peter O'Toole, Richard Harris, and Oliver Reed—his case is different because of when and how he drank. As opposed to those more glamorous if ultimately no less tragic cases, Newton didn't drink after the war—he drank and drank to dangerous excess during it. In other words, whereas the bad behavior of younger actors could be understood as a reaction to and expression of emerging postwar prosperity after years of war and economic austerity, the same prosperity that forms the loosely permissive backdrop for films such as *The Knack . . . and How to Get It* (1965), *Darling* (1965), and *Alfie* (1966), Newton's drinking during a time of total mobilization—a time when eating, sleeping, talking, and not talking were seen as part of the war effort—could be understood both as a failure of will or "lack of moral fibre," and as a performed and costly Falstaffian resistance to the social logic of total war. That is not to say that his drinking problem was different from what came before or after war; rather it could have *looked* like something different during wartime. We saw this anxiety in the work of wartime Shakespeareans who felt it necessary to reject Falstaff and his sack-drinking lack of restraint all over again. We can see it also in

Cyril Connolly's 1938 identification of drink as one of the artist's "enemies of promise": "Drink is available and there are still artists who drink to excess out of the consciousness of wasted ability, for drunkenness is a substitute for art; it is in itself a low form of creation."[139]

Although one does not want to exaggerate the wartime stigma against heavy drinking, it was in fact the case that between World Wars I and II, the consumption of both beer and spirits in Britain had decreased drastically: "Between 1919 and 1939 consumption remained at historically low levels, though with variations reflecting the state of the economy and employment."[140] In a 1943 review of Mass Observation's *The Pub and the People*, George Orwell writes, "The Mass Observers . . . have no difficulty in showing that there was extraordinarily little drunkenness in the period they were studying: for every five thousand hours that the average pub stays open, only one of its clients is drunk and disorderly."[141] As a result and as opposed to the previous war, there was no real outcry against drinking during World War II because, as John Burnett remarks, "National efficiency was not now threatened by drunkenness and industrial unrest, and in these circumstances government could regard reasonable supplies of beer (as of tea) to civilians and the forces as an aid to national morale at a time when many foods were rationed."[142] In a way that recalls my larger argument about official as opposed to unofficial eccentricity: "The conviviality of beer drinking," writes James Nicholls, "had considerable purchase at a time when notions of traditional sociability were being harnessed as a defense against the cultural and military threat of the German war machine."[143] Seen in light of this relatively moderate and prosocial attitude toward drinking, Newton's aggressive, antisocial, and atavistic drunkenness could have read as something very different from ordinary, culturally sanctioned drinking. In other words, by the time of *Henry V*, Newton had begun as an actor and a man to bear an excessive significance that must have contributed to his vexed appeal to directors as a character actor, particularly in films—such as *Henry V* and *Odd Man Out*—that reflected more or less explicitly on the experience and the costs of life during and after wartime.

There is another, related significance to Olivier's decision to cast Newton as Pistol, one that becomes clear at the film's end. After Agincourt, after the deaths of Falstaff, Nym, Bardolph, and, it is at last revealed, Mistress Quickly, and after Pistol's final humiliation at the hands of Fluellen, Newton turns to face the camera to deliver Pistol's parting speech.

> Doth Fortune play the strumpet with me now?
> News have I that my Nell lies dead

I' th' hospital of a malady of France.
And there my rendezvous is quite cut off.
Old do I wax, and from my weary limbs
Honour is cudgelled. Well, bawd I'll turn,
And something lean to cutpurse of quick hand.
To England will I steal, and there I'll steal:
And patches will I get unto these scars,
And swear I got them in these present wars.[144]

The scene is notable for a few reasons. First, this is the only moment in the film's naturalistic third act when an actor turns to the camera in order to address to the audience directly. As already described, Olivier represents both Henry's soliloquy on the eve of Agincourt and Falstaff's dying memory of Hal's rejection as voiceovers spoken while the camera lingers closely on their pensive faces. His handling of those moments would seem to suggest the film's adherence to naturalistic rules governing the impermeability of the fourth wall. It is for that reason all the more striking that, between his beating and his departure, Pistol turns to the camera in order to engage the audience directly. This helps in part to solidify Newton's late place in the tradition of the clown or the Vice; as I said before, what differentiated the clown from other types of performances was exactly his tendency to break the performance's frame to improvise and to stake a claim as an actor or celebrity as much as a character. And, while Pistol's brief speech is not

"To England will I steal, and there I'll steal."

especially marked as a clown's moment in Shakespeare (unlike, for instance, Kemp's epilogue at the end of *2 Henry IV*), Olivier treats it as if it were one; he strengthens and updates the connection by bringing a cartoonish, Looney Tunes quality to Pistol's speech and, even more, to his scampering exit offstage and out of the film. The script directs: "The music starts as Pistol scurries off and disappears in a barn. . . . Pistol emerges from the other side of the barn with a pig under his arm and cockerel in his hand. He runs up the hill away from us and disappears."[145]

Newton's late turn toward the audience represents the culmination of an exaggerated theatrical logic that has run like a countermelody throughout *Henry V*. For, while Olivier's three stylistically distinct acts work like a tacitly progressive aesthetic history that takes us from the unapologetic and open theatricality of 1600, through the framed totalities of the Limboug brothers, to the antitheatrical cinematic naturalism of 1944, Newton's Pistol remains resolutely the same—the clown, the fool, the parasite—despite the demands of political and aesthetic history. We could see this resistance as another aspect of Olivier's scholarly project in *Henry V*. Trying to come to grips with an apparent shift in Shakespeare's dramaturgy that coincides with the departure of Kemp and the death of Falstaff, Olivier maintains the exquisitely theatrical Pistol as a homeopathic excess that might both embody the older style of theater and, with its disappearance, fully usher in a new style. That said, Olivier also seems to see that the very logic of the scapegoat or parasite that would allow for that rejection also makes that rejection necessarily incomplete and encourages us to understand what remains and why. In other words, at the same time that Olivier's film makes a difficult argument about what needs to be sacrificed in the service of this total war, it also acknowledges the real costs of that sacrifice. Like other wartime works discussed here, the film seeks via the figure of Pistol to make two apparently distinct arguments: one makes a case for the undeniable necessity of this war and the other a case against war as such. Pistol thus emerges as an anamorphic hinge that connects and separates the rabbit and the duck of total war. The film attempts to manage at the level of style a position that many were trying to manage during World War II: how to be really and honestly both for and against war.

When the fourth wall falls at this late moment, Pistol isn't addressing just any audience; he is addressing a war-weary audience in 1944. What could Pistol have to say to 1944? What's most important about this moment is that Pistol's final message, delivered at once at the end of the battle of Agincourt and near the end of the war, is reflection on what happens when men come home from war. And it is, indeed, a message different in kind from Henry's exhortation that his men imagine themselves a "band of brothers," trading war stories as veterans, grizzled and beloved at home. As opposed to the image of the scarred and noble old soldier, Pistol invites us to imagine the soldier returned home as a problem, as—in the spirit of Newton's whole performance—someone or something excessive and troubling that cannot be readily reabsorbed into everyday life. Something like this, of course, has always been true of war. As Homer and then Tennyson imagined, an experience as violent, as absolute, as epic as war must have unsuited many men for a life at home, a life "centered in the sphere/ Of common duties." This is perhaps why it takes Odysseus so long to come home and why Achilles never comes home at all. Shakespeare seems to have had something similar, if decidedly and pointedly less epic, in mind when he imagined Pistol's degraded homecoming. Joel Altman points to a contemporary 1598 Parliamentary "proclamation authorizing summary execution of incorrigible [beggars and vagabonds]. . . . Specifically mentioned were those 'coloring their wandering by the name of soldiers lately come from the wars.'"[146] James Shapiro writes: "Overlooked in the spectacle of Henry's (and Essex's) imagined homecoming is the largely suppressed and unhappy story of the return of war veterans like Pistol. . . . Through bitter war veterans like Pistol, Shakespeare also hints at the corrosive and unavoidable national cost of the Irish war."[147] And Rabkin adds: "[O]ur regret is for more than the end of some high comedy: it is for the reality of the postwar world the play so powerfully conjures up—soldiers returned home to find their jobs gone, falling to a life of crime in a seamy and impoverished underworld that scarcely remembers the hopes that accompanied the beginnings of the adventure."[148]

The soldier coming home was no less a problem in 1944. Although there is little evidence to suggest that war veterans were really more violent or antisocial than individuals otherwise affected by World War II, a moral panic around the solider, his training, and the imagined difficulty of his reentry into ordinary life began to gather steam early in the war.[149] In newspapers, magazines, and popular films the image of the poorly adjusted or, indeed, the sociopathic veteran appeared again and again. The *Daily Mail* suggested that perhaps "men 'trained in the use of lethal weapons [had lost] some of their normal inhibitions against the taking of human life.' 'They've been trained in lawlessness, ordered to behave like thugs, and decorated for doing it . . . what do you expect?' was (as the *New Statesman* suggested) by 1946 becoming conventional wisdom."[150] Another observer noted "that 'paratroops have been trained as all-in-wrestlers and boxers, and Dacoits who can kill by the quick twist of a cord. Yet,' he mused, 'we shall expect all these lads to be well-behaved and docile post-war.' *Good Housekeeping* magazine warned its readers that their homecoming husbands had been transformed into 'mechanized men, trained to do one thing only—kill the enemy.'"[151] In other words, in 1944 Pistol's direct address to the camera would not only have read as structural recognition of the minorness of the minor character or as a reflection on the life of the early modern camp follower but also as a warning or, indeed, a threat delivered directly from a figure conjured out of late war and then early postwar anxiety. In other words, to see Pistol in 1944 was to see an excess that was more than merely formal; it was to see the figure of a soldier who in a very real sense could not come home but nonetheless does come home.

Unfit to Serve

Olivier's *Henry V* is, indeed, splendid propaganda. It is also one of several films that were released near the end of the war or after the war that work to represent the difficulty that men and women had adjusting to life after the losses and social dislocations of the war. We might think of Powell and Pressburger's *A Matter of Life and Death* (1946), where Squadron Leader Peter Carter survives a crash landing only to find that he had suffered brain damage. As a result, he needs to work through an elaborate and impossible fantasy of a court case in heaven before he can truly live again on earth. Carol Reed's *Odd Man Out* (1947) and *The Third Man* (1949) both work to embody the position of someone whose actions or commitments have unsuited them for everyday life. In the first case, James Mason's character Johnny is an IRA fighter just out of prison; an apparently hysterical case of blindness interrupts bank robbery, which in turn makes him a fugitive not only from justice but also from other people. In *The Third Man*, Harry Lime's absurd role as the mysterious third man at the scene of his own faked death reveals the degree to which the necessary complicities of wartime threatened to put people at odds with the world and with themselves: "Who is the third who walks always beside you?"[152] In Powell and Pressburger's uncharacteristically noir *The Small Back Room* (1949), David Farrar plays Sammy Rice, a military researcher whose loss of a leg has driven him to self-pity and alcohol; he, too, appears to have been broken by the war. In Cavalcanti's *They Made Me a Fugitive* (1947), Trevor Howard plays an RAF veteran whose desperate thrill-seeking leads him to join a gang of crooks smuggling and selling war rations. While the "they" of the title ostensibly refers to the double-dealing members of his gang who frame him for murder, it might equally refer to a whole culture that sent him emotionally unprepared to war. A similar and surprising case can also be made about David Lean's *Brief Encounter* (1945), as I will demonstrate in the next chapter.

The world that Pistol resists is thus a propaganda world, a world with little time for a magnificent ruin of a man like Robert Newton. As I have suggested, Robert Newton was not a product or a symbol of postwar affluence. Unlike Richard Burton, Peter O'Toole, and Oliver Reed, he did his drinking during wartime, and, as many of his directors knew, it resulted in a particularly chaotic and deeply self-destructive kind of unfitness. This is complicated by the nature of total war, a kind of war that saw not only combat but also all manner of civilian activity as a direct, if obscure part of the war effort. To choose unfitness—to choose to be unfit to serve—during a time of total commitment and total war is arguably to live a self-destructive argument about war that would have been impossible otherwise to make. In other words, what Olivier saw in Newton was a great actor whose notoriously bad behavior acted as an implicit interpretation of Shakespeare's character and thus his whole play. Casting is, in these terms, an aspect of cinematic technique and thus of cinematic form; in this instance, casting works tacitly against a totalizing view of both war and cinema that Olivier's film might seem otherwise to support. The world of total war is the world of a young, charming, and callow king, a king who would feign fellowship, execute prisoners, and pursue war for its own sake. It is also a world with little room for the drunks, the clowns, and the soldiers who neither return as heroes nor have the decency simply to die. And it is, as Olivier and his film understand, a world from which, Falstaff, Pistol, Will Kemp, George Robey, Orson Welles, and Robert Newton would not go, or at least not quietly.

3

Celia Johnson's Face

Before and After *Brief Encounter*

encounter, *n.*: A meeting face to face; a meeting (of adversaries or opposing forces) in conflict; *hence*, a battle, skirmish, duel, etc.

—*Oxford English Dictionary*

I didn't think such violent things could happen to ordinary people.

—Laura Jesson in *Brief Encounter* (1945)

Is *Brief Encounter* a war movie? Maybe, maybe not. Although Lean made his film during the war and released it right after, it is set just before and thus cannot represent the war directly. As Antonia Lant puts it, "Its diegesis is fastened both to that 'so-called peace and civilization' of the winter before the outbreak of war, and to the time of the audience's present, that is, 1945."[1] *Brief Encounter* is thus not about the military, although a couple of thirsty soldiers show up to offer some much needed comic relief. Its main male characters—the husband, the lover, and the lover's disapproving friend—are not in uniform, although Laura Jesson (Celia Johnson) and her husband, Fred (Cyril Raymond), idly imagine a naval career for their young son Bobbie. It is not about the Blitz, although Lean filmed exterior shots on the west coast of England in part to better observe the blackout. It is not about mourning, although its main character, Laura Jesson, wanders past a war memorial at a moment of poignant personal dejection. Although Lean himself talked about *Brief Encounter* in relation to the wartime rise of British cinematic realism, the film's reception has mostly accepted the war's absence from the film and steered clear of it as a significant context; with some important exceptions (most notably Lant's essay) postwar critics focus instead on its old-fashioned sexual politics, its very English atmosphere of barely managed repression, and its considerable command of cinematic technique. So, although *Brief Encounter* is not about war because it is set just before its beginning it is also all about war insofar as the war, present in its absence, contributes to its tense, expectant, and mournful mood; if it seems that *Brief Encounter* is not about war, war is nonetheless all about—around, near, adjacent to—it.

The film's complicated temporal relation to the war is reflected in its equally complicated narrative structure: the film begins at its end, six weeks after its protagonists first meet; it then flashes back to the start and makes its way back from that beginning to the end of the affair with which the film began. The film's compressed play of before and after is thus another version of the self-consciously involuted narrative designs of both *Colonel Blimp* and *Henry V*, films that, as I've argued, put narrative and cinematic pressure on the difference between past and present in order to make difficult arguments about the experience of war. However, where those films deal in wide, obviously historical timespans (1902, 1918, and 1942; 1415, 1600, and 1944), the events of *Brief Encounter* take place less than a decade before the film's time of release. That said: if only a few years separate *Brief Encounter*'s setting from its appearance, those years were filled with a violence that would have made the suburban plenty of Laura's world seem like a paradise lost. "Lights are blazing, trains run on time, chocolate is purchased without coupons": these are relatively trivial instances of what divided the setting of *Brief Encounter* from the time of its arrival in cinemas.[2] So, although its past would have looked uncannily like its present to audiences in 1945, references to the war and its effects would in fact have been as anachronistic to *Brief Encounter* as a wristwatch on a Roman gladiator. Despite all this, I want to argue that *Brief Encounter* is not only a war film but also Lean's best war film, a war film that uses cinematic technique to make important and difficult arguments about war, arguments that are present throughout the film but especially in the film's most characteristic shot: a recurring close-up of Celia Johnson's face. In other words, I want to suggest that that film exploits technical aspects of cinema in order to think about the experience of war and the pressure that war puts on life before, during, and after. Once again, these techniques, arguments, and ideas are embodied with surprising and poignant economy in a shot of Celia Johnson's face.

Screen Memories

That face: it is, after all, the beginning, middle, end, structural center, and emotional heart of *Brief Encounter*. In David Thomson's words, "The film's core is Laura's aching experience, and that is how it hangs on Celia Johnson's crushed gaze."[3] After accepting the role, Johnson wrote to her husband:

Celia Johnson's face.

"It will be pretty unadulterated Johnson and when I am not being sad or anguished or renouncing I am narrating about it. So if they don't have my beautiful face to look at, they will always have my mellifluous voice to listen to. Lucky people."[4] Although she writes with characteristic irony, she was right—both about our good luck and about her huge centrality to the film. *Brief Encounter* is almost entirely structured around Celia Johnson's face, her voice, and her character's thoughts. Laura Jesson, the middle-aged woman whose chaste extramarital affair is the film's subject, is not only the focus of *Brief Encounter*'s slight plot but also that plot's apparent point of origin. The film is told mostly in flashback, as a memory unfurling within Laura's mind: "In short, what we get, throughout the film, insists that it is Laura's view of her brief liaison with Alec, how it was for her then, how it is for her now."[5] The film begins at its end with Laura's final meeting with Alec Harvey (Trevor Howard), the doctor with whom she has had her brief and doomed encounter. She then returns home to sit by the fire and her husband Fred and to mull silently over (and thus to narrate) the events of the previous few weeks: she meets a man when he helps remove "a piece of grit" from her eye; she falls in love with him and he falls in love with her; they realize that they can't abandon their families and so they part; he goes to South Africa and she goes home. At this point, Laura emerges from her reverie and returns to the present, putting us back more or less where we began.

Lean signals the initial passage from the narrating present of Laura's living room to the narrated past of the film's plot with a dissolve that momentarily brings the railway café—the site of the film's most important past action—seemingly *into* the present of the Jessons's living room. The sequence is technically daring for a number of reasons: it takes immediate and disorienting liberties with the film's chronology, not only signaling—as it surreally projects a static living room into or onto a bustling train station—that we've entered the interior space of Laura's memory but also suggesting that, under the right conditions, the past can overwhelm the present. The dissolve also briefly doubles Laura, letting us watch her (frame right) watch herself drinking tea (frame left). As we watch her watching herself, it seems either as if the present Laura—the back of her head cast in shadow and her face apparently illuminated by the reflected light of the remembered image—has taken a seat in the cinema alongside the movie-going audience or as if her head and eyes have themselves become a sort of projector, casting what ought to remain unseen—thought, memory, the past—onto the surface of the present. It is, writes Charles Barr, "precisely as if she were watching, or summoning up her own story on a cinema screen."[6]

Lean and the film's cinematographer, Robert Krasker, manage the scene with a strangely insistent skill. The present Laura's head is lit from above, which both helps to frame her and to produce the projective-memory effect I describe; because, however, the café's overhead lamps provide a credible natural source of that light, past and present are, if only for a moment, brought impossibly into the same physical space. As if emitted from an

The dissolve

already dead star, the six-week-old light from the café somehow finds its way to her head and face in the present. The shot thus manages both to ignore and to observe one of the "sacred commandments" of cinematographic naturalism: that any light in a shot needs to come from an explicit or implicit but nonetheless physically tenable source.[7] Insofar as it bleeds over from the past into the present, the shot's light is an embodied if ephemeral form of anachronism; it is an example of what Gérard Genette calls *achrony*: "an event we must ultimately take to be dateless and ageless."[8] Cutting across the divide between past and present, the shot's light makes an argument about the complication of past and present even as it falls out of the temporal order that otherwise organizes *Brief Encounter*.

The light is thus something like the cut that is not a cut (the no-cut) that I see at work in *The Life and Death of Colonel Blimp*; and just as the cut's absence allows *Colonel Blimp* to embody while it undermines the naturalized presentism of a total war culture, here the light calls attention to itself as cinematic technique and helps to reveal one of the stylistic seams that hold a film and an idea about history together. It is also something like Olivier's decision to cast Robert Newton as Ancient Pistol in *Henry V*, a decision that accentuated the untimeliness of Shakespeare's character and offered that character as an immanent and unruly alternative to the film's otherwise "splendid" propaganda. Put differently, the shot allows the timelessness of cinematic technique *as* technique to erupt into the represented time of the film. More than just another instance of what some viewers took as Lean's mania for technique, the shot is a strongly realized—even overdetermined—form of what Walter Benjamin referred to as the "dialectical image": "It's not that what is past casts its light on what is present, or what is present its light on what is past; rather, image is that wherein what has been comes together in a flash with the now to form a constellation."[9] As we will see, this dialectical eruption or image is characteristic of *Brief Encounter* and its critical relation to cinema, history, and war.

Face Time

As a result of the complex, unstable, and pervasive tension between past and present that runs through the film, the close-ups of Celia Johnson that punctuate and bookend the film are called upon to do a tremendous amount of structural and emotional work, work that was lost on neither Lean nor Johnson. Johnson wrote to her husband, Peter Fleming: "I am scared stiff of the film and get first-night indijaggers before every shot but perhaps I'll get over that. It is going to be most awfully difficult—you need to be a star of the silent screen because there's such a lot of stuff with commentary over it—it's terribly difficult to do."[10] Lean saw Johnson's often tacit but always communicative performance as exemplary: when you watched Johnson act, he said, you saw that good acting "is, in fact, thinking."[11] Roger Manvell writes, "She looks quite ordinary until it is time for her to look like what she feels."[12] The performance is all the more remarkable once one realizes that her voice-overs were recorded later and added to the film and that much of *Brief Encounter* is, in fact, Celia Johnson simply and silently sitting and thinking and feeling in front of a movie camera.

The shot is aesthetically assured. Johnson is sharply lit and held in shallow focus, a fact that draws attention to her face and allows the room behind and the round-backed chair on which she sits to dissolve into indistinct darkness. Her face is shadowed, pale, tired, and filmed in hard light without the softening effects of either makeup or lens diffusion; the viewer's eye is drawn to that face's "imperfections" (a mole, a creased forehead, a vein snaking across her temple) as well as to her huge, sad, deeply set, and downcast eyes. Her face appears at the end of a subtly deliberate tracking shot not unlike the one Olivier used to pull in toward the face of his ruminating king; as the camera slowly approaches, the lights behind Johnson dim almost imperceptibly, bringing her face, hair, shoulders, wide collar, and slightly labored breathing into greater relief. Because the shot's lighting thus lingers over the minor details of her face, hair, and dress, it says that she is not only ordinary but also *real*. Lean in fact understood this as an especially British realism; he wrote in 1947 that "British audiences enjoyed" films like *Brief Encounter* because they "were about people like themselves—people they understood. But, above all, they were so 'real.'"[13] This desire for a "documentary realism" was, as Lean saw, partly a result of the war: "During the war . . . films were shot on location, actors abandoned theatrical for more natural mannerisms, and a newsreel-like style was employed to photograph the action. There was no doubt, according to Lean, that *Brief Encounter* was in the vanguard of films representing the new postwar realism."[14]

Even so, some of the effects Lean achieves exceed the demands of the film's putative realism, passing over into something more mannered and extreme. For instance, the low-key lighting style that Krasker employs throughout the film often appears more film noir than kitchen sink.[15] A scene is lit in a low-key style when "the ration of key to fill light is great, creating areas of high contrast and rich, black shadows"; with low-key lighting, faces and foreground objects are brightly lit, while the background and its stuff remain in shadow. Indeed, classic accounts of noir's visual style seem readymade for *Brief Encounter*: "the constant opposition of areas of light and dark . . . characterizes film noir cinematography. Small areas of light seem on the verge of being completely overwhelmed by the darkness that now threatens them from all sides. Thus faces are shot low-key, interior sets are always dark.'"[16] These terms apply to the shot I've been looking at as well as to many others in the film; and *Brief Encounter*'s stylistic debt to film noir goes beyond its handing of Celia Johnson's face. Night shots of the train station where Laura and Alec meet seem better suited to the nightmare Vienna of *The Third Man* than to the suburbs. Lant writes, "As Laura scurries through the streets, Milford is transformed from a humdrum, daytime shopping center into a rain-slicked, nighttime no-man's land."[17] At other points, the film opts for an almost expressionist visual style. A woman's mouth is shot at an inappropriate scale and with apparently unmotivated, dreamlike intensity; objects like umbrellas and hats loom in the foreground with Hitchcockian menace and produce an effect of scalar imbalance that Siegfried Kracauer associated with American "terror films" immediately after the war: "People emotionally out of joint inhabit a realm ruled by bodily sensations and material stimulants, a real in which dumb objects loom monstrously high and become signal posts or stumbling blocks, enemies or allies. This obtrusiveness of inanimate objects is infallible evidence of an inherent concern with mental disintegration."[18] So, despite the fact that the film is without murders, gumshoes or *femmes fatales*, it frequently relies on the visual language of noir—in the words of David Thomson, "this women's picture looks noir."[19]

An Ordinary Woman

There is an apparent disconnect between *Brief Encounter*'s content and its style. On the one hand, Coward's script takes pains to stress the ordinariness of Laura and her life. She borrows her books from Boots, eats her lunch at the Kardomah, and listens to Rachmaninoff on BBC radio in the evening; she embodies, in other words, an experience that was modern but not modernist, middlebrow but not stupid, ordinary but not mundane. Self-identified as an "ordinary woman," Laura is something quite other than the "problematic individuals" of film noir or the eccentrics that I've been tracking throughout this book: "It all started on an ordinary day in the most ordinary place in the world, the refreshment room at Milford junction."[20] On the other hand, the film toggles between an evenly lit cinematographic style appropriate to the ordinary world of Milford Junction and one that evokes the stylistic and psychological extremities of expressionism. Instead of pursuing a naturalistic or documentary transparency, *Brief Encounter* again and again calls attention to style as style. Why does the film handle its avowedly ordinary stuff with a style so extraordinary?

We might begin by looking at the film as a sort of technical exercise or essay, as Lean's effort to use his film's relatively slight plot as an occasion for experiment and the refinement of his still developing craft. The film was both praised and blamed early on for its apparent willingness to pursue technique for its own, inorganic sake. According to André Bazin, "Nothing could be more tightly structured, more carefully prepared, than *Brief Encounter*—nothing less conceivable without the most up-to-date studio resources, without clever and established actors."[21] In the eyes of Jean Queval, David Lean "seems to be only interested in those exceptional subject matters that flatter the super-technician."[22] David Thomson writes that "Lean easily gets overcalculated."[23] We might also make a more generous case and say simply that there is in fact enough of a thematic overlap between *Brief Encounter* and noir to motivate Lean's style: although it "is not often listed among the *noirs*, . . . it is a film about traps, feeling guilty, and being imprisoned against your nature."[24] The film might be taken in other words, as a sort of domestic noir, a style of film that overlays the stylistic charge of film noir onto an ordinary but no less intense personal experience; *Brief Encounter* might, in that case, be taken as a gentler cousin to "noir weepies" like *Mildred Pierce* (1945), which Lant invokes as an appropriate historical and stylistic counterpart to *Brief Encounter*.[25] We might also, as I have begun to suggest, look to ways in which the style of *Brief Encounter* is appropriate to a wartime content that its odd temporal structure must not allow.

The Great Hiatus

Brief Encounter is set just before the war but was released just after, which makes the film a strange kind of period piece, an oddly foreshortened historical film that looks back to a time before the war. What's complicated about this is, after all, that *Brief Encounter*'s past is different from but still so very close to its present; with only a few years separating the film's setting from its release, it would have been difficult for audiences in 1945 to gauge the historicity of its characters, its manners, or its fashions. Of course, the availability of rationed items would have struck viewers; one critic praised the film for its "extraordinary feat of projection . . . by setting the picture in pre-war days and providing—out of the rigors and shortages of post-war life—all the proper accoutrements of the past, including chocolate buns."[26] Some of Lean's other attempts to mark the past as past are subtler: "The reason David put up with that outlandish peaked hat which Celia Johnson wears in the film was to signal both the date and the fact that she was meant to be provincial. 'Now, of course, people say, "Oh, that hat. It dates the film." Well, it was meant to.'"[27] Lean, of course, misses the point here. When people in the 1960s said that the hat "dates" *Brief Encounter,* they meant that it seems tied to the general time of the film's release—a midcentury England that struck later viewers as improbably repressed—and not to its very particular setting in the years or months immediately preceding as opposed to those immediately following the war. For instance, in 1984 John Russell Taylor praised Lean's film for its inadvertently ethnographic qualities: "At this distance of time *Brief Encounter* assumes another, rather surprising quality—that of a documentary insight into a vanished scene, a vanished way of life."[28] For Lean, however, the hat was not something that came from another age; it was rather a visual index of historical differences that were both minor and immense. It was the visual trace of an effort to make a film that could represent the brief but no less enormous historical difference between the before and the after of World War II.

After all, it was only the onset of the war that made "the winter of 1938–39" into such a distinct and coherent period, into what the philosopher of history Reinhart Kosseleck understands as a historical "event," "a discernible unity capable of narration."[29] If, however, we need the event in order to narrate history, which is to say to organize history into a series of things that happen before and after other things, we also need a sense of before and after in order first to imagine the event. It is the event that allows us to narrate history. Events are history's smallest unit of narrative measure and thus need to exist before they can be put into a sequence. In order to identify the event as smallest unity, however, one needs already to have a concept of before and after: "A minimum of 'before' and 'after' constitutes the significant unity that makes an event out of incidents."[30] You need the event before you can have before and after, and you need before and after before you can have the event. What leads us to this vicious circle is an important third term, the excluded middle—that which falls between before and after and makes the event possible.

We might look here to the psychoanalyst Jean Laplanche's notion of "afterwardness." In an effort to account for the apparent reversibility of psychic causality in Freud, for the fact that early experiences lead to later symptoms and that later knowledge can make earlier experiences differently significant or even freshly traumatic, Laplanche argues that what makes psychic life available to psychoanalytic interpretation is the structuring fact that "two scenes [are] linked by associative chains, but also clearly separated from each other by a temporal barrier which inscribes them in two different spheres of meaning."[31] In psychoanalysis, it is this temporal barrier, this period of structural latency that makes interpretation possible; not itself an event, the barrier that separates before and after is what allows psychic history to mean something; Lacan called the latency period "the source of the construction of [the subject's] entire world."[32] For Benjamin, the narration of history requires a similar barrier: "The present determines where, in the object from the past, that object's fore-history and after-history diverge so as to circumscribe its nucleus."[33]

In *Brief Encounter*, that temporal barrier or divergence—invisible but necessary to the making of sense—is the war. We might think here of F. R. Leavis's habit of referring to World War I as "the Great Hiatus" or the title of David Jones's 1937 long poem about his experience of World War I: *In Parenthesis*.[34] Saint-Amour writes about the interwar years as just this kind of a middle, a parenthesis caught between the experience of one war and the anticipation of another: "in the immediate wake of the First World War, the dread of another massive conflict saturated the Anglo-European imagination, amounting to a proleptic mass traumatization, a *pre*-traumatic stress syndrome whose symptoms arose in response to a potentially oncoming rather than an already realized catastrophe."[35] We might also think about the moment in *Colonel Blimp* when Clive learns that World War I has come to an end. He sits on a battlefield with his man Murdock and, as the distant shelling stops, birds begin to sing. Between the end of one sound and the beginning of the other, the world is held suspended in a brief but no less felt pause.

For Benjamin, this ability to think about the relation between the event, its before, and its after—to think, in other words, historiographically—was partly derived from the cinema: "The first stage in this undertaking will be to carry over the principle of montage into history. That is, to assemble large-scale constructions out of the smallest and most precisely cut components."[36] Cinema was, of course, more than a convenient analogy for Benjamin; at its best, cinema was for him an immanent form of critical thinking: "By close-ups of the things around us, by focusing on hidden details of familiar objects, by exploring commonplace milieus under the ingenious guidance of the camera, the film, on the one hand, extends our comprehension of the necessities which rule our lives; on the other hand, it manages to assure us of an immense and unexpected field of action."[37] Insofar as cinema relies on the relation between "small components"—shots—and what comes between them—cuts—it is itself a concentrated mode of thinking about the interaction of events and what comes between them. Cinema, in other words, is not like the practice of history—it is the practice of history. This is, of course, to follow, as Benjamin did, the great Soviet theorists in putting montage at the heart of cinema; V. I. Pudovkin wrote, "the material in film-work consists of pieces of film, and . . . the composition method is their joining together in a particular, creatively discovered order."[38] Benjamin's contemporary Marc Bloch was thinking in similar terms about film and history in 1930: "Since life is nothing but movement, could we not consider that grasping history through the regressive method is akin to unrolling the last reel of a film from its end, expecting to find gaps in it, but intent on respecting its mobility?"[39] Bloch would revisit this figure just before he was killed by the Gestapo in 1944: "Here, as elsewhere, it is change which the historian is seeking to grasp. But in the film which he is examining, only the last picture remains quite clear. In order to reconstruct the faded features of the others, it behooves him first to unwind the spool in the opposite direction from that in which the pictures were taken."[40] What changed between 1930 and 1944 was Bloch's commitment to the image; whereas history had been like cinema in 1930, it simply *was* cinema in 1944. Insofar as both history and cinema depend on a difficult relation between only theoretically minimum units (historical events or cinematic shots) and what connects and separates them (the temporal barrier or latency period or the cinematic cut) it makes sense—as it made sense to Benjamin and Bloch—to think of cinema in general as a form of history and, more to the point, as a form of historiography.

This developing relation between cinema and historiography between and during the wars has important consequences for *Brief Encounter*. First, it helps us to better see how the film is *about* war; without the war as the excluded but nonetheless necessary middle that makes the difference between its past and present (the time of its setting and of its release), the film couldn't make what stylistic sense it does. Second (and not paradoxically), because both the fact of that middle and the tenuousness of that difference are so foregrounded in the film, anachronism becomes a key aspect of the film's structure at several levels, including plot, style, and dialogue. Lean, perhaps an editor before all else, understood cinema's ability to manage time and made that ability one implicit subject of his films. In other words, the possibility of confusion between before and after in the film—what we might call the afterwardness of *Brief Encounter*—is what gives the film, as well as its characters and objects, its peculiar and powerful significance. It is, in other words, exactly along the line of a historical and cinematic divide between before and after that the film is a film importantly and critically about war.

War Timing

The war stands in its absence as the film's structuring middle, as that which makes its stylistic negotiation of before and after possible. A noir style is in that case both appropriate and inappropriate to the film; it is appropriate to the wartime moment of its production and inappropriate to its prewar setting. Like the impossibly naturalistic light source that leaps from Laura's memory into the space of her present, style in *Brief Encounter* cuts across what should distinguish past and present. More than mere anachronism, the film's appropriately inappropriate or inappropriately appropriate style is a sort of scandal, an eccentric disturbance that keeps the film from settling comfortably into either past or present. In this way, *Brief Encounter* is best read as a film about time and about the formative pressure that war exerts on the shared social experience of time.

David Lean got his start as an editor and several of his films bear traces of an editor's central preoccupation with the cinematic management of time. This is especially true of Lean's several war films: *In Which We Serve* (1942), *This Happy Breed* (1944), *The Bridge on the River Kwai* (1957), *Lawrence of Arabia* (1962), etc. Like *Brief Encounter*, these films are historical films, and Lean relies throughout on a cinematic concept of history. Instead of simply representing historical events, Lean treats history as if it were cinema, as if real relations between past, present, and future, between cause and effect, between intended and unintended consequences ought to be seen as aspects of a cinematic syntax: cut, dissolve, close-up, fade. As Antoine de Baecque puts it, "Special effects, framing, editing, Technicolor, superimposed images, slow motion, flashbacks, split screens, looks-to-camera . . . all these tools have a history . . . and all have also played a role in history."[41] Because Lean's chosen type of history is military history, these issues appear with an especially sharpened focus; like filmmakers, war planners look to the past to understand the present and, indeed, to shape the future. This is, as we will see, something that Lean understood and that informs the structure of his war films and, somewhat more obliquely, the self-consciously anachronistic structure of *Brief Encounter*.

Take, for example, *In Which We Serve* (codirected by Lean and Noel Coward). The "in" of the film's title, taken from *The Book of Common Prayer*'s "Forms of Prayer to be Used at Sea," works on several related levels. It refers to the whole of the Royal Navy and thus its larger military purpose: "Be pleased to receive into thy almighty and most gracious protection the persons of us thy servants and the Fleet in which we serve."[42] It also refers to a particular ship, the HMS *Torrin*. The film opens with a single line of narration, read by Leslie Howard, who acts the part of the chorus in *Henry V*—"This is the story of a ship"—and archival newsreel footage of a ship under construction. Showing the corporate labor that goes into the *Torrin*'s construction helps to underline the film's analogy between the ship and its sailors and the ship of state and its citizens; in both cases, to be "in" something is to be part of an endeavor that trumps personal differences, an idea that the government was keen to convey in a time of total mobilization. The *Torrin* thus functions both as a representative of British naval might and as an enclosed space that lends the film a dramatic and political unity necessary to effective propaganda. Coward and Lean take pains to fill the ship with a cross-section of British society. After the ship is attacked and sunk by German planes, its survivors gather around a floating ring in order to await rescue. They represent a neatly inclusive range of socioeconomic types: there's the upper-crusty Kinross, the middle-class Chief Petty Officer Hardy, and the working-class Ordinary Seaman Shorty Blake. United "in" the space of crisis, the film's different characters both maintain the visible marks of their respective classes and transcend those differences in the service of a shared enterprise.[43]

Once the sailors are gathered around the floating ring, the film begins to offer their individual stories in a series of flashbacks that radiate out from that realized narrative hub. Coward and Lean got the idea for the flashback structure from *Citizen Kane,* which Lean encouraged Coward to see: "from *Kane* [Coward] got the idea of the flashbacks. Quick as a knife, he took the narrative, cut it up, introduced this Carley float, which was a sort of raft all these ships carried, and he used the men clinging to the Carley float to jump from one part of the story to another."[44] Like spokes emanating from a wheel, these different lines of the past are brought together in the film to make an argument about the leveling social logic of total war: in a war that affects everyone, everyone's story matters.

Politically effective, this radial device also creates an oddly suspended aesthetic effect; on the one hand, the cyclic structure of the flashbacks makes it difficult to track the film's intersecting timelines. Is Shorty's story exactly or only roughly contemporary with Kinross's? Would it be possible to identify the shared social and historical space that these different stories inhabit? Indeed, the sailors' memories occasionally lapse into a sort of metaleptic disorder where one character's memories somehow originate *within* the diegetic frame of another character's memory; as Bert Cardullo puts it, "although a flashback begins in the context of one person's memories, it often ends in the middle of another's."[45] On the other hand, these ambiguities don't matter much to the politics of *In Which We Serve.* No matter how different the experiences of its characters, the film always and necessarily returns to the shared national space and narrative present of the circular life raft. The point of the film is not to keep different stories straight; it is rather to convey a shared sense of the pressure that war exerts on individuals and groups, a pressure that subordinates the idea of before or after to the larger feeling of being "in" something; "the interwoven flashbacks underline the film's theme: in general, the unity of all England in the face of the Nazi threat during World War II."[46] Lean uses a cinematic technique embodied in the image of a circular raft to convey both the experience of and a possible psychic reaction to that state of political suspension.

We might also consider *Lawrence of Arabia* (1962) and its famous and impossibly long shot of Omar Sharif coming out of the desert as Sharif Ali. Lawrence, making his way to meet Prince Faisal in order to figure out "his intentions in Arabia," stops with his Bedouin guide at a desert well. The two take a moment to fill canteens and drink before the guide spots a rider in the distance. At first, the rider appears as little more than a speck in the wavering eye of a desert mirage. Slow minutes pass between the actor's first appearance as a dot on the horizon and the moment when he comes close enough to shoot Lawrence's hapless guide, Tafas. The shot is justly famous both for its tensely dramatic effect and for its technical achievement. The cinematographer Freddie Young remembers, "We had Omar Sharif go practically out of sight until he was a little pinpoint in the distance and David told him to ride straight towards the camera, and we shot a thousand feet. Nobody had done it before and nobody had done it in color in 70mm."[47]

Ali's emergence from a mirage also makes for one of *Lawrence*'s several subtle cinematic puns; a mirage is an illusion that results from the way light plays across space. It is, in other words, a lot like cinema, a fact not lost on Lean. The object of one of Lean's most accomplished cinematic shots would, in that case, be the cinema itself. Lean makes a similar joke with another of the film's most famous shots: our first view of the desert comes in the form of a bravura cut from a match that Lawrence blows out to an image of the

Easy stages.

sun rising over the desert. This type of cut is called a match cut because it "matches" an object in one shot with a different but similarly positioned object in another, in this case the match's flame with the rising sun. So, Lean uses a match cut with a match. (Powell and Pressburger use a similarly spectacular match cut from a falcon to a war plane at the beginning of *A Canterbury Tale.*) Lean goes on to underline his joke with an uncharacteristic and, I think, forced technical error; as the sun comes fully into view, a lens flare appears in the upper-left corner of the screen, an effect that runs against the aridly perfect visual style of the film as a whole. That the image of the sun's rise is uncharacteristically marred by a lens flare underscores Lean's broader interest in using cinema to capture cinema; a lens flare is, after all, one of the only ways a camera can take a picture of itself. As D. A. Miller says about the appearance of a flare in another conspicuously perfect film, "*Psycho*'s lens flare, to take this uniquely well-documented instance, purposely invites us to metacinematic reflection; it is a sort of cameo of the apparatus."[48]

Ali's emergence from the mirage—agonizing in its length—thus establishes an idea about time, motion, and history on which the film draws again and again (Lean repeats the effect later with Lawrence's long ride out of the Nefud with the fallen Gasim). Not only are we confronted on several occasions with what the play between space and time means for military strategy (Lawrence's impossible march across the Nefud to take the Turkish stronghold at Aqaba, his trek across the Sinai Peninsula to alert the higher-ups in Cairo that Aqaba has fallen, his lone walk from Syria to Jerusalem), but the film also uses that experience of palpable duration to imply an idea about history. The film is filled with meditations on the making of history as experience, record, and ideological spectacle; this is especially clear when it comes to thinking about the tortured relation between particular tactics and European strategy in the Middle East; for, while the film would seem to be about World War I, it is more persuasively about later conflicts in the Middle East that had their origin with Lawrence's "small beginning." As Scott Anderson argues, the "small" acts, "hidden loyalties," and "personal duels" of a few passionate men—a bookish, largely untrained British soldier (Lawrence), an oddball Prussian spy (Carl Prüfer), an American oilman (William Yale), and a Romanian Zionist (Aaron Aaronsohn)—"helped create the modern Middle East and, by extension, the world we live in today."[49] Indeed, characters in *Lawrence* are often compelled to argue for the durational and strategic elasticity of historical cause and effect when it comes to the world-historical significance of local events. When General Murray derides the Middle Eastern campaign as "a side-show of a side-show," the diplomat Dryden responds, "Big things have small beginnings, sir"; when asked how he will make the huge distance between Darra and Jerusalem, Lawrence responds, "in easy stages"; and, when he works to convince Ali to make the trip across the Nefud to take Aqaba, Lawrence points across the desert and says, "Aqaba is over there. It's only a matter of going." In each case, the film makes an embodied, step-by-step (or frame-by-frame) duration—time as it is projected into and across the reality of space—into a palpable and important aspect of war and history, into something like the palpable viscosity of events that Clausewitz refers to as "friction":

> The difficulties accumulate and end by producing a kind of friction that is inconceivable unless one has experienced war. Imagine a traveler who late in the day decides to cover two more stages before nightfall. Only four or five hours more, on a paved highway with relays of horses: it should be an easy trip. But at the next station he finds no fresh horses, or only poor ones; the country grows hilly, the road bad, night falls, and finally after many difficulties he is only too glad to reach a resting place with any kind of primitive accommodation. It is much the same in war.[50]

The friction or resistance offered by the textured realism of space (a road, a field, a desert) congeals time, turning it into something gummy and real. It is the specifically cinematic reality of that time that preoccupies Lean in *Lawrence of Arabia*, a film that does as much as any to make one feel time as it hardens into official history. Because the film makes this process of ideological reduction palpable, it stands both as a modern epic and as a challenge to ideological work which makes modern epics epic. With this, *Lawrence of Arabia* emerges as something like the long works of interwar encyclopedic modernism that Paul Saint-Amour sees as pitted against the totality of epic: "Set beside such an epic premise, the fragmentariness and internal fissuring of long modernist fictions begin to look less like the flaws through which a longed-for totality seeped away and more like a critical refusal of epic's all-too-vital political logic."[51] As opposed to relying on the fragment, though, *Lawrence* instead uses the self-conscious drag of its temporal style to render cinematic time into something clotted and palpable; Lean's long long shots defamiliarize an experience of wartime and national history that the epic would seek to make natural and inevitable.

In *Lawrence of Arabia* and *In Which We Serve*, Lean uses formal devices—long takes in and of the desert in *Lawrence*, the radial flashbacks that emanate from the survivors' ring in *In Which We Serve*—to embody different ideas about history and experience during wartime. One can find similar figures in Lean's other war films: the bridge as a figure for the collapse of instrumental into noninstrumental time in war in *The Bridge on the River Kwai* (1957); the lyric poem as figure for what would but finally can't escape the ersatz totality of total war in *Doctor Zhivago* (1965); and the very idea of years "between the wars" as a figure for the retroactive narrative logic of national character in *This Happy Breed* (1944). Part of what makes these figures work is the fact that these films are so obviously about war. What, then, about *Brief Encounter*? What does its form, its style, its sense of cinematic technique have to say about war?

The Bomber Always Gets Through

Brief Encounter has a complicated relation to its war. Because of the temporal dissonance between its setting and its release, the film cannot be about war in any direct way. Like it or not, though, the war was all about—which is to say physically and psychologically around or proximate to, before, during, and after—*Brief Encounter*. Whatever the film's content, it was the product of and was viewed in the immediate wake of a home front experience that had altered life in Britain and beyond; where it was made, how it was made, and how war-weary audiences who first saw it were conditioned by the material and psychological conditions of the home front. The experience of the home front during World War II was unlike that of previous wars. Because the war was understood as conceptually total and thus as a war in which states self-consciously committed the totality of their military, economic, and social resources to war, civilians were increasingly understood—and, more to the point, *understood themselves*—as acceptable targets of military violence. This situation was exacerbated by technical developments in aerial combat that further undermined the distinction between civilian and soldier.[52] As Guilio Douhet, air war's first theoretician, saw it in 1921, aerial combat would make all future wars total wars: "No longer can areas exist in which life can be lived in safety and tranquility, nor can the battlefield any longer be limited to actual combatants. On the contrary, the battlefield will be limited only by the boundaries of the nations at war, and all of their citizens will become combatants, since all of them will be exposed to the aerial offensives of the enemy. There will be no distinction any longer between soldiers and civilians."[53] With "Bomber" Harris and Curtis LeMay, the London Blitz, the Allied bombing of Lubeck, Munich, and Mainz, the firebombing of Japanese cities, and, at last, the atomic bombing of Hiroshima and Nagasaki, World War II did all it could to realize the terrible promise of Douhet's prediction. As a result, death, displacement, and deprivation became a part of normal civilian life in Europe and beyond: "only in Britain and Germany did military losses finally outnumber the civilian death toll; in total more than 19 million non-combatants were killed across Europe."[54]

The logic behind and justifications for aerial bombing shifted over the course of the war as planners became increasingly focused on the psychological and moral as opposed to the physical effects of destruction; whereas early British attacks on Germany focused on the destruction of military and then industrial targets, by October 30, 1940, Churchill both acknowledged and believed that "the civilian population around target areas must be made to feel the weight of war."[55] Arthur Harris, the head of Bomber Command, put it more directly: "It should be emphasized that the destruction of houses, public utilities, transport and lives, the creation of a refugee problem on an unprecedented scale, and the breakdown of morale both at home and at the battle fronts by fear of extended and intensified bombing, are accepted and intended aims of our bombing policy. They are not by-products of attempts to hit factories."[56] Later, it became clear that bombs were surprisingly inefficient when it came to killing individuals: "British planners had assumed that for every metric ton of high-explosive bombs dropped on a city, about seventy-two people would be killed or injured. The actual rate turned out to be only fifteen or twenty casualties per ton."[57] Strategy then shifted again as bombs were instead used to "de-house" urban populations; as one of Churchill's advisors put it, "People don't like to have their homes destroyed. [They] seem to mind it more than having their friends or even their relatives killed."[58] After the war, Fred Ikle, a RAND Corporation analyst studying the effects of the bombing, determined that a population wouldn't become fully demoralized until "about 70 percent of a city's homes were destroyed."[59] (Ikle would go on to help plan for the social and military consequences of a US-Soviet nuclear war.) As opposed to World War I—where what Paul Fussell refers to as the "ridiculous proximity" of a world more or less untouched by war heightened the ironic contrast between home and front—World War II's home front wasn't a place of respite removed from the violence of localized combat; during the Blitz, Mass Observation captured one "grizzled, elderly Cockney" declaring, "We're in the front line! Me own home—it's in the Front Line."[60]

As a result of this mix of factors, total war altered the look, feel, and sound—which is to say the felt reality—of everyday life in Europe and elsewhere. Massive military mobilization had altered the demographic make-up of whole populations. Bombs dropped night after night blocked roads, leveled buildings, altered the structure of cities, and changed the nature of the sky. Once more or less neutral, the sky had become a reminder of danger; as Orwell famously put it in 1941: "As I write, highly civilized human beings are flying overhead, trying to kill me."[61] Aerial bombing seemed to alter and indeed to pervert the very order of things: "And suddenly everything was submerged in the milky light of the netherworld. A searchlight behind me was sweeping the earth at ground level. Frightened, I turned around, and then I saw that even nature had risen up in hatred against herself. Two trunkless pines had broken through the peaceful trance of their existence and turned into black wolves avidly leaping after the bloody sickle of the moon, which was rising before them. Their eyes gleamed white and foam dripped from their snarling mouths."[62]

Less disastrous, but maybe more important to cinema were the blackouts that anticipated and accompanied aerial bombing and for a time changed the very meaning of light and dark: the home front was "given imaginary unity—by the blackout ordered to defend Britain's cities against aerial attack. . . . As one military historian notes, 'Blackout was one of the ways in which the totality of this total war declared itself for it was universally imposed in Germany, France, Italy, the UK and elsewhere.'"[63] The war also altered the European and British soundscape as bombs and planes—like the Stuka Ju87 dive bomber and, later, the V-1 rocket—were designed to maximize not only physical but also psychological damage. Marc Bloch described their "strictly acoustic" effects during the Nazi invasion of France in 1940: "Nobody who has ever heard the whistling scream made by dive-bombers before releasing their load is ever likely to forget the experience. It is not only that the strident din made by the machines terrifies the victim by awakening in his mind associated images of death and destruction. In itself, and by reason of what I may call its strictly acoustic qualities, it can so work upon the nerves that they become wrought to a pitch of intolerable tension whence it is a very short step to panic."[64] The war's effects on the home front were, of course, materially devastating; life, property, and mobility were lost on a grand scale. Less measurable but no less significant were the ways it altered the physical, psychological, and sensory nature of everyday life in Britain and Europe: the British psychoanalyst Edward Glover reflected in 1940: "[T]he whole atmosphere of modern war is likely to revive those unreasoning fears that the human race has inherited from its remotest ancestors: gas masks that make us look like strange animals; underground shelters; rumours and suspicions; enemies overhead and unseen; wailing sirens; creaming air bombs, and vast explosions in the night."[65] An effect of this alteration of reality was that the nature of realist representation also changed; what rated as real in a world of total violence and sensory extremity was different from what would or could have been believed only a few years before—which brings me back to *Brief Encounter*.

New Sensations

How does *Brief Encounter* represent this reality, the reality of a world rewritten at an existential level by the experience of total war? Because the film is divided between the before of its setting and the after of its production and release, this question is doubly significant. In other words, if the home front experience of total war had indeed altered or at least added to the meaning of light, dark, sound, hunger, sleep, and so on, then a "realistic" portrayal of the recent past might need to project aspects of the postwar present onto the prewar past in order to be convincing. We need to remember that a twenty-year-old viewer of *Brief Encounter* in 1945 might have had difficulty remembering a world where the reciprocal meaning of light and dark hadn't been affected by the necessity of blackout; what would constitute a realistic representation of the recent past to such a viewer? In this way, we might see *Brief Encounter*'s complicated representational management of past and present as a response to the traumatic discontinuity of war: "On an experiential level," writes Eelco Runia, "discontinuity is the extent to which a particular event wasn't supposed to happen, the extent, that is, to which the event was at odds with the worldview from which it emerged. Consequently, to come to terms with a traumatic event means to establish a worldview from which the traumatic event stops being 'impossible.'"[66] As I have been suggesting, because the war had become part of what was real, the film had to rely upon that war for its structure, its style, its significance, and for the terms under which it succeeds or fails as an instance of cinematic realism. So, if it couldn't refer directly to the war, it had nonetheless to rely on the war because war had become proof of something real that exceeded the experience of war itself; and as we've begun to see, because the film can't represent the war and its world as content, it instead approaches the war and its effects as film style. In this way, *Brief Encounter* offers another example of what, in the introduction and following Adorno, I refer to as the late eccentricity of the British war film, as a resistance appearing both as an impacted style and in moments of aesthetic eccentricity or stylistic excess that gave paradoxical expression to a war that would not be represented directly.

We might look, for instance, to the film's management of sound. One of the first sounds we hear is the whistle of the express train as it races through Milford Junction during the opening credits. The sound is insistent, shrill, loud, and something other than what one expects from a train; indeed, the sound is loud enough that it seems for a moment impossible to overtake and to drown out the film's extradiegetic score. A species of what Gérard Genette refers to as metalepsis, the sound is similar to moments "when an author (or his reader) introduces himself into the fictive action of the narrative or when a character in that fiction intrudes into the extradiegetic existence of the author or read . . . such intrusions disturb, to say the least, the distinction between levels."[67] Insofar as the sound crosses over from the represented world of the film out into the world of the soundtrack and thus the world of the camera, the theater, and the audience, it does something similar to the light that crossed over from past to present in the sequence described above. In other words, because the sound exceeds its relation to any represented content, it instead announces itself as technique; as a result of its nervy sound and its place on the edge of the film's diegetic frame, the whistle seems calculated both to index and to produce anxiety.

Indeed, the first instance of this whistle not only doesn't sound much like a train but also doesn't sound like other trains in *Brief Encounter*—with one important exception: toward the end of the film, Laura, bereft at having lost Alec, runs onto the train platform and nearly commits suicide. Lean adopts something close to a surrealist style here: he once again drops the lights behind Celia Johnson's face as she thinks or, rather, panics in the face of a fresh and unspoken loss, the shift in contrast giving her face an expressionist emphasis; the sequence suggests that the relationship's end leads nearly to a breakdown, a fact that appears to infect the camera, which responds with an odd, crazy tilt; finally, as Laura runs out to the platform's edge, the film's first whistle returns as a high-pitched externalization of the hysteria that once again nearly overtakes both Laura and *Brief Encounter*. The fact that the whistle is a late repetition of the film's opening suggests a correspondence between mental breakdown and the limits of *Brief Encounter*'s cinematic form (what Thomson calls "the dysfunction between a stiff upper lip and a mind turning to jelly"); because its first appearance seems to break the film's diegetic frame, its second appearance suggests a significant relation between the limits of aesthetic and psychological coherence.[68]

Lean foregrounds the shrillness and the intensity of the train's whistle in a way that underscores the degree to which the acoustic world had also been mobilized during the war; because the sound seems both at the film's opening and at Laura's moment of crisis to overwhelm the film's soundtrack and, in some impossible sense, to drown out the whole of its world, it stands as a sensory equivalent to an experience that had traumatically undermined differences and distinctions that had once promised, however ineffectually, to keep war at bay. And like weapons that were designed to take military advantage of what Marc Bloch called their "strictly acoustic qualities," Lean's whistle recalls the degree to which the war had turned hearing into a form of practical psychological warfare. Harold Nicolson captured the overwhelming sound of the Blitz in his journal: "I have never heard such a variety of sounds—the whistle of the descending bombs, the crash of anti-aircraft, the dull thud of walls collapsing, the sharp taps of incendiaries falling all around."[69]

Sidney Giliat does something similar—if somewhat clumsier—with *Green for Danger* (a 1947 film that again stars Trevor Howard). In many ways a classic procedural—there's a murder, a locked room, and a mordantly funny detective—the film relies on the regular sound of "buzz bombs" to provide atmosphere and increase suspense; although they do that important work, they and the war are otherwise oddly extraneous to the film. Put differently, *Green for Danger* understands the war as a complicated but normal part of life, as a backdrop against which other, sometimes bad things happen; it thus counts on the same effect that the V-1 flying bomb's designers did: that the psychological effects of the bomb and its sound could do as much damage as the bomb itself. Fritz Lang makes similar use of the Blitz-as-backdrop in his 1944 film noir *Ministry of Fear*, in which a stray bomb functions as little more than a convenient if especially violent plot device. In *Brief Encounter*, Lean's use of the train's whistle makes it into something more than an externalized sign of Laura's heightened emotional state or a material symbol of the separation that the train will facilitate; rather, it suggests ways in which the acoustic world had been made significant as a means of creating internal and incapacitating states of anxiety, a fact that mirrors the war's larger collapse of front and home front, outside and inside, soldier and civilian. What had been most personal—the senses and our private experience of them—had been brought forcibly into the public world of war. In each of these films, the sound of war has become an emotionally significant but nonetheless regular part of the real world and thus necessary material for a successfully realist representation.

Lights Out

I've already talked about how the film's darkened palette might be interpreted as an effect of and response to Britain's experience of blackout. In addition to the familiar emotional resonance of the film's high-contrast look, its play between light and dark helps Lean to imagine an incomplete symbolic relation between war and its end. Although it was the case that the lights would come back on with war's end, the new emotional and aesthetic stakes of the cinematic relation between light and dark would nonetheless retain some of its wartime significance. Take, for example, Lean's first truly postwar film, *Great Expectations* (1946). Although the film's first half follows Dickens's novel fairly closely, it moves further and further from its source at it goes on. This is most striking at the film's conclusion. Dickens's novel ends on a famously ambiguous and shadowy note: "I took her hand in mine, and we went out of the ruined place; and, as the morning mists had risen long ago when I first left the forge, so, the evening mists were rising now, and in all the broad expanse of tranquil light they showed to me, I saw no shadow of another parting from her."[70] In Dickens, the day is waning as Pip takes Estella's hand, a fact that raises the darkling possibility that the lack of parting's shadow has more to do with the failure of the light than with any real hope for the future. Lean, however, has Pip return to Satis House, which has been burned but not destroyed in the fire that kills Miss Havisham. Estella has taken over the house and, as she sits in Miss Havisham's darkened rooms, seems ready to take her places as a lonely and bitter recluse. Pip runs to the window and tears down the heavy drapes that keep Satis House shrouded in darkness: "I have come back, Miss Havisham! I have come back—to let in the sunlight!" Light streams in through the windows, waking Estella from her ethical doze and encouraging her to take Pip's hand and, presumably, to take it once again in marriage.

This conclusion makes tacit but unmistakable reference to the war's end. First, Lean's turn to Dickens for his first postwar film allows him to situate his cinema in a longer and victorious national tradition; the implied cultural continuity between England's rich literary history and its contemporary cinema points to Britain's longevity and survival, an idea that Olivier had explored during the war with *Henry V*. Second, Lean's revision is important in and of itself; the absent presence of what Dickens had imagined as a fully ruined house would of course have reminded viewers of the many, many structures that had been bombed and burnt into rubble during the blitz. Because he both invokes and swerves from the available image of the bombsite, Lean is able to engage in a complicated and allusive form of mourning as he simultaneously invokes and disavows the freighted and familiar image of the wartime ruin.[71] More particularly, the tearing down of drapes would have been significant in itself to audiences who had lived through blackout and who would only recently have been able to remove the thick blackout curtains that kept indoor light from streaming out into the world. The shot thus directly aligns postwar liberation with the aesthetic promise of the cinema: as the light streams through Miss Havisham's room, illuminating dust motes along the way, it would have evoked the light of a projector throwing its image onto the screen from behind and above the audience. Turning Satis House into both a memory of war and a movie theater, Lean aligns the promise of the immediate postwar period with the cinema itself.

This image of light streaming in *Great Expectations* is also a reference to several related scenes in *Brief Encounter*. On Thursdays Laura goes to the pictures and sits in a darkened cinema while light streams overhead and onto the screen. The cinema is Laura's space of independence and freedom from the pull of home, husband, and children; it is an alternative to and an escape from everyday domestic demands. The cinema is also where she and Alec go together as they begin their courtship. The imagined films that they do or can see are all love stories: *Flames of Passion, The Loves of Cardinal Richelieu, Love in a Mist*. The cinema is thus a space of "high romance." Indeed, the lines that she recalls from Keats's sonnet "When I Have Fears" in order to help Fred with his crossword puzzle also refer to nearly cinematic effects of light and dark: "When I behold, upon the night's starred face,/ Huge cloudy symbols of a high romance,/And think that I may never live to trace/Their shadows, with the magic hand of chance." Keats imagines the world as a play of shadow and light projected across a surface, that is, a magic lantern that would stand as a precursor to the cinema. As Laura indulges in a waking dream of a possible life with Alec—dancing, riding in a convertible, strolling on a cruise ship's deck—her fantasies, middlebrow indices of high romance, seem to be cast like light onto the window of her train compartment; and, as discussed, Lean lights the moment when Laura begins to remember the past as if that past were projected from her mind onto a screen. Lean again and again aligns cinematic light with the possibility of escape. (Powell and Pressburger achieve a similar effect in *A Canterbury Tale*, where light streaming through a gap in Thomas Colpepper's window is both a dangerous index of his guilt—he *is* the Glue Man!—and a figure for his hope for a British future that would organically depend on the British past, a link underscored by his use of a magic lantern in his lectures on local history.) In the case of both *Brief Encounter* and *Great Expectations*, cinematic light cutting through the darkness represents an escape from conditions associated with the war; it would have read both as a figure for the end of blackout and as a reminder that the cinema had been one of the few forms of entertainment—one of the few forms of escape—available to ordinary people during wartime.

However, whereas the heritage drift of *Great Expectations* makes the gesture feel sincere (if clumsy compared with the downbeat beauty of Dickens' ending), *Brief Encounter* ultimately seems less sure about cinema as a form of therapy or escape. After all, most of the movies that the film invents for Laura to see or to think about seeing look pretty bad; the joke trailer Lean makes for *Flames of Passion* stirs violence, sex, exotic locales, and a leering ape into an unsavory stew. To escape into a film like *Flames of Passion* is to deny reality; indeed, Lean hoped that films like these—canned, overblown, gauzy—had become less possible in Britain after the war:

> The outbreak of war in 1939 introduced an entirely new phase in the history of films in this country. The British public, starved of almost all the other forms of escapism, flocked into the cinemas, and picture grosses beat all previous records. *But* in their everyday lives these same audiences were being brought face to face with reality: the life-and-death reality of the blitz. They knew what it was like to be frightened, and they knew that death came with a whistle and a roar, not with fifty violins and a heavenly choir. The Hollywood romances didn't seem so convincing. The over-dressed stars were living in a dream world which had no connection with the reality of clothing coupons and blackout.[72]

Brief Encounter is in fact a film appropriate to this new sense of reality, which is to say that the experience of war put Lean and his cast and crew in a position to have a better grip on reality as such than filmmakers of the pre-war era. *Brief Encounter* thus complicates what it means to think of cinema as a form of escape (from war, from fear, from life); it also suggests that the war would remain an influence on cinema even after its conclusion. If the real became more real as a result of the war, then we shouldn't imagine that the war can simply be left behind or burnt away with cinematic light like Dracula or the ghost of Miss Havisham. In other words, whereas *Great Expectations* seems to end hoping that the war and its darkness are truly over, *Brief Encounter* suggests that the difference between before and after war might, after all, be harder to maintain.

Duck! Rabbit, Duck!

We might think of another, better film that Laura and Alec see on one of their Thursdays. Appearing before the feature is an unnamed Donald Duck cartoon that represents one of the film's few moments of unalloyed and guiltless pleasure; the screenplay describes them as they watch the film: "They are both laughing and are obviously very happy."[73] The cartoon—minor, antic, anarchic—seems to offer the couple a real escape that the hack melodrama of *Flames of Passion* could not; in 1947, Lean called Walt Disney "surely the most original movie-maker ever."[74] Insofar as cartoons are only light, color, and sound, they come close to an ideal of pure cinema, and in *Brief Encounter* they seem for a moment to stand in for cinema's most liberating potential. "The Disney world," writes Neal Gabler, "is a world out

At the movies.

of order: all traditional forms seem not to function. And yet the result is not a nightmare world of pity and terror, a tragic world, but a world of fun and fantasy."[75] Donald might, in this case, be taken as a figure of what Scott Bukatman calls "animatedness," a concept I invoked in relation to Robert Newton's Ancient Pistol; figures of animatedness—Ko-Ko the Clown, Gertie the Dinosaur, Daffy Duck—channel aggression into "mobile," "kinetic," "vital," and "unruly" forms of resistance.[76] "In some respects," writes Gabler, "Donald Duck seemed to offer audiences both a vicarious liberation from the conventional behavior and morality to which they had to subscribe in their own lives and which the Duck clearly transgressed and, since he usually got his comeuppance, a vicarious revenge against the pretentious, unattractive, and ornery at a time when the entire world seemed to be roiling in anger and violence."[77] And just as the fictional director John Lloyd Sullivan comes to see Disney comedy as a source of authentic respite from real suffering at the end of Preston Sturges's *Sullivan's Travels* (1941), so does Lean seem to see in Donald Duck an authentic and therapeutic alternative to the constraints of Laura's everyday life.

There is, though, something strange about the film's otherwise exuberant response to the cartoon. At its conclusion, Laura admires Donald's "dreadful energy and his blind frustrated rages." Alec describes the cartoon in terms even more apocalyptic: "The stars can change in their courses, the universe go up in flames, and the world crash around us, but there will always be Donald Duck."[78] There is an element of violence and anxiety to *Brief*

Encounter's understanding of the cartoon, a conscious blurring between light and dark that *Great Expectations* works more directly to differentiate. And, indeed, descriptions of Mickey and Donald as joyously and even a little dangerously ludic are more appropriate to the Disney cartoons of the thirties. By 1940, the meaning of Mickey Mouse had already begun to shift with *Fantasia*; whereas Mickey had been an anarchic and occasionally violent figure in 1928's *Plane Crazy* and *Steamboat Willie*, over the next decade animators made his character increasingly cute (plumper with wider, more visible eyes) and more benign. Seen across the threshold of war, Mickey thus meant two very different things: plain craziness in the thirties followed by a cuddly return to order.

Donald Duck's evolution is even more striking. Although he was also made to look cuter, unlike Mickey, he became no more human: "Ollie Johnston [a Disney animator] reminisced that in the shorts, as Mickey Mouse became more humanoid, Goofy and Donald became more preposterous and inhuman."[79] Donald also remained fundamentally angry, and in 1942 he became the most visible representative of Disney's effort to assist the war effort: "Donald was deemed . . . suitable for wartime conversion and thus was featured in a remarkable array of war-related films. . . . The most notable of [these] efforts was . . . produced for the War Department, 'Der Fuehrer's Face' (1943), which won an Oscar for best short subject and may have been the single most popular propaganda short produced during the war."[80] In it, Donald dreams that he lives in Germany ("Nutzi Land") and works as a sort of slave in a munitions factory; at one point, he stands at his conveyor belt and falls into a kind of hectic trance as he is obligated to "Heil Hitler" before an endless series of photos of "Der Fuehrer." Although it is pretty shocking to see Donald Duck in a Nazi uniform (a fact that the Disney corporation tacitly acknowledged by keeping the cartoon out of circulation until 2004), in its context, "Der Fuehrer's Face" worked to suggest a playful and distinctly American alternative to totalitarian thinking in several of its forms: Disney's comic superabundance as an alternative to the fixed and official cultural forms of National Socialism, Donald's "dreadful energy" as an eccentric alternative to the rationalization of the factory floor, and the aggressive minorness of the cartoon form in general as an alternative to the bad equivalencies of administered culture. In other words, whereas Donald Duck represented innocent if antic entertainment in the mid-1930s, by 1945 he would have been firmly associated in American and British imaginations with the war; and although the language that Laura and Alec use—dreadful energy, crashing worlds, the universe in flames—would have seemed inappropriate to the duck of the mid-1930s, it would have been perfectly

Dreadful energy.

appropriate to the duck who had thrown tomatoes at Hitler and—painted as he often was on the nose of both bombers and bombs—rode firebombs to earth as they fell on Tokyo and Dresden.[81]

Both appropriate and inappropriate, the cartoon reflects a logic that runs throughout *Brief Encounter*. The single figure of Donald Duck is, in other words, significant in two incommensurate ways. In the context of the 1930s, he represents a space of play, an escape from everyday life into a ludic world of possibility. As such, he seems to offer Laura and Alec their purest moments of pleasure; their affair, a brief escape from everyday life into a space of play, is like the cartoon—delicious, free, ephemeral. In the context of 1945, however, Donald Duck's "dreadful energy" could have conjured the more dreadful energy of bombs, guns, and war. What's important here is the fact that both versions of the cartoon are simultaneously at work in *Brief Encounter*; Donald thus appears as another version of Wittgenstein's "duck-rabbit" (a Donald Duck Rabbit): although the anarchic innocence of the prewar period and the sharper violence of the postwar period are both aspects of his image, they remain at odds because they are of different times. The temporally divided structure of *Brief Encounter* means that we have to take Donald as another gestalt figure, which, like the light that Lean streams in from the past to the present or like a noir style that is at once appropriate and inappropriate to the film's content, functions differently as it shifts from one historical context to the other and thus points to the specificity of both. Donald Duck is, in other words, an embodied form of critique in

Brief Encounter, a figure that resists that which would keep prewar and postwar worldviews separate. His "dreadful energy" needs in that case to be understood in three ways: there is the 1930s "dreadful energy" of pure play; there is the 1940s "dreadful energy" of the war and its violence; and there is the third "dreadful energy," the energy of that which would exceed either historical context, an energy (reminiscent, perhaps, of Empson's version of the pastoral) that threatens critically to unbind a history that would keep the past separate from the present in order to keep the war in its place.

All by Myself

Donald Duck, the anachronistic darkness of noir, a light that streams from out of the past into the present: all of these are figures of a kind of untimeliness that appears everywhere in *Brief Encounter.* There are many more. Think of Lean's famous use of Rachmaninoff. Although its familiarity has made it hard really to hear what the Piano Concerto no. 2 is doing in the film, it is in fact another of these in-between gestures. We are, of course, meant to understand that Laura's admiration for the Second Concerto holds Laura suspended between her innate aesthetic sense and her limited cultural access, between her good taste and few opportunities to satisfy it. Rachmaninoff indeed felt himself to be a figure trapped between moments. Long seen as both a kitschy classicist and a forward-thinking modernist, in 1939 Rachmaninoff was a man out of time: "I feel like a ghost wandering in a world grown alien. I cannot cast out the old way of writing, and I cannot acquire the new. I have made intense effort to feel the musical manner of today, but it will not come to me."[82] This in-betweenness was already there in Rachmaninoff's musical thinking in 1900 when he composed the Second Concerto; it is, I think, most audible in a tension between Rachmaninoff's melodies, which tend to go for big and maybe obvious effects (it is, after all, intensely hummable), and his harmonies, which are pianistic, knotty, close, and ambiguous. The piece thus changes tone and key frequently, giving Lean an opportunity to toggle quickly between the high romance of the melody and the contrapuntal uneasiness of its harmonic setting; like the duck, the light, and the dark, *Brief Encounter*'s Rachmaninoff means two different and incommensurate things at once.

We might think of another of the film's songs. One day, as Laura walks through Milford Junction in the first flush of love, she hears music: "The sun was out and everybody looked more cheerful than usual. There was a barrel organ at the corner by Harris's. It was playing 'Let the Great Big World Keep Turning.'" The song catches her ear for a number of reasons. Of course, its lyric is one that anticipates the film's doomed love affair, "Let the great big world keep turning/Nevermind if I've got you." There is, however, more: "Let the Great Big World Keep Turning" was one of several popular numbers written for the 1916 musical *The Bing Boys Are Here. The Bing Boys*, which follows a pair of countrified brothers—Oliver and Lucifer Bing—as they make their way amidst the lures of London, played for much of 1916 and featured the music hall great George Robey as Lucifer. Although *The Bing Boys* does not refer directly to its war, its success was nonetheless tied up with wartime experience, both in the trenches and on the home front:

> A tank commander asked Robey for *Bing Boys* posters to decorate his tank "next time we go into action"; and [the producer Oswold] Stoll received hundreds of requests from "France, Salonika, and Mesopotamia" for the one representing Robey and Lester "each with a girl on their knees." The show was alleged to "put a new vitality into trench-tired boys," which received an unconsidered twist in Wyndham Lewis's short story "The War Baby" where a subaltern and his girl, going to the Alhambra fed on war-wine and kisses, found that "Robey, with his primitive genius, flattered the mood of the evening."[83]

The "primitive genius" of Robey and *The Bing Boys* thus was not only a temporary escape from war but also a sort of critical response to it. In other words, if World War I seemed to begin in an atmosphere of willfully unreflective sincerity, the music hall represented an endangered form of comic truth-telling; in 1922 and after the death of Marie Lloyd, T. S. Eliot would wonder "why that directness, frankness and ferocious humor which survive in her, and in Nellie Wallace and George Robey and a few others, should be extinct, should be odious to the British public, in precisely those forms of art in which they are most needed, and which, in fact, they used to flourish."[84] (Hitchcock makes a similar reference to the radical and residual honesty of the music hall in *The 39 Steps* with the figure of Mr. Memory, a man who not only remembers everything—the past as plenum—but also cannot tell a lie; he must as a result die along with his art at the film's end.) That bits of that very British and nearly extinct past come to Laura as she drifts through her day makes sense in the context of the film's wartime interest in understanding the relation between past and present; like Rachmaninoff and Donald Duck, the tune is a bit of foreign matter, a cultural survival seemingly indigestible to and out of sync with the world of *Brief Encounter*. And, as we know, Robey's portrayal of Falstaff does something similar in Olivier's *Henry V* and thus introduces yet another level of intertextual and historical complexity into those few notes of music; they manage, if we listen closely enough, to evoke World War I, the decline of music hall, the "ferocious humor" of George Robey, Robey's appearance as Falstaff in the previous year's *Henry V*, and, indeed, Falstaff himself as a figure of carnival resistance. And, like Olivier and Robey's Falstaff, what the notes can mean seem entirely to exceed one or the other structure put in place to contain them.

The invocation of British music hall also helps to account for one of the film's larger generic discontinuities. Much of the film's comic relief comes in the form of interactions between Myrtle and Albert, the flirting, bickering couple who work at the train station and represent a bawdy, proletarian alternative to Laura and Alec's tasteful encounter. Critics have tended to see their performance as a sharp and awkward intrusion into the film's otherwise muted, middle-class realism: "The only weaknesses are the synthetic Cockneys in the synthetic station buffet . . . , the comedy of the lower orders once more rendered in caricature."[85] Joyce Carey and Stanley Holloway do play their roles with a broad gestural relish that seems at odds with the film's overall quiet: "Albert! Now look at me Banburys—all over the floor!"[86] If, however, they can seem like too much—even Lean found them "embarrassing"—they perform an important function: they return a nearly extinct and maybe wholly imaginary "directness, frankness, and ferocious humor" to a world that seems to have lost precisely these qualities. Like "Let the Great Big World Keep Turning," they are another form of comic survival, another untimely presence that puts the time of *Brief Encounter* briefly and critically at odds with itself; and because that comedy could be understood in 1945 as well as 1916 to be an effect of and reaction to the political and social demands of wartime, its return marks another point at which *Brief Encounter* tacitly argues for its own complicated relation to war and its aftermath.

Violent Things

Released immediately after the war and mixing the memories of war time and a time before war, *Brief Encounter* makes an oblique case for violence's presence in everyday life: "I didn't think," Laura muses, "such violent things could happen to ordinary people."[87] Audiences in 1945 would surely have been able to identify with her feeling of surprise and resignation in the face of this new and terrible discovery; after all, years of total war had acquainted many ordinary people with "violent things," a fact that breaks into the film partly in the form of several morbidly funny tonal shifts. As Laura and Fred discuss whether they should take their children to the zoo or to the pantomime, Fred jokes that they should take them to neither: "We'll thrash them both soundly, lock them up in the attic, and go to the pictures by ourselves."[88] Later, when Alec invites himself along to the cinema with Laura, he offers an off-color explanation for why he's not wanted back at the hospital: "Between ourselves, I killed two patients by accident this morning. The matron is very displeased with me. I—I simply daren't go back."[89] And late in the film, Laura overhears Myrtle gossiping with her employee Beryl about her ex-husband: "You can't expect me to be cook, housekeeper, and charlady all rolled into one during the day, and a loving wife in the evening just because you feel like it. Oh, dear, no. There are just as good fish in the sea, I said, as ever came out of it and I packed my boxes then and there and left him." When Beryl asks what happened next, Myrtle responds cooly: "Dead as a doornail inside three years."[90] These are, of course, just jokes—however, they also gesture toward an idea that neither the characters nor the film can acknowledge directly: that life really would be easier without patients, without children, without husbands, without other people. A more serious example: as Laura's talkative acquaintance, Dolly Messiter, rattles away, Laura thinks, "I wish you'd stop talking. I wish you'd stop prying and trying to find things out. I wish you were dead—no I don't mean that. That was silly and unkind. But I wish you'd stop talking."[91] Jokes, off-color remarks, stray thoughts: as Freud taught us, all these point to what might be working beneath the only apparently still waters of everyday sociality. Or, as Alec's friend, Stephen Lynn puts it after nearly walking in on Alec and Laura in the midst of their inevitably thwarted assignation: "You know, my dear Alec, you have hidden depths that I never even suspected."[92]

This suspicion—that the surface of ordinary life conceals hidden depths—connects *Brief Encounter* with a number of other films that deal more obviously with the insinuation of violence into the ordinary. The best example—and one possible source for Lean's explicit focus on the "ordinary"—is probably Hitchcock's *Shadow of a Doubt* (1943). There, the unexpected appearance of a family's beloved Uncle Charlie in bucolic Santa Rosa, CA, leads to the revelation that he is in fact the "Merry Widow Murderer," a cold-blooded serial killer on the run. If, though, we would see him as an extraordinary and alien intrusion into an otherwise ordinary existence, his famous speech to his niece (also Charlie) makes a different case:

> You're just an ordinary little girl, living in an ordinary little town. You wake up every morning of your life and you know perfectly well that there's nothing in the world to trouble you. You go through your ordinary little day, and at night you sleep your untroubled ordinary little sleep, filled with peaceful stupid dreams. And I brought you nightmares. . . . Do you know the world is

> a foul sty? Do you know, if you rip off the fronts of houses, you'd find swine? The world's a hell. What does it matter what happens in it?

As played by Joseph Cotten, Uncle Charlie is handsome, upright, and charming. He is welcomed into the Santa Rosa community, invited to dinners, and asked to make toasts and give speeches to ladies' clubs. The real ease with which he blends in with the ordinary people of Santa Rosa suggests that, in the end, his violence might not be an exception to the rule; indeed, his apparently telepathic connection with his young niece—the "ordinary little girl"—suggests that he has, in fact, been a part of the ordinary all along. As is often the case in Hitchcock, the ever-present possibility of violence disrupting the lives of ordinary people suggests indeed that mayhem, murder, and violence, or at least their possibility, are not the exception but rather the rule. Insofar as *Brief Encounter* is also built on the knowledge that violent things happen to ordinary people, it is a quiet but appropriate cousin to films such as *Shadow of a Doubt* and Orson Welles's *The Stranger* (1946), the melodramas of Douglas Sirk and Nicholas Ray, and, in time, the rotten Americana of David Lynch.

Unknown and Yet Well Known

That said, there are also other, more specific moments of unease that gesture less obliquely toward the historical catastrophe that occupies *Brief Encounter*'s tacit structural center. There are, for instance, the film's several quiet gestures toward military life: the appearance of the two drunk and disorderly soldiers in Myrtle Baghot's cafe, Laura's conversation with Fred about a naval career for their young son, and her largely unmotivated nighttime visit to a World War I memorial. Understanding the difference between the time of the film's setting and its release makes one realize that those soldiers will indeed see combat, that young Bobbie might someday fight and die in a war, and that men like Fred and Alec may yet be called upon to serve. Seeing these possibilities alongside the war memorial makes the tragic aspect of the film's temporality all too clear: although the film's characters dream about the future at the time of the film's prewar setting, by 1945, the time of the film's release, things would have been different. Some or all of these men and women could be dead, their homes destroyed, their families—which the film does so much to protect—scattered, displaced, or ruined. In this way, the war memorial offers a sort of before-and-after mourning; like the war itself, the war dead are part of what the film both relies on and occludes.

This sense of the fragility of things, of a fraught compromise that might always stand between the seeming calm of ordinary everyday life and an extraordinary violence that always stands either just outside or, in fact, at its very core, gives us a better sense of *Brief Encounter*'s more and less coded relation to war. In addition to the historical allusions, the quiet but clear symbols, and the points of cultivated formal ambivalence, there is this basic truth to the film: that having an affair, that wanting things that exceed or undermine the apparent stability of the everyday is always a matter of assessing the relation between liberty and security. As Antonia Lant writes, the personal and logistical pressures that war had put on romantic relationships, the idea of family, and the responsibilities of mothers were part of "the history to which David Lean's *Brief Encounter* inevitably belonged as it presented a mother's choice between emotional and sexual fulfillment outside marriage, and obligation to her husband and family: a choice between risk and security."[93] On the one hand, as is the case with both *Colonel Blimp* and *Henry V*, the film can thus be read as a personal argument for the national need to suspend freedom, pleasure, and risk in the name of security, to see that war's lesson was that a supreme crisis meant that values associated with Clive Candy, Falstaff, and a certain idea of England—irony, chivalry, humor—had to be given over and at least temporarily forgotten in the face of an ultimate crisis, a fight for national survival. On the other hand, each of these films also suggests that the choice between freedom and security might be a false one and that, if the violence and loss associated with risk is not necessarily opposed to the security of the everyday and instead lurks somewhere at its core, we need to think twice before choosing security over freedom in the name of avoiding violence because violence is perhaps an aspect of security in even its most ordinary forms. This knowledge—that freedom is hard and security might not save us—doesn't make things easier either for Laura or for Britain; but, in the nature of all knowledge, its seemingly insuperable difficulty and the awful responsibility it places on *those who know better* makes it no less vital and no less true.

Close-Ups

I've already made the case that Celia Johnson's face is the undeniable structural and stylistic center of *Brief Encounter*: It bookends and contains the flashbacks that make up most of the film's plot; it is a concentrated example of the film's whole cinematographic style; and it sets and sustains the film's emotional tone. I have yet to state, however, what this image meant before, after, and in the midst of war: what does Celia Johnson's face mean? In *Painting with Light* (1949), a handbook that otherwise offers few absolute rules, the cinematographer John Alton writes: "*feminine close-ups or portraits should always be beautiful.* In films they are the jewels of the picture, in stills, the decorations of the desk or home. A picture can be beautiful, yet have mood and feeling too. Therefore, even in scenes which call for mood, for special feeling, it is the rendition of feminine beauty we strive for and attain by keeping the key low."[94] Limited direct light, professional make-up, lens diffusion: these are the tools typically used to beautify women's faces in classic Hollywood cinema. They are also the techniques that *Brief Encounter* studiously avoids; Johnson's face is highly key-lit, it is presented more or less without makeup; and its eccentricities—a vein, or a mole—are thrown into relief. Although no one would deny the beauty of Celia Johnson's face, that beauty comes in a form that seems, once again, more appropriate to another kind of film. So, what does this particular and particularized face mean?

It seems clear that Lean was in part thinking about Carl Theodor Dreyer's *La Passion de Jeanne d'Arc* (1928). Lean would have seen Dreyer's early film as well as 1943's *Day of Wrath*, both films that, as Dreyer told Roger Manvell soon after the war, depend on the centrality of the face: "'I watch the face,' he says; 'it is the face that matters'. . . . Close-shots are the essence of Dreyer's technique; his camera works on the faces of his characters."[95] One can feel Dreyer's influence on *Brief Encounter*, particularly in Lean's effort to capture Johnson's abstracted, yet focused stare inside and into the past. Indeed, the implicit association between Johnson and Renée Jeanne Falconetti (the actor who played Dreyer's Jeanne) continued to be felt after *Brief Encounter*. Johnson's next major role was Saint Joan in a 1948 Old Vic production of Shaw's play. Director John Burrell must have had *Brief Encounter* in mind when he cast Johnson (she tended before *Brief Encounter* to play light comedy, so playing Joan represented a distinct departure). There is, in that case, an odd circuit of influence at work here: Dreyer influences Lean, who films Johnson as if she were Joan; Shaw's *Saint Joan* reminds Burgess of Dreyer's *La Passion de Jeanne d'Arc*, which, in turn, reminds him of *Brief Encounter*, which encourages him to cast Celia Johnson as Joan. In a way that begins to feel familiar, the faces of Jeanne d'Arc and Laura Jesson seem threaded together in a strangely complex play of before and after.

As in *Brief Encounter*, Dreyer's close-ups exploit an uncomfortable tension between the cool precision of his film style and the almost unbearable emotional intensity of Falconetti's performance; as Bazin puts it, "Herein lies the rich paradox and inexhaustible lesson of this film: that the extreme spiritual purification is freed through the scrupulous realism of the camera as a microscope."[96] Aside from its intensity and beauty, what most distinguishes Dreyer's close-ups of Falconetti's face are their resistance to a conventional cinematic economy of shot/reverse shot: "Dreyer avoids the shot-reverse

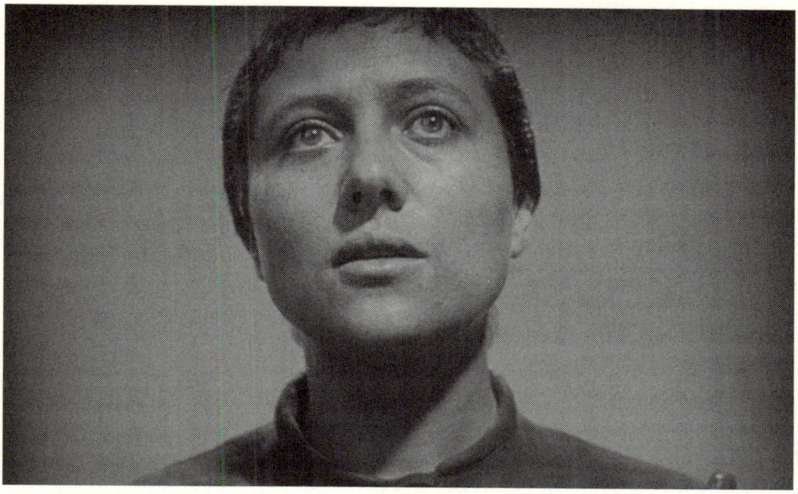

Jeanne d'Arc.

shot procedure which would maintain a real relation between each face and the other. . . . He prefers to isolate each face in a close-up which is only partly filled, so that the position to the right or to the left directly induces a virtual conjunction which no longer needs to pass through the real connection between people."[97] When the camera looks at Falconetti, she seems to look past or through it. This is evidence of the film's commitment to the difficult reality of the spiritual; the film uses Jeanne's intense focus on something beyond the frame not only to suggest something about her faith but also to force the viewer to confront belief as a real—or even realist—encounter with what cannot be represented. In order to complete the cinematic circuit of these shots, a viewer (or a camera) would need believe in (or at least suspend disbelief in) the ineffable object of Jeanne's attention; it is because of this spiritual realism that Deleuze takes *La Passion de Jeanne d'Arc* as a precociously modern film, as a film in which "subjectivity, then, takes on a new sense, which is no longer motor or material, but temporal and spiritual: that which 'is added' to matter, not what distends it."[98]

What makes Dreyer's modernity "precocious" for both Bazin and Deleuze is that it comes before 1945, before the devastation and loss that came to light at the end and immediately after the war with revelations about the camps and the Holocaust. This is what motivates both Deleuze's analytic move from the movement-image to the time-image and, more recently, Antoine de Baecque's account of "the modern turn" in cinema, "which," for him, "grew out of an attitude of critical assimilation of the inheritance of the past: consisting both of the fact of the existence of the extermination camps, as seen in the striking footage of 1945, and of a history of cinema whose affiliations . . . were no longer straightforward and no longer consisted of direct genealogical lineages."[99] Central to de Baecque's "modern turn" is a recurring shot of a staring face that seems both to see the enormity of history and atrocity directly and to offer history as something that, embodied in the single human face, needs to look back: "History itself is staring at us."[100] As a result, de Baecque follows both Bazin and Deleuze in seeing the war as a turning point in the history of cinema; because of its role as witness to the opening of the camps in 1945, the cinema became essentially connected with a new capacity and a new responsibility, one that he sees at work in the postwar look-to-camera close-up. While one could simply say that the films to which he refers—Welles's *The Stranger* (1946), Bergman's *Summer with Monika* (1953), Rosselini's *Journey to Italy* (1953), and Resnais's *Hiroshima mon amour* (1959)—also owe a debt to Dreyer's work with Falconetti, there's more at stake here. (One could, of course, add to de Baecque's list: the concluding still of Jean-Pierre Léaud in *Les 400 coups*, the mad stare of mother/Norman at the end of *Psycho*, the painted eyes of the Greek statues in *Contempt*, Julianne Moore gazing at her reflection in *Safe*, and so on.) Rossellini, Bergman, Resnais, and others thus adopt the structure of Dreyer's spiritual realism, of Jeanne's look into the infinite, in order to develop a historical cinema capable of witnessing the enormity of real and material events and traumas that nonetheless resist aesthetic representation; the postwar encounter with the enormity of what happened during World War II takes the form of a disenchanted but structurally intact version of Dreyer's mysticism, a look that retains the intensity, the distance, and the eloquence of Dreyer's Jeanne in the absence of spiritual guarantees.

To take another example: Carol Reed's *The Third Man* (1949) pursues in a darker, less ambivalent way many of the themes that I've been looking at over the course of this book. And, like *Henry V* and *Brief Encounter*, it engages directly—far more so—with the difficulty of living in a postwar period that seems unable to distance itself from war. The design of the film, its sharp and strange camera angles, its lingering interest—real because of the intensity of its care and surreal because of the nature of its object—in the alien landscape of occupied, bombed-out Vienna, its queasy mix of comedy, tragedy, and something altogether less legible: all these come together to make an argument about the enormous pressure that war puts on the experience of history as meaningful. As Carol Reed puts it in his arch opening monologue, "I never knew the old Vienna before the war with its Strauss music, its glamor, and easy charm."[101] In the immediate postwar period, *then* has little or nothing to do with *now*. This frank disconnect between past and present is there in the film's fraught relation to an especially fraught moment in cinematic history. As I mentioned in relation to *Colonel Blimp*'s no-cut, the war period represented for both Bazin and Deleuze a moment when filmmakers turned away from the founding logic of montage to depth-of-field cinematography. For Bazin, in particular, the sustained and deep shot appeared better able than the cut to address the deepening moral and historical crises of life during and after wartime. De Baecque points to Bazin's commitment to "the sequence shot and the pan shot, which, by avoiding any cut in the take, and thus the pitfalls of editing, are the most ethical formal acts of cinema, in that they appear to be a mechanical copy of the real . . . the least manipulated and least manipulable image that can render reality visible, and especially its supreme ordeal: the corpse, the work of death."[102] (As de Baecque also points out, Hitchcock made a similar argument when he advised cameramen to use "slow pans, with the camera moving right and left on a tripod to capture" the whole truth of the Holocaust for Sidney Bernstein's unfinished 1945 documentary about the opening of the camps; because people wouldn't *want* to believe what they were seeing, they would, he thought, see the cut as evidence of exaggeration or fabrication.)

It makes sense in that case that *The Third Man* divides its style between two different modes. On the one hand, and this is signaled by Welles's deferred presence, Reed and Robert Krasker (who, once again, was cinematographer for *Brief Encounter* and, uncharacteristically, *Henry V*) rely on deep, static shots of the interiors and exteriors of Vienna, shots that give the eye opportunity to try to comprehend the degree to which the old world has been physically altered by war. Although Reed was, contrary to some accounts, wholly responsible for the look of the film, it does owe much to the example of Welles, whom Bazin and Deleuze saw as representative of the mid-century move away from montage. On the other hand, Reed does rely on an exaggerated set of cuts at a few key moments, namely two chase scenes through bombed-out Vienna and especially Harry Lime's last frantic run through the sewers. Although that last scene is brilliantly and frenetically cut, its parts don't add up to something more, a fact that puts Reed's film at odds with classic accounts of montage as a synthetic logic. Indeed, as opposed to offering some larger idea about the scene's topography, the cuts seem rather to divide and redivide space in a way that resists consolidation, leaving the city and the film in fragments. Put in different terms, Reed's cuts result in a form of montage that gestures toward but ultimately bypasses the hopes of Pudovkin and Eisenstein for a rigorously overtonal montage, a montage that would produce a third idea out of the formal or thematic tension between two shots. That third idea, the soul of an older, more optimistic, more politically possible cinema is revealed in the chase scene as hopelessly residual, as a trace or stylistic specter that lingers on after its use had been obliterated by events. Montage's overtonal third idea haunts the film like Plato's third man, the recursively ghostly figure one needs in order to relate the real to the ideal, the no-thing or no-one that is nonetheless required for other things to make sense: "Who is this third who always walks beside me?"[103] After the war, montage *was* the third man.

More pertinent here are a number of shots that anticipate the hollowed-out stares to which de Baecque points in Resnais and Rossellini and that recall Celia Johnson's earlier staring face, a face that seems to look significantly and intently at nothing. In the first shot, the caretaker at Harry Lime's apartment turns away from a window after promising to meet Holly Martins and to give him evidence about Lime's death. As he turns, he appears to see and stare in surprise at someone or something. Reed holds the shot of the man's still face for a few agonizing extra beats. Although we never see what he sees, we can tell that the object of his gaze means him no good; and, indeed, he turns up dead a few scenes later. Even more significant is a shot of Holly Martins staring into the crib of one of Harry's infant victims, a child that is disastrously affected by a mix of meningitis and Lime's tainted penicillin. Once again, Reed withholds the object of Martins' gaze, leaving the horror of the child's suffering to our already primed imaginations. Although an earlier montage dramatizes Calloway's careful, bit-by-bit presentation of evidence that makes the case for Harry's guilt, it is an all-at-once sight of someone's suffering that ultimately convinces Martins to act. And it is the sight of him seeing what we cannot see that is meant to make undeniable his responsibility to do something, indeed, his responsibility to kill his friend Harry. Welles's presence in the film implies a connection between this half-withheld moment and a scene in Welles's own 1946 film, *The Stranger*, where a young wife is compelled to watch footage from the concentration camps in order to convince her that her husband is, in fact, a Nazi in disguise. Welles's dramatic use of witnessing is far less subtle than Reed's, but, as he later told Peter Bogdanovich, "I do think that, every time you can get the public to look at any footage of a concentration camp, under any excuse at all, it's a step forward."[104] Although Reed pointedly withholds the sight of death, he gives us, as Lean did four years earlier, a look at someone looking significantly at *something*.

Brief Encounter comes after the mystical innocence of Dreyer and before the weary cynicism of Reed (as well as Rossellini, Bergman, and Resnais); it might seem in that case to lack either the gravity or the historical position to *see* what they were able to and, indeed, had no choice but to see. *Brief Encounter* is thus influenced by the "modern turn" that one can begin to trace in the more forward-thinking corners of noir, in the early films of Italian neorealism, in the "spiritual realism" of Dreyer; and, yet, it appears crucially before the distribution of the camp footage that, for de Baecque and others, fundamentally changed cinema's formal meaning as a medium as well as its ethical relation to history. If, in that case, Lean's shot seems to put his film in the middle of a larger tradition of films that foreground cinema's special capacity for looking at history, what is it that *Brief Encounter*, Laura Jessson, and Celia Johnson are looking at? What are we looking at when we look at her looking? Or, to put it in the larger terms of my argument, what, after all this, is *Brief Encounter* about?

A Brief Something

Brief Encounter was not the title of the play Noël Coward produced in 1936; back then, it was called *Still Life*. While that title worked for Coward's play and while a "still life" is sort of like a "brief encounter," it nonetheless felt wrong for the film Lean had in mind: "'There was a terrific hunt for the title,' said David. 'I remember Noël saying, "We've got to think of a good title for this." It was obviously going to be a small film. "A brief something—something short." Noël, Gladys Calthrop and I had various guesses, all bad, and it was Gladys Calthrop who suggested *Brief Encounter*.'"[105] Why *Brief Encounter* instead of *Still Life*? For one, the painterly connotations of "still life" might run against the stylized medium specificity of *Brief Encounter*. Indeed, the film has, as I've been suggesting, a special concern with the idea of duration and, more particularly, in the different ways in which cinema can convey the passage of time. There's another suggestive aspect to the title; although "encounter" can refer to the "fact of meeting with (a person or thing), *esp.* undesignedly or casually," its primary sense is a "meeting face to face; a meeting (of adversaries or opposing forces) in conflict; *hence*, a battle, skirmish, duel, etc." What is a *Blitzkrieg* if not a brief encounter? That said, while I'm of course interested in the possibility that Lean, Coward, and Calthrop would have stumbled upon a title that could also be applied without alteration to a film explicitly about World War II, what's more important here is the idea of an encounter as a necessarily fraught face-to-face meeting. As I have argued, what both distinguishes the film's signature shot of Celia Johnson's face and connects it to the Dreyer before and the Reed after is the fact that it is a shot of a woman seemingly looking at nothing; another way to put it is to say that each of these films and *Brief Encounter* rely on one half of a classic shot/reverse shot sequence, which, according to David Bordwell, "in its prototypical form . . . [is] predicated on a two-person, face-to-face encounter."[106]

If shot/reverse shot is in fact tied to the "two-person, face-to-face encounter," the half shot/reverse shot sequence we get with the lone, looking face is something like a "shave and a haircut" without the "two bits"; in other words, the felt formal integrity of the anticipated whole makes what's ultimately missing as palpable in its absence as the feeling of a phantom limb. My question then can be framed in these terms: if *Brief Encounter* offers us one half of a shot/reverse shot sequence, if it suggests through its form an absent or unrepresentable content, what would that content be? I'll conclude by offering four readings of what's on the other side of Celia Johnson's brief cinematic encounter. The first is my most conventional and thus my most abbreviated reading. *Brief Encounter* is a love story, a fact that has gone slightly missing in the pages that have come before. As Laura sits by the fire and thinks about the previous weeks, she thinks of Alec, her lost lover, and of the future she could have had but renounces for her husband and children. In this way, the shot draws on one of the most familiar uses of the matched eyeline reverse shot in classic Hollywood cinema; bringing men and women together within the conventional and thus comforting rhythm of shot and reverse shot allows us to imagine the couple as a form; and, indeed, most of the film's uses of the sequence feature Laura and Alec in the midst of their courtship, their conversations, and their final separation. A formal figure for the melancholy and thwarted outcome of their brief encounter, the absent reverse shot is a way of suggesting the degree to which Alec, the lost amorous object, continues *to inform* and to structure Laura's thoughts and feelings; and, insofar as the film suggests that Laura will be able to return to an ordinary life with her family, it relies on the shot to turn melancholia into socially productive mourning. In these terms, we could see the shot as a clever but ultimately minor variation on the classic vernacular.

Scared of Your Wife, Soldier?

My second reading follows the first, but with an important, ideological difference. We could assume that Lean is using the shot/reverse shot sequence to suggest something about the real presence of the couple as a social form, which, because it is a form, can be efficiently expressed in the stuff of film content and film style. Instead of seeing the lover Alec as the shot's lost object, however, we might instead see Lean as offering a larger postwar analysis of the couple. If a completed shot/reverse shot sequence is an efficient cinematic equivalent to the complementary heteronormative couple, a broken shot/reverse shot sequence could give shape and affective force to that couple's failure. *Brief Encounter*, one of the first films in England to deal directly with ordinary middle-class adultery, could, in other words, be taken as a comment on the postwar fate of companionate marriage. Celia Johnson's face—melancholy, beautiful, singular—might in that case be all that's left of the couple.

In the second half of the forties, marriage in Britain seemed to have become one of the war's unintended casualties. Husbands had been separated from wives for months and years, and newspaper correspondence columns were filled with requests for advice and consolation from men and women who worried that one, the other, or both would have been changed beyond recognition: "The *Daily Mirror* received so many inquiries from worried servicemen approaching demobilization that it ran an article—'*Scared of your wife, soldier?*'"[107] This fact coupled with the physical and psychological pressures of war led to a generalized social anxiety about the institutional stability of marriage: "Nothing like it has ever been seen in our social history before . . . [it is] a modern matrimonial landslide."[108] There was, of course, some real reason to worry insofar as divorce and adultery became more regular or at least more visible facts of British life. Carol Smart writes, "in 1946 the divorce rate reached a peak of 41,704 petitions, a level it was not to reach again until 1967"; and Alan Allport adds, "two-thirds of the record number of divorce petitions in 1946 and 1947 cited adultery as the cause for the marriage's breakdown."[109]

That said, the public response to that demographic shift might be better understood as a form of "moral panic."[110] Kenneth Howard imagined in his *Sex Problems of the Returning Soldier* (1945) that the war had damaged the sexual confidence of British husbands:

> He is constantly on the alert for any sign in letters from home of waning affection or other sentiments. Every possible shade of meaning is read into the most innocent sentences . . . he is apt to be surly and suspicious, to imagine that someone is trying to usurp his place. His awareness of his own sexual desires and temptations and his own possible weakness add to his suspicions . . . remember that nothing makes anxiety more acute and more intolerable than a feeling of helplessness, an inability to "do something about it."[111]

More luridly, the war's end led to more popular if largely unfounded fantasies of bigamy, violence, and murder: "In the eighteen months that followed the end of the war in Europe, scarcely a Sunday went by without at least one story in the *News of the World* about a returning serviceman killing or assaulting his errant wife or her lover—or, in a few cases, being preemptively killed by them before he could act himself."[112] As Allport goes on to argue, these "*crimes passionnels*" captured the imagination not because they were all that common—they in fact were not—but rather because they spoke, however incoherently, to a feeling that the gender and sexual relations that had underwritten marriage in Britain had been altered—maybe irreparably—by the social and military demands of total war. *Brief Encounter* has thus to be understood in relation to the larger terms of this panic. Shortly after the film's release, Lean was accosted by "a rather horsy" man: "I would like to express my disapproval of you. I am exercising the greatest restraint in not hitting you. . . . You showed that lady—Celia Johnson I think is her name—considering being unfaithful to her husband. Do you realize, sir, that if Celia Johnson could contemplate being unfaithful to her husband, my wife could contemplate being unfaithful to me?"[113]

In part, these anxieties were the result of shifts in women's participation in and authority over social and economic life on the home front; this was the case both within the frame of the family where women were often the only authority figures left as well as within the larger civilian workforce and, indeed, the military itself: "The Second World War led to a labour shortage of immense proportions. Women were the obvious reserve of noncombatant labour, either by transfer from industries not considered essential for the war effort or from inactivity. They were encouraged, and then coerced, into industry and into the Auxiliary Services in ever-increasing numbers between 1940 and 1943."[114] Historian Mark Mazower writes, "the war itself had profoundly altered traditional gender roles, disrupting family ties and providing women with new tasks and challenges outside as well as inside the home."[115] Although historians differ on the long-term social and economic effects of women's increased role in the wartime workforce in Britain, it is nonetheless clear that the shift contributed to immediate postwar anxieties about what had been imagined as a "normal" family. Lant writes, "Mothers (and fathers) lost children through evacuation, drafting, enemy action, and by being forced, by the difficulty of daily conditions as a single parent, to give them away for fostering."[116] How, it was asked, could the family return to normal when total mobilization had altered the very coordinates of normal life?[117]

These worries were expressed both in returning British soldiers' concerns about being out of place in a Britain that had changed almost beyond recognition and in the disappointment of women who were encouraged to return to traditional roles after the war; for instance, women who were dismissed from mixed-gender antiaircraft batteries felt betrayed: "The government, the army and the ATS [Auxiliary Territorial Service] did their best to dampen the liberating effects of the mixed battery experience. Women were channeled back into acceptable female roles. One gunner recalled how, 'When the war was over and things began to run down, life got very dull. Girls who had been part of anti-aircraft gun teams were redirected into jobs as storewomen on our depot and lost their rank and quite understandably were resentful.'"[118] Of course, a lot of propaganda was directed toward mitigating these effects, and it is along these lines that one can see a difference between wartime and postwar British cinema.

For instance, *In Which We Serve* worked partly to manage anxiety about the increased presence of women in the workforce and the resulting changes in gender and sexual relations by taking pains to imagine different modes of sociality for men and women during wartime. One can see this in a set-piece speech that Alix, Captain Kinross's wife (also played by Celia Johnson), gives at Christmas dinner:

> What we will deal with is the most important disillusion of all, that is, that wherever [a wife] goes there is always in her life a permanent and undefeated rival—her husband's ship—whether it be a battleship or a sloop, a submarine or a destroyer, it holds first place in his heart. It comes before wife, home, children, everything. Some of us try to fight this and get badly mauled in the process. Others, like myself, resign themselves to the inevitable. . . . It's extraordinary that anyone could be so fond and so proud of their most implacable enemy, this ship. God Bless this ship and all who sail in her.[119]

On the one hand, Alix displays an unusual sort of social authority; as she offers her toast from the head of the table, she stands in for the film's several strong female figures, characters who are represented both as surviving and managing the home front while the men are away. On the other hand, she accepts a diminished role within the family, accepting that there are things—ideals, identities, ships, and crews—that take precedence over the couple. The film thus offers a case for a set of social values that had been redefined—bent but not broken—by the shifting priorities of total mobilization.[120] Another aspect of this project appears in a later scene when the Torrin stops to pick up a group of men stranded and wounded at Dunkirk. Battered and bloody, they gather in the ship as Shorty (John Mills) makes his way through the crowd feeding men cocoa and biscuits by hand when they are too wounded to do so themselves. The scene is remarkable for the unproblematic, unanxious way in which it represents homosocial intimacy and caring between men. As previously mentioned, *In Which We Serve* directs its propaganda toward a particular end, the effort to imagine a Britain that might transcend socioeconomic, ethnic, and gender differences in the service of total war. As a result, the film imagines a version of life both in and out of the military that comes close to a kind of utopia, a fact apparent in the unselfconsciously loving atmosphere of the Torrin in particular and *In Which We Serve* in general. The question, of course, is whether this utopian vision—in part a temporal effect, as I suggested earlier, of being *in* war—can outlast the war itself.

Taken as a postwar film, *Brief Encounter* and its highly strung atmosphere suggest both a desire to return to things as they were (or as some wished they had been) and an anxious knowledge that such a return is impossible.[121] This is partly visible in the increasingly sneaky nature of Alec and Laura's relationship. The film is, as others have suggested, suffused with a sense of guilt that seems often to border on paranoia. On her way out of the cinema with Alec, Laura says, "We crept out before the end, rather furtively, as though we were committing a crime. The usherette at the door looked at us with stony contempt."[122] Later, as she considers her thwarted rendezvous with Alec in Stephen Lynn's apartment, she comes across a policeman; passing him, she thinks: "I walked away—trying to look casual—knowing that he was watching me. I felt like a criminal."[123] In both cases what feels like judgment is more likely guilt internalized. In other words, whereas Lean's earlier film approached sociability and its possibilities with a charming looseness, *Brief Encounter* sees the social world as darkly repressive. In the words of Richard Dyer, "This sense of guilt, shame and unhappiness is all-pervasive."[124]

Second, whereas *In Which We Serve* could represent a caring intimacy between men without anxiety, *Brief Encounter* features a deeply uncomfortable exchange between men. After taking Laura back to a borrowed flat, Alec is interrupted by the early return of his friend and the flat's owner, Stephen. Laura escapes out the back before he enters, but leaves her scarf behind, which Stephen finds; he then scolds Alec with curious intensity:

> I am the one who should apologize for having returned so inopportunely—it is quite obvious to me that you were interviewing a patient privately—women are frequently neurotic creatures, and the hospital atmosphere upsets them. From the rather undignified scuffling I heard when I came into the hall, I gather that she beat a hurried retreat down the backstairs. I'm surprised at this farcical streak in your nature, Alec—such carryings-on were quite

unnecessary—after all, we have known each other for years and I am the most broad-minded of men.[125]

As many have noted, aspects of the scene—the shared apartment, Stephen's disappointment, his hurt—suggests that Stephen and Alec are or were more than friends. However, as opposed to *In Which We Serve*'s open displays of homosocial care, *Brief Encounter* represents Stephen's attachment to Alec as something strange and slightly toxic. Alec: "You're very angry, aren't you?" Stephen: "No, Alec: not angry. Just disappointed."[126] The conversation is one of the few moments in the film that is not focalized through Laura's character; she runs out the back before he enters the room and thus never even gets to look at him. His appearance is, in other words, *impossible* insofar as the whole of the film's plot is meant to be the retroactive working of Laura's memory; it is thus either a narrative lapse on Lean's part or a fantasy on Laura's. In either case, Stephen's desire (whether for Alec or against Laura) is presented as something structurally liminal and needlessly symptomatic. As opposed to the war film's effort to encourage new modes of sociability and care under the sign of total mobilization, the postwar film works incompletely and anxiously at the level of form and content to police relations that had been treated or at least imagined in more open terms during wartime.[127]

One way, in that case, to see Lean's broken shot/reverse shot sequence is to take it as a form in miniature of a traditional couple that has been put under threat by the social fallout of total war. Changed gender roles, prolonged absence, and the trauma of war posed all manner of threats to a normative ideological structure that seemed somehow inappropriate to the postwar world. The other side of that new world is, at least at moments, marked by panic, guilt, paranoia, and repression; indeed, this reading would take usual complaints about *Brief Encounter*—it is prudish, repressed, in denial—to a sort of logical extreme. The broken shot/reverse shot sequence, in that case, would be a stand-in for the broken couple, and the lone, melancholy shot of Celia Johnson's face would be a figure for the ruin of that couple once ordinary life had been altered, opened, and then closed up once again by the physical and social violence of total war. This leads me to a third, more allegorical reading of the shot.

You've Been a Long Way Away

While we should, indeed, see Lean's truncated sequence as a reflection on the instability of social relations between men and women after the war, there's more going on here; although the film participates in or perhaps draws on postwar anxieties about sex, it also exceeds them and offers a critical take both on what's become of desire after the costly freedom of wartime and on the experience of war and its aftermath. Some of what's additionally at stake here comes across in the film's last lines. After reliving the whole of her short affair with Alec, Laura wakes up to find that Fred has been watching her with more attention and perspicuity than we would have expected from her kind, genial, and apparently dull husband. He comes to her side as she weeps and asks, "Whatever your dream was—it wasn't a very happy one, was it?" After she responds, "no," he gets the film's last word: "You've been a long way away . . . thank you for coming back to me."[128] The lines signal Laura's second and final return to the family; she's already returned in body, but, having worked through the previous weeks in memory—having, in other words, more or less mourned Alec—she returns now in heart and mind. The words are also curious because it's hard to say just what Fred means. Does he know what she's been thinking about? Has he seen it—as we have—projected across her face? If Fred somehow knows what's going on—if he somehow knows what we know—then he is not simply an unromantic foil for the passionate Alec. The film can then suggest that Laura loses less by returning home; indeed, what she gains at the film's last moment is renewed respect for her husband's character and intelligence. Finally surprising Laura with a perceptiveness equal to her own, Fred's last lines might at last turn *Brief Encounter* into something akin to Cavell's comedies of remarriage, mature films that get the couple "*back* together, together *again*."[129] One contemporary critic "admired Cyril Raymond's performance as 'the homely husband' precisely because he had 'masculine' control enough to listen to Laura's tale without revealing that he had heard it: he 'suspected more than his emotions showed.'"[130] If, however, he doesn't know and is instead just the same sweet, dull Fred, then the return home is less satisfying and no less melancholy; the marriage will continue but only in the shadow of Laura's structuring dissatisfaction. That Lean leaves this moment in a state of suspension is another moment at which it declares its quiet relation to the more obviously ambiguous ambiguities of classic art-house cinema.

There is, however, something else slightly off about Fred's last words. Why is it that he casts Laura's waking from her reverie as a return from "a long way away"? What distance does he imagine? And how has she come home? What's odd here is how appropriate these lines would sound if they had been spoken to a soldier coming home from the war. Indeed, one way to make sense of the film's last lines and the singular shot of Celia Johnson's face is to see *Brief Encounter* as a phantasmatic inversion of another dimly imagined film, one in which Laura is not the almost adulterous wife, but rather the soldier husband just come home; the film might, in other words, be read as a sort of contrapuntal dream of war, an effort to cloak a latent story of violence and loss in the manifest garb of an "ordinary" woman's brief affair: "I didn't think such violent things could happen to ordinary people." That is, in the nature of good and democratic propaganda, Lean's film could be understood as an understated but not unavailable story of a soldier's homecoming, of return and repair after the trauma of war.

There are several aspects of the film that support the notion that Laura stands in for a soldier just returned from war. She travels by train from one station to the next. And her drift past a war memorial at a moment of emotional need, an unfeminine cigarette in hand, suggests a just buried and poignant emotional relation to the war. Most telling, though, is her face, which resembles other notable moments of cinematic witness; indeed, her blank yet full middle-distance stare seems to conjure the obscure transparency of a look at war: "The eyes had grown larger and transparent, as they appear in icons. The cold, meanly divisive window glass was shattered, and through the wide openings the infinite behind man wafted unhindered into the endlessness before him and hallowed his countenance for the passage beyond time. Let us cast this visage as a constellation into the sky, to remind us of our last chance before everything turns into a faceless mass."[131] Hans Erich Nossack's comparison of people looking at war with religious icons anticipates Alexander Nemerov's discussion of the icons that appear in Val Lewton's home front films: "Icons do not tell stories but rather aspire to put us in the presence of the being they represent. Instead of deep spaces permeated by far-flung actions, they give us a flattened space, virtually a non-space in which static figures solemnly demand the viewer's direct engagement."[132] Nemerov's description also doubles as a good reading of Celia Johnson's face, a face that looks out from the shallow space of a close-up and demands from the half-space of a shot without its reverse shot that someone or something else look back. Indeed, her look not only suggests that the enormity of war might be best represented in the faraway stare of a woman looking at nothing but also resembles looks that were often associated with the soldier's experience of war trauma or, as the earlier war had it, shell shock. Laura's hollow stare into an objectless middle distance, in that case, should be understood in relation to the film's other blatantly symptomatic moments: she falls suddenly into both laughing and crying jags; she has unexplained headaches and fainting spells; and, most suggestively, her situation brings her to the very brink of self-destruction: "I meant to do it, Fred, I really meant to do it—I stood there trembling—right on the edge."[133]

If, in other words, we treat *Brief Encounter* as a sort of dream, as an effort to represent the war via a series of condensations and displacements, we can see Laura as a representative of a historically specific psychological response to war. In World War I the psychological effects of combat were treated as shell shock, an amphibious diagnosis that refused to decide whether soldiers' trauma had a physical or psychic origin. By the time of World War II, however, the rise of a specifically British psychoanalysis had led to a surer, if still problematic consensus that war indeed affected men's minds. At best, this understanding led to progressive efforts like the development of a group-therapy technique at Northfield Military Hospital; at worst, it led to a further demonization of war trauma, as in the case of the RAF's blanket diagnosis, LMF, or "lack of moral fibre." In any case, once seen in this context, Laura's response to the affair resembles symptoms reported by soldiers returning home—"fatigue, headache, depression, anxiety, and difficulty sleeping."[134] More to the point, Laura's post-affair disposition seems to rhyme in both form and content with the experience of coming home. One soldier, Lieutenant George Chippington, wrote of war's end as if it indeed were the end of an especially intense love affair: "After so many years of the excitements and dangers of the campaign and the sufferings and privations . . . the sudden full stop to all purposeful activity out of its very emptiness, has created an overpowering sense of isolation. I am now as it were a mere spectator doomed forever to stand off-stage while others act out the drama in which I no longer have a role."[135] Another, Lieutenant H. C. F. Harwood, wrote, "I have never felt like committing suicide in my life, but at that moment I can truthfully say that I came very near to it."[136] "I meant to do it, Fred, I really meant to do it."

Laura's place in the one half of the shot/reverse shot sequence that I have been describing does in fact suggest a profound isolation, a sense of being cut off from the world of the family and the community as a result of a knowledge that she has but cannot communicate; although Chippington's secret is the special experience of combat and Laura's an affair that she cannot share with her husband, the effect is the same: both are exiled from the social as a result of what they have come to know but cannot communicate. The soldier's experience of being doomed to watch the world from the distant and passive perspective of the spectator is Laura's experience as it is conveyed both by her structural relation to the story of *Brief Encounter* and, more evocatively, by her face, by a recurring shot of Celia Johnson's face that allows us to watch someone else watching something of which she can no longer be a part. This helps to account for the power of this shot; to see Celia Johnson's large, melancholy eyes looking at what she can neither have nor forget is to see in barely distorted form what would have been all too familiar to audiences in 1945; as one returning soldier puts it, "My eyes were those of a captive on the run, expressing a suspicious fear as if being hunted." Or, as Laura puts it, "I felt like a criminal."[137]

A Bit of Grit

The face of Celia Johnson thus variously reflects the psychic and social traumas of wartime. In one reading, the shot offers a diagnosis of British society after the war. Because of displacements and necessary shifts in the distribution of gendered labor, an old (and always incomplete) understanding of companionate marriage was no longer tenable. Johnson's long look at the blank space where another ought to be is in this way an eloquent, conservative, and ultimately melancholy response to a world fundamentally altered by war. In another reading, the shot offers a formal description or embodiment of a historically specific version of war trauma. Unlike the previous war, World War II put psychic life, emotional experience, and memory at the heart of its diagnostic accounts of war and its effects. In this case, the wide, sad eyes of Celia Johnson represent—as if filtered through the distorting but revealing logic of the dream—what it would look like to look at someone looking at war. If war is too much to look at directly, looking at someone else looking and suffering might be the next best thing. Both readings are, I think, right; and both treat the shot as a more or less distorted representation of the historically specific content of the postwar and home front experiences of World War II. However, still more can be said about Johnson's performance and about *Brief Encounter*; for example, how this shot not only reflects a particular historical experience but also challenges cinema's potentially critical relation to history and to war. In other words, *Brief Encounter*'s signature shot is perhaps best read as an embodied argument about cinema *in* history and about cinema *as* a particularly powerful form of historical reckoning.

What does Celia Johnson in fact see when she looks off into space in *Brief Encounter*? One deceptively simple answer is that she sees a camera. To make this film, Celia Johnson spent many hours looking directly at a camera, and the resulting shots make up, I maintain, the film's emotional and structural core. This centrality and the difficulty of her performance were not lost on Johnson and Lean and his crew. Johnson, as I mentioned, claimed to be terrified by the camera's singular attention, and Lean was amazed by her ability to *think* on camera. One of the film's cameramen reported: "You can do anything with her. Stick lamps under her nose, she's got such technique, nothing bothers her."[138] It is telling that Johnson's "technique" is understood as a sort of resistance to the emotional imposition—

the bother—of the camera. The Mitchell 35mm camera that Lean used for *Brief Encounter* is an imposing thing, made even more so by the need to encase it in its large, matte-black sound-dampening "blimp." And, because Johnson was not made-up and filmed without diffusion, the feeling of the camera's close and heavy scrutiny would have been all the more palpable. The camera is not simply a recording device in *Brief Encounter*. It is rather an important and material—if implicit—part of the film's emotional field; insofar as it could or did cause her bother, which she in turn had to suppress, the camera effectively becomes a part of Celia Johnson's face.

The film thematizes the eruption of the apparatus—as camera, as film style, as cinematic technique—into the fiction of the film several times over the course of the film. For instance, Laura meets Alec when she gets a bit of grit in her eye, a fact that calls material attention to the eye as lens as well as bodily organ; the vicarious discomfort one feels at the sight of Alec dragging his handkerchief across her eye rhymes with the awkwardness of being reminded from within the illusion of a film that lights, cameras, and members of a film crew are all present "behind" the image. The bit of grit returns later in the film in one of its most famous scenes. Early in their courtship, Alec tells Laura about his "special pigeon," the research area that he hopes to pursue in addition to his work as a general practitioner: "my specialty is pneumoconiosis. . . . [The] slow process of fibrosis of the lung due to the inhalation of particles of dust."[139] He goes on to list different particulates—coal dust, metal dust, stone dust—that can compromise the body's tenuous natural integrity. What we are supposed to understand throughout this conversation, however, is that while they speak of inhaling bits of grit, they are in fact acknowledging their attraction to each other. Whereas the first appearance of grit calls attention to the eye as a physical instrument and thus to the cinematic apparatus, in the case of the second, the self-consciously euphemistic nature of their conversation—where grit stands for the material force of sexual desire—calls attention to the film's reliance on artifice and writerly technique. At both levels, the bit of grit emerges as a figure for the eruption of technique as a sort of matter into the thematic space of the film.

Most striking in this regard is the scene of Laura and Alec's last encounter; in the midst of their final conversation, they are interrupted by Laura's talkative acquaintance Dolly Messiter (which brings us back to the film's opening scene and the film almost to a close). In order to represent Laura's feelings of disappointment and abstraction, Lean shifts from a high-key to low-key lighting style, bathing her face in increasingly harsh direct light while allowing the fill to dim and the background to fade into darkness.

A bit of grit.

The moment is notable both for its ultimate effect and for the fact that one can follow the lights dimming as an obviously contrived process: "When I was directing *Brief Encounter* we experimented with an extreme technique of emphasis. In the closing scenes of the picture, when Celia Johnson is sitting in the railroad station and listening to the train that is taking her lover away for the last time, we took down the lights of the room behind her and even faded out the voice of the woman talking to her, so that all the emphasis was on her face and the sound of the departing train."[140] In a sense, the cinematographic change of emphasis is a culmination of the film's visual logic, a shift from the film's putative domestic realism to an exaggerated chiaroscuro more appropriate to *The Cabinet of Dr. Caligari* or *The Third Man*; it is, in other words, late visual proof of a stylization that had been at work all along.

Lean then follows with something even more radical. After Alec leaves and Laura understands that he is not coming back, the camera—focused again on Johnson's face—slowly but spectacularly tilts in sympathy with Laura's own feeling of falling apart. Lean slowly rotates the camera clockwise, which produces the effect of the world turning in a counterclockwise direction. In the background we hear the sound of the approaching express, a high, wavering noise that seems once again almost to leap out of the film's frame. The effect is potent because it doesn't feel limited to Laura's experience of the moment; rather it feels like Laura's anxiety has somehow bled out from the fiction of the film and infected the camera, the actor, and

An extreme technique of emphasis.

the audience. It is a moment of emotional intensity powerful enough to tear the barrier that would keep the world of *Brief Encounter* separate from our own: "the camera tilts over, making her seem drunk or distraught as she goes to meet [the express]. It's a calculated effect, and Lean easily gets overcalculated—but in this case the vibrato works just because the image seems to be willed by the actress."[141]

This brings me to my final reading of Celia Johnson's face and *Brief Encounter*. Whereas Dreyer and Reed used the broken shot/reverse shot sequence to suggest the presence of something too big for cinema—the spiritual realist experience of the divine, the enormity of history itself—Lean does something different but no less ecstatic. The *almost* "overcalculated" encounter between the camera and Johnson's face instead calls attention to the necessary split between actor and character, between the face of Laura Jesson as she gazes abstractly into the recent past and the face of Johnson as she looks almost directly into the camera's lens. This split—made palpable at moments like the one I just described—is the film's most concentrated embodiment of the historiographical logic described in this book. Insofar as the split makes visible the actor playing Laura Jesson, it also smuggles in that actor's very few previous film roles—Alix Kinross, the wife of a Naval captain whose ship is sunk in *In Which We Serve*; and Ethel Gibbons, a woman we see live and suffer through two world wars in *This Happy Breed*. Like the unmotivated and uncanny reappearance of the color red in each of *Colonel Blimp*'s three acts, the face of Johnson cuts across Lean's early films, creating points of impacted and uncanny stylistic overlap that in turn call attention to the historically compressed nature of wartime itself: "It is," writes Greil Marcus, "a curving time made by the way actors carry roles with them through the careers, each role, if the actors can burn at the core, bleeding into every other."[142] What we see when we see the face of Celia Johnson is both the face of Laura Jesson and the face of an actor who looked at a camera that had previously looked at her while she was looking at the experience, the costs, and the waste of war.

The doubled logic of the shot thus forces us to confront a formal and temporal divide between the time of the film's action—its setting in the before of the late 1930s, and its appearance on screens in 1945. More precisely, because the staring face of Johnson is felt at moments like these to be in both places or times at once, it properly exists as a critical or historiographical comment on the relation between the past and the present. As Lant writes, the film seems to know that "the recent past of Britain was hard to formulate, for its heritage of rationing, illegitimate births, strikes, and urban destruction and its memories of death and partings were still very much of the present."[143] In the most material of ways, the war's past refused to stay put. What makes Johnson's face a figure for the tragic perspective discussed here is not only that it stands as a tacit witness to the waste of war but also that it acknowledges the violence of the past as always possible in the present, that violent things do indeed happen to ordinary people, and that the only way maybe to prevent or mitigate violence in the future is to admit as much now.

Epilogue
Derek Jarman's War

> . . . the pity of war, the pity war distilled.
>
> —Wilfred Owen, "Strange Meeting" (1919)

> AMYL: Shit.
> MAD: What's up, Amyl?
> AMYL: I've broken my Winston Churchill mug.
> MAD: Don't worry, we'll stick him together.
>
> —Derek Jarman, *Jubilee* (1977)

I have argued that some films made in Britain during World War II offer an opportunity to think differently both about what it means to represent wars from within wars and about what it means for something to be *about* something else. World War II posed special representational challenges to filmmakers and others: because of its logistical enormity, the unprecedented scope of its destruction, its conceptual status as total, and the way it seemingly remade the very stuff of everyday life through aerial bombing, blackouts, rationing, and the logistical demands of total mobilization, World War II put terrific pressure on and created new critical opportunities for aesthetic and specifically cinematic representations. Light, dark, sound, silence, music, work, play, sleep, sex, food, belief, virtue, and truth all meant or could mean other, surprising things when seen from within the real and the conceptual ambit of total war. As a result, the films I have discussed rely both on moments of stylistic excess or eccentricity that call attention to the medium-specific resources of the cinema and on a range of ideologically loaded and historically specific ideas about eccentricity as a national value. At the same time that one can track an official, propaganda version of wartime eccentricity (the cherished and "little" eccentricity of the English), one also encounters darker, unofficial, or critical versions of eccentricity—

moments of aesthetic and ideological excess that call attention to logical contradictions immanent to the concept of total war.

Although we often remember World War II as a singular moment of national unity in Britain, it was in fact characterized by a shared experience of intellectual and emotional ambivalence about the value and significance of war, an ambivalence that demanded different approaches toward both war's forms and its content. On the one hand, the war was widely recognized as a necessary and just war, a war that had to be fought if European civilization were to survive. On the other hand, the fresh memory of the Great War and its absurd waste made ridiculous the idea of any unambiguously good war. Kingsley Martin, editor of the left-leaning *New Statesman*, wrote in 1940 that Churchill misunderstood the British people's "feelings when he talked of this as the finest moment of their history. Our feelings are more complex than that. To talk to common people in or out of uniform is to discover that determination to defend this island is coupled with a deep and almost universal bitterness that we have been reduced to such a pass."[1] Although Martin's feelings of complexity were of course particular to his situation, they are, I think, nonetheless representative of contradictions and compromises that were immanent to the war; Martin later wrote, "I combined in myself many of the inconsistencies and conflicts of the period which long tried to reconcile pacifism with collective security, and a defence of individual liberty with the necessity of working with Communists against Fascists."[2] As I have shown, a range of attitudes toward the war took a singularly doubled form: we would have to suspend our values—fair play, good sportsmanship, moderation—in order to save those values. The films I discuss all engage with the question of how productively to portray, as Cyril Connolly put it, "a war of which we are all ashamed and yet a war which has to be won."[3]

I have also argued that these films—*The Life and Death of Colonel Blimp*, *Henry V*, and *Brief Encounter*—use the specificity of cinema and cinematic style to come productively to grips with this necessary doubleness and to imagine cinema as a form of historical reckoning especially appropriate to the complexities of total war. Although cinema is not the only medium capable of critically relating the history of World War II, and although World War II was not necessarily absolutely different from other wars, its specificities and the medium of cinema came together in Britain in the 1940s to enable an especially canny kind of cinematic thinking. More to the point, these films work at the level of form and style to develop aesthetic strategies that could accommodate that real and necessary doubleness without falling into any number of available but inappropriate patterns: bad faith, mute resignation, sterile paradox. These films thus mobilize a productive and eccentric tension between narrative content and film style in order to develop a pragmatic aesthetic that could both recognize the specific necessity of this war and the larger shame and "original violence" of war as such. As a result, they both refuse to reify war into an epic or simply memorial experience and force an imaginative confrontation with war's root causes; they explore, in other words, a human tendency toward aggression that would seem to exceed the historical terms of any war in particular. As Powell and Pressburger, Olivier, and Lean try to understand, to repress that aggression or to understate its effects seems in itself to turn history into either tragedy or farce. This, for obvious reasons, is a difficult and dispiriting argument to make during wartime; it is nonetheless a necessary argument, and the achievement of these films is that they managed to make it in the midst of war.

Despite their considerable critical and historical power, these films fell largely out of favor after the war. This is partly the result of broader shifts in British cinematic tastes in the 1950s and after:

> A decade that began with the new government scheme to promote British film-making, by rewarding producers with a share of the so-called Eady Levy (named after a Treasury official) on cinema admissions, ended with two seemingly interminable comedy formulae—the "Carry On" and "Doctor" series—firmly entrenched as the routine diet of British audiences. . . . Declining attendance, cinema closures (and conversion to bowling alleys or bingo halls), the rapid spread of television, spurred on by the introduction of ITV—all of these can be pasted together into a highly selective, though familiar, picture of British cinema sunk in torpor before the arrival of the Angry Young Men (or Northern realists), who would transform it into a world-class contender in the early sixties.[4]

With the end of the war, the particular value and aesthetic complexity of the British war film became harder to see both as the war was inevitably reduced to an official memory of shared sacrifice and as critical energies were turned increasingly toward what the Angry Young Men saw as the enervating, emasculating, and unheroic effects of relative postwar affluence and the society that administered it. We can see this in films like *Saturday Night and Sunday Morning* (1960), *This Sporting Life* (1963), and *The Loneliness of the Long Distance Runner* (1962), in which Colin Smith, the lonely runner of the film's title, self-destructively and self-consciously falls between the cracks of new American-style consumerism, working-class resentment at the paternalism of the welfare state, and a crisis of masculinity marked by the withering-away and eventual death of his father, a figure both for a more recognizably English working class and for a decaying generation that really fought and thus really remembered the war. Like the other films that I've looked at, *The Loneliness of the Long Distance Runner* relies on the comparative significance of particular faces: Colin's pinched and largely inexpressive glare, the hollowed-out look of his father's face moments after death, and the unused gas masks that Colin and the other Borstal boys are forced significantly to disassemble for scrap. However, whereas the faces of Roger Livesy, Celia Johnson, Robert Newton, and Laurence Olivier embody the richly doubled and critical character of these films, the blank countenances of Richardson's film seem to deny the possibility of real significance in the postwar period.

The Angry Young Man's break from the values and styles of the 1940s in Britain took different but related forms in the following decades: in light Godardian reflections on late capitalist surface and spectacle in swinging-sixties films such as *Darling* (1965), *Blow-Up* (1966), and *Alfie* (1966); in the apocalyptic images of exaggerated or threatened masculinity in glam, proto-punk, and punk films such as *A Clockwork Orange* (1971), *The Man Who Fell to Earth* (1976), and *Quadrophenia* (1979); in the class-conscious agitprop of Ken Loach or the late kitchen-sink realism of early Mike Leigh; as well as in the development of a stylized postimperial aesthetic in films such as *My Beautiful Launderette* (1985), *Mona Lisa* (1985), *Playing Away* (1986), and, later, *The Crying Game* (1992). We could think, too, about Ealing comedies, Hammer horror, the Bond franchise, British gangster pictures, the heritage film, the British rom-com, feel-good films such as *The Full Monty* and *Billy Eliot*, the lock-stock-and-lad films of "Cool Britannia," and so on. Although these films are all very different, they share an origin both in explicit reactions to the sexual, economic, and political displacements of the postwar period and in tacit reactions against the style and substance of the wartime cinema of the 1940s. Put differently, changes in British society after the war as well as cultural shifts in attitudes toward the war and its generation made it difficult to appreciate the aesthetic and critical achievement of the films discussed here, films that came to be seen as overly patriotic, hokey, merely eccentric, aesthetically aberrant, or oddly prudish. They are films that, with varying degrees of aesthetic success, try to reject, forget, or overcome the war; and insofar as they are efforts to forget war, they are, of course, about war, too.

Derek Jarman was one of the first British directors to look explicitly to the war cinema of the 1940s for aesthetic and technical inspiration. This is, in part, a result of where his personal history falls in relation to the larger history of twentieth-century Britain. Jarman was born in 1942 and his father was a bomber pilot for the RAF, an experience that left a violent mark on his and his son's life. Although Jarman came of age as an artist and as a gay man in the 1960s, the war and its character remained a strong presence in his thinking and his films:

> Old RAF flying jackets, loaded pistols, medals and wartime souvenirs. They became my inheritance. I have never been anti-military in the way that some are, how could I be? My father fought a hard war. He fought Hitler, prosecuting the war with a violence that proved uncontainable. I don't know how to solve that, but without men like my father the war would not have been won! After it was over, he carried on the war. It had destroyed his world. He had many friends who were killed, he laid his life on the line but survived. A terrible sadness invaded his life; at the end he became a kleptomaniac, and stole what he felt had been stolen from him.[5]

For Jarman, the war was thus never entirely a thing of the past; it was rather an inheritance, a symptom, a problem, a violence uncontainable by history or by life. Unlike filmmakers who would try either to reject the war as a lie or to manage it as memorial, Jarman works to articulate a complicated relation to the war, its necessity, and its shame that recalls the complex position of the wartime films discussed here. As a result, Jarman was able to look back to and draw inspiration from filmmakers such as Powell and Pressburger (as well as from Kenneth Anger and Pier Paolo Pasolini) at a moment when that was not at all an obvious move. He wrote in 1984: "[T]here is only one English feature director whose work is in the first rank. Michael Powell is the only director to make a clear political analysis in his films, his work is unequalled. *The Life and Death of Colonel Blimp* is the finest English feature, and *A Canterbury Tale* and *A Matter of Life and Death* are not far behind."[6]

One can see Jarman's debt to Powell, Olivier, and Lean in a number of ways: in a paradoxically radical traditionalism that mixes a melancholy appreciation for England's past with a sharply experimental sense of social critique; in his characteristic mix of cool-headed political analysis and self-consciously overripe romanticism; in his sensitive ability to wed cinematic images and cuts with music and sound; in his pervasive sense that the violence of the present—in his case the social, homophobic violence of the Thatcher years—should not and cannot be seen as different in kind from the violence of the past. Indeed, this sense of a past war continuing to assert itself in the present runs throughout Jarman's films. We might think of his use of explicitly historical settings in films such as *Edward II*, *Caravaggio*, and *Wittgenstein*; in each case Jarman takes, understands, and expands on techniques that Olivier and Powell and Pressburger used in their historical—or, rather, historiographical—films not only to imagine the long and darker cultural history of England but also to radicalize that history by forcing the past into critical contact with the present.

This takes a couple of different forms for Jarman. On the one hand, we can think of these films as a species of antiheritage history film. Unlike the Merchant-and-Ivory model, Jarman's presentations of the English past don't offer it as a comfortably other place. Instead, he enlivens luminously queer moments of political conflict, aesthetic achievement, and philosophical investigation in order to show how our culture—at its best—has been and remains more than a little queer all along. One aspect of Jarman's crucial influence on the New Queer Cinema of the 1990s is his use of the historical film to imagine and to trace a queer counterhistory of European culture. On the other hand, each of these films also works to show how the history of violence that would seem to be about its states of emergency—periods of civil unrest in early modern England and renaissance Italy, World War I, World War II, the collapse of the British welfare state under Thatcher, a long history of homophobia, the AIDS crisis—are in fact part of a continuous history that needs to be understood in terms of a critical and comparative historiography. In a way that once again recalls the films I've considered over the course of this book, Jarman's films are an instance of a historical project that Walter Benjamin understood in similarly cinematic terms fifty years before: "Historical materialism must renounce the epic element in history. It blasts the epoch out of the reified 'continuity of history.' But it also explodes the homogeneity of the epoch, interspersing it with ruins—that is, with the present."[7] And, indeed, more than any other filmmaker in Britain, Jarman's cinema and, in particular, his early cinema is a political cinema of ruins.

Jubilee (1978) opens with a scene in which Queen Elizabeth I asks the court alchemist, John Dee, to entertain her with a vision of England's future. He then conjures an angel, Ariel, who in turn reveals a future England run by punks, shock troops, and insane television execs. The shift from the present to the past is, at first glance, striking. Elizabeth's drawing room is lit in a stark chiaroscuro style that recalls the paintings of Caravaggio while anticipating Jarman's later experiments with black-box settings (in, for instance, his *Caravaggio*); however, as the film cuts suddenly to the dystopian future promised by the angel, a bombed-out, smoking London bathed in an even and harsh light, the shift seems to mark out a difference in kind

Churchill's Mug.

between the past and the future. As the film continues, that difference becomes more and more obscure. Jenny Runacre, the actor who played the renaissance queen returns as Bod, the cruelest and most cunning member of the girl gang that wreaks havoc throughout the film. In an early scene the gang's resident intellectual (Jarman's script refers to her as a "historian of the void"), Amyl Nitrate, offers a brief history lesson—asking, among other things, "Was Winston Churchill a hero?"—just before inadvertently shattering her commemorative Winston Churchill mug; when Elizabeth and John Dee look forward, Amyl looks back, throwing the film's status as prophecy and history into question.[8] Also, insofar as the film is a comment on the 1977 Silver Jubilee that stands proudly alongside The Sex Pistol's "God Save the Queen" and The Clash's "1977," *Jubilee* is not only a comment on a particular queen; it is also a comment on a mode of political sovereignty that directly links the violence of the past, present, and future. It "gazes," writes Michael O'Pray, "back into the past from the standpoint of contemporary England and then proceeds to create an image of the future."[9]

Jarman shot some of *Jubilee* in parts of London that still bore the scars of the Blitz. At first glance, his future London thus resembles other period future-shock films that imagine a tomorrow in which cities have degenerated into different versions of a Hobbesian wilderness, including *Planet of the Apes* (1968), *The Omega Man* (1971), and *Logan's Run* (1976). However, whereas those films imagined a canned future on storyboards and Hollywood backlots, Jarman pointedly looked for his future in the tenacious ruins of World War II. If the critical force of Jarman's film comes from its efforts to put an apparently sacred past into contact with a profane present, its London physically embodied a present unable to manage, memorialize, or undo, or, indeed, effectively to sacralize the past. Indeed, this London of significant and significantly forgotten rubble, of a present that can't escape its past is Jarman's London. Jarman's ruined London returns even more poignantly in *The Last of England* (1989), a film which blends Super 8 scenes of another future England run by shock troops in balaclavas, riot cops, and barking German shepherds with found documentary footage of people walking to work, of fascist rallies, and of teeming cityscapes as well as with home movies of him, his sister, mother, and father during and after the war. As I said, Jarman's father was an RAF bomber pilot, and the film is, among other things, an attempt to come to grips—as Powell and Pressburger, Olivier, and Lean did years before—with the difficult idea that a war could be both necessary and evil, and that violence tends to run past its ostensible historical and psychological bounds. Thinking of an apparently bucolic scene of him playing ball with his mother and sister, Jarman remarks: "[T]he film triggers memories. I see the camouflage, the barbed wire, and the H-blocks of my childhood; my sister Gaye, and myself playing ball on the lawns of RAF Abingdon, where my father was Station Commander—I'm six years old, it's the summer of 1948."[10]

Jarman transferred all of these different types of film—different types that evoke the play between his memories of war and its aftermath—to

London's burning.

video, edited his film in that format, only to transfer it all back to 35mm stock. This was an incredibly laborious process in 1989. As a result, the film mixes its media, its histories, and its often violent imagery into a beautifully and erotically blurred continuity, a method that nicely embodies the film's larger, complex sense of history as a set of confrontations between only apparently distinct types of desire, violence, loss, and, perhaps, recompense. As a result, *The Last of England* is Jarman's most explicitly archeological project, one that sees the past, present, and future as sites to uncover and confront; instead of a trowel and brush, however, Jarman uses the aesthetic resources of cinema and, in particular, video to upset the memorial quiet of history. In addition to the distressed and fragile homogeneity of the film's multiply transferred look, Jarman used the specific resources of video editing to cut time in a way that would have been impossible with film; this is especially visible in the film's extended scene of an apocalyptic disco that seems to announce the apparent end of things with its volatile mix of sex, violence, and death: "The images in the disco are not arbitrary, although there is an element of chance in the way they rattle along. The cutting is staccato, and aggressive. It would not be possible to cut film this way, although theoretically you might attempt it. 1600 cuts in six minutes. The sequence crashes into the film unexpectedly, the pace is relentless. It should wind the audience. Why do I want to do this?"[11]

Much of the film centers on the apparently aimless activity of a few tattooed boys as they wander through the persistent past-future rubble of London docks, masturbating, doing drugs, breaking rocks, setting off flares, and so on. In one striking scene, a shirtless boy beats, kicks, and finally grinds himself against a large reproduction of Caravaggio's *Amor Vincit Omnia*. Insofar as the moment forces together a high point of the late renaissance, the lingering ruins of World War II, and the conceptual last of England, it is characteristic of Jarman's political and aesthetic blend of the radical and the conservative: "Jarman's hatred of Thatcherism was partly because her particular brand of Conservatism wasn't actually conserving anything. Nevertheless, he remained deeply suspicious of the heritage industry, declaring an equal hatred for the way the Elizabethan past might be used to 'castrate our vibrant present.' His historical films were always meticulously researched but always included startling anachronisms such as the Frisbee in *Sebastiane* or the typewriter in *Caravaggio* which opened up the possibility of a living relationship between past, present, and future."[12] As with the wartime films I've looked at over the course of this book, Jarman's films rely on anachronism as an especially powerful cinematic tool. Indeed, the London that Jarman films, a London that is a palpable mix of its wartime

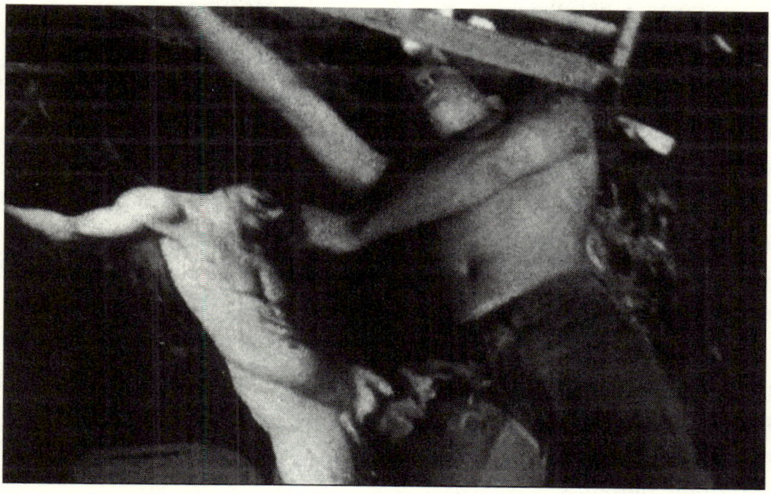

Boy with Caravaggio.

past, its broken present, and the future that seems the likely and tragic result of that present, stands as a powerful argument about the historical and social tenacity of violence: "In *The Last of England* the devastation wrought by Margaret Thatcher's social and economic policies is represented as a continuation of the Blitz as London burns before being reduced to rubble."[13]

Jarman's most explicit reference to the cinema of the 1940s comes with *War Requiem* (1989), which is set as a kind of music video to a 1963 recording of Benjamin Britten's piece of the same name. The film opens with a visibly frail Laurence Olivier in his final film appearance as the quasi-allegorical Old Soldier (he died only a few months later); a Nurse cares for Olivier's character, adjusting his lap blanket and rolling him down the path of what appears to be a veterans' rest home. As they move down the path, he fiddles with some medals, trying shakily to pin them to his cardigan zip-up sweater; we hear Olivier in voiceover, weakly reciting lines from Wilfred Owen's "Strange Meeting":

> Yet also there encumbered sleepers groaned,
> Too fast in thought or death to be bestirred.
> Then, as I probed them, one sprang up, and stared
> With piteous recognition in fixed eyes,
> Lifting distressful hands as if to bless.
> And by his smile, I knew that sullen hall;
> By his dead smile I knew we stood in Hell.

The poem and the medals appear to evoke disparate, violent memories and thoughts in the Old Soldier as Jarman cuts to found footage of explosions, fires, stretchers, men carrying the wounded and the dead through trenches. Having, at last and with the help of the Nurse, pinned the medals to his chest, the Old Soldier looks directly into the camera, staring out toward the audience as memories, fantasies, and nightmares of the war begin to unfurl in a mix of 35mm, Super 8, and found documentary footage; his memories are somehow mixed in with what appear to be the experiences of the dead Owen and are juxtaposed with religious visions, quasi-allegorical passages, the wars of several decades as they were or would be seen on TV. The apparent disorder of the Old Soldier's thoughts, as expressed in Jarman's quick, disconcerting cuts, rhymes cannily with the "diabolic" harmonic interval (the tritone, flattened fifth, or "diabolus in musica") upon which Britten's score largely depends.

In Britten's *War Requiem,* that tritonic interval both suggests the essential, timeless discord of war and, because it falls between more familiar tonalities, stands as yet another example the rabbit-duck effects that I've been tracing throughout this book. The tritone is, indeed, an importantly ambiguous effect within Western music, an amphibious harmonic relation that both resists and, in resisting, calls attention to the structure of conventional tonality. In Britten, it works to balance without resolving different aspects of war: its beauty and its squalor, its imagined order and its practical futility, its opportunity and its waste, its necessity and its great shame. Indeed, Britten's own experience of the war offers another example of the doubleness I've described. Although Britten and his lover, Peter Pears, were pacifists and conscientious objectors, he understood his resistance to violence in the characteristically fraught structural terms of total war; he wrote in a 1942 statement with which he refused both combatant and noncombatant service: "I realize however that in total war, it is impossible to avoid all participation of an indirect kind but I believe I must draw the line as far away from direct participation as possible."[14] Like the wartime filmmakers discussed in this book, Britten understood World War II's totality as a conceptual as well as a practical problem, one that he later sought to encode in the pull between a large and frankly lovely sense of order and a necessary, particular, bedeviling dissonance in his *War Requiem.*

Commissioned for the late reopening of Coventry Cathedral after its destruction in the war, Britten's piece uneasily mixes the traditional Latin Mass of the Dead with Wilfred Owen's World War I poetry in order to commemorate and criticize the violence of World War II; like the tritone, Britten's broad and almost cinematic assemblage of nearly but finally not incommensurate parts into a single act of remembrance invokes the official or memorial generality of war alongside the irreducible particularity of its violence and its loss. As Heather Wiebe writes, "The worldly experience of war arrives as if conjured from the space of the bell's tritone, like a film close-up revealing the nature of this disruption."[15] Like the reconstructed cathedral—a new structure built around the paradoxically preserved ruins of what had been destroyed in 1940—Britten's requiem uses a variety of quasi-cinematic tools—sudden shifts in volume that create the feel of close-ups, stylistic juxtapositions in the score and the libretto that create the critical effect of montage, and a tritone that invokes the more broadly anamorphic possibilities of cinema—to upset the *official* war memorial's tendency not to help us remember but rather to let us forget.

It is clear that this is part of what Jarman heard in Britten's piece, and his initial close-up of an aged and frail Olivier works to connect his film to the formal logic of Britten's score as well as to the wartime films discussed in the previous chapters. Olivier's presence as the quasi-allegorical Old Soldier recalls Powell and Pressburger's effort to embody the similarly archetypal figure of Colonel Blimp, an aging warrior invoked to help understand a larger history of violence. Olivier was Powell and Pressburger's first choice for the role of Clive Candy; they turned to Roger Livesey only when Churchill's government refused to give Olivier leave from the Fleet Air Arm to make the film. As a result, Jarman seems in *War Requiem* to make good on the counterfactual promise of *The Life and Death of Colonel Blimp,*

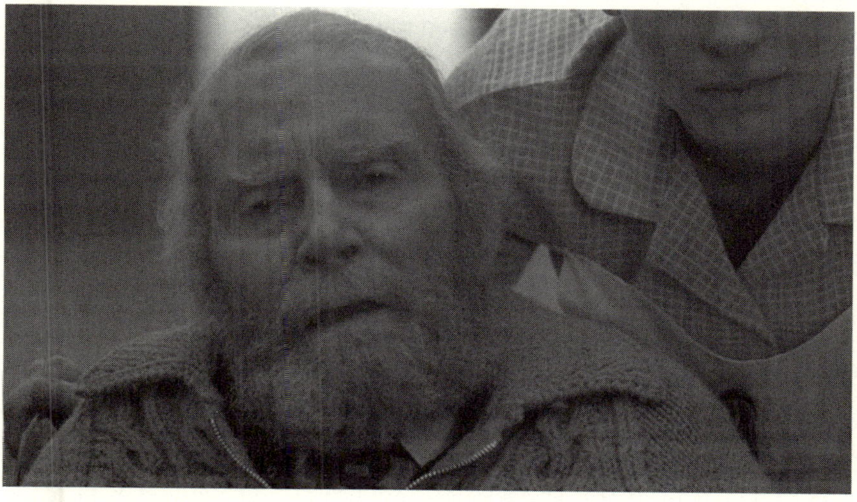

The world at war.

imagining what might have happened if the government and the world had seen Powell and Pressburger and their films more clearly. Olivier's look into the camera accompanied by a voiceover also recalls Olivier's own shot of Henry's vigil on the night before the battle of Agincourt in *Henry V*, a scene that attempts to synthesize exteriority and interiority, the theater and the cinema, the actor and the character, the body of the man and the idea of a king. Here, too, we listen as a voice quietly registers what's happening behind a more or less static image of a face, a relation that promises some kind of compromise between inside and outside, past and present, memory and experience. That said, Olivier's appearance in *War Requiem* also offers another, more critical account as it focuses our attention on the bodily particularity of the actor, in this case on the heartbreaking spectacle of Olivier's really dying body, which brings to mind not the ideal presence of the hero-king-star but rather the excessively present, already ravaged body of Robert Newton as Pistol. As I argued, Newton's unruly particularity provides a kind of counterpoint to Olivier's ostensible effort to imagine and embody national unity in the body of the king. And, finally, like Lean's *Brief Encounter*, *War Requiem* relies on the face for its narrative structure. As with Celia Johnson's melancholy stare, Olivier's face both authorizes and undermines the film's coherence as an account of war and its effects. And, just as her face stood as a point where the past and the present of war were forced critically together, Olivier's resists the tendency to memorialize war and thus to reduce it to a past understood as officially different from the present. Because it brings together the history of war and the history of cinema in Britain, Jarman's casting of the aged Olivier is an argument about cinema, war, and the relation between the two.

Jarman identifies, shares, and adapts an argument about war and history that runs through my discussion of the films of Powell and Pressburger, Olivier, and Lean, an argument about the temporality of war and the character of its violence. Although the first half of *War Requiem* is filled with images associated with the memory and the memorialization of World War I—trenches, poppies, and Tommys—it turns in its second half to a more general and difficult argument about war. After following the winding path of the Old Soldier's thoughts for over an hour, Jarman cuts abruptly back to Olivier's face. Once again staring directly into the camera, he ushers in a late series of *almost* timelessly violent images: cities burning, fantasies of ritual sacrifice, and, most strikingly, documentary footage taken from other wars, including World War II, the Vietnam War, the Soviet war in Afghanistan, and civil wars in Africa. These images are brutal, and, while they bear the traces of their particular moments in space and time, they are cut together

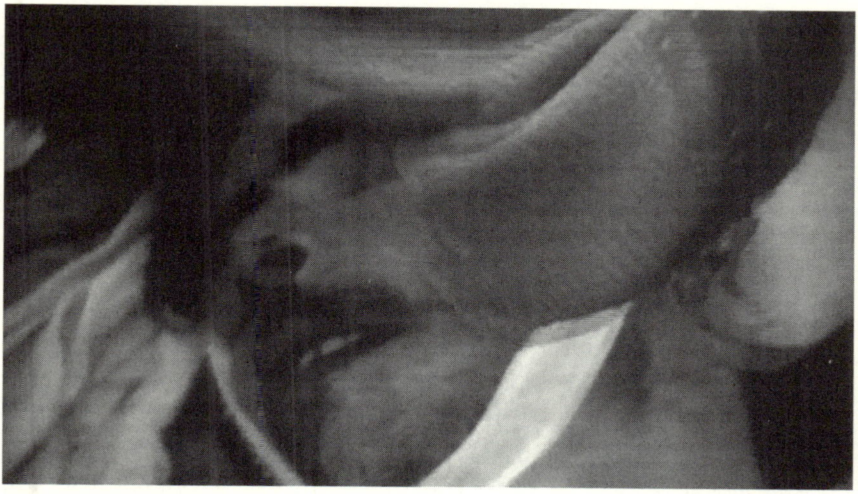

The pity of war.

in such a way as to identify what remains tragically the same from war to war: the degradation, the loss, the reduction of persons to things, and an overall sense of the tremendous, tragic waste of war.

Like the films discussed in this book, Jarman's *War Requiem* is both an effort to reckon with and to represent a particular experience of a particular war and a meditation on general modes of human violence that must exceed the terms of any one war. The film thus brings together several different registers: a sense of commemoration, an enigmatic personal and aesthetic "reparation" for personal loss, a feeling of outrage at the horror of war, and a pointed if tacit response to the AIDS crisis in Britain as well as to Jarman's own recent diagnosis. Jarman discovered he had the disease while making *The Last of England*, and he dedicated *War Requiem* "In my heart . . . to all those cast out, like myself from Christendom. To my friends who are dying in a moral climate created by a church with no compassion."[16] Later, he both complicated and clarified his sense of the film's contemporary significance: "So, yes, it is my AIDS film . . . but it's not. I leave that to others. The film's as ungrounded as possible so it remains an open situation, so people can put their own interpretation on parts of it."[17] Jarman thought of *War Requiem* as a film with its own particular and particularly difficult relation to *aboutness*, a relation that emerges from the uncertain space between Britain's long military past and the social violence of its present. It is a film *about* World War I, World War II, the Vietnam War, and the war in Afghanistan, just as it is a film *about* war poetry, beauty, and love; memory, religion, and

Thatcher's rise; the collapse of the welfare state, homophobia, the AIDS crisis, and more. The film works, in other words, to reveal ideological, psychic, and historical tensions that emerge when wars are memorialized and the human tendency toward violence is imagined as merely atavistic, as backward, as someone else's or some other time's problem. As Jarman saw in the midst of his own political emergency, violence against bodies, against ideals, against futures isn't limited to this or that war; and, insofar as he pursues that argument cinematically, he draws on techniques, styles, and ideas that Powell and Pressburger, Olivier, and Lean developed in their own deeply self-conscious wartime films. This ability to think both about a particular political situation and about the nature of violence and history writ large is, I maintain, the real and specifically cinematic achievement of some films made in Britain between 1939 and 1945; and although this sense of cinema's critical capacity was made possible by the particular experience of World War II, it has not been and must not be limited to this or that war.

Acknowledgments

I had to learn a lot to write this book. As a result, I have a lot of people to thank. First, thanks to Fred Nachbaur and Kurt Piehler for considering the book and then including it on Fordham's list. The care and intelligence with which they approached the proposal, the readers' reports, and the manuscript itself meant a great deal to me and helped me to see it through. Thanks, too, to Eric Newman and Will Cerbone, who helped to oversee the editorial and production processes. They make it seem easy. I can't say enough about Michael Koch's copyediting. He read the manuscript with attention and intelligence and made *War Pictures* a much better and clearer book. I also need to thank the anonymous Press readers for their sharp, directed, and generous comments on the manuscript: both saw things about the book that I wouldn't have seen without them. Wendy Xin and Luke Terlaak Poot offered detailed and scrupulous assistance getting the manuscript into shape at a key moment. Evan Winchester did fantastic work chasing down leads (especially on Robert Newton) early on.

A number of friends and colleagues read and commented on some or all of the manuscript at different stages of its development. Four in particular read and commented on the manuscript, helping me to write a much better book than I could have otherwise: my many conversations with Cathy Gallagher about the manuscript and about the spoken and unspoken compromises that underwrote the war were invaluable; her thinking about the war and, in particular, the anxieties that characterized its early days is a shaping influence throughout. David Miller read the manuscript at a critical moment and helped me to see and embrace what it was really all about. Alexander Nemerov encouraged me not only to write about eccentricity but also to let some of my own eccentricities to come a little closer to the surface. Alan Tansman showed me late in the game how much I could gain by cutting; he made the book sharper, smarter, and shorter—a gift to us all! Several others read and commented on parts of the book, often giving guidance and encouragement when I needed it most: Dan Blanton, Mitch Breitwieser, Eric

Bulson, Jeff Knapp, Paul Saint-Amour, and Linda Williams. Who could ask for better, smarter, more sensitive, and more humbling readers?

Special thanks go to Alex Nemerov (again) and Sue Zemka, whose brilliant responses to my essay on *Brief Encounter* in *ELN* encouraged me to think in better and broader ways about Celia Johnson's face.

Given the time I managed to take with this, I've had the chance to discuss its ideas and arguments with many others who have improved the book in ways they may or may not recognize: Elizabeth Abel, Charlie Altieri, Julia Bader, Julie Carr, Ian Duncan, Eric Falci, Josh Gang, Steve Goldsmith, Donna Jones, Celeste Langan, Jos Lavery, Colleen Lye, Maura Nolan, Derek Nystrom, Katherine O'Brien O'Keeffe, Doug Pfeifer, Ben Robinson, Mary Ann Smart, Garrett Stewart, Elisa Tamarkin, Bryan Wagner, Alex Woloch, and Adam Zucker.

Thanks, too, to the participants at the events where I presented parts of the book: the "Shape of the I" conference in Boulder, Colorado, 2012; the UC Berkeley Consortium on the Novel, 2011 and 2013; and the Musical Pasts Consortium in London, 2016. Thanks also to the Townsend Center for the Humanities for making possible the graduate and undergraduate courses that I organized with Alan Tansman. The brilliant students and colleagues in those two classes did much to make me see what might be valuable about work like this. Parts of chapters 1 and 3 were published in modified form in *Critical Inquiry* 35, no. 1, and *ELN* 49, no. 2, respectively. Thanks to both journals for publishing those earlier pieces and for allowing me to use heavily revised versions of that material here. Thanks also to British Pathé for permission to use the images of Halifax in Berlin that appear in Chapter 1.

Many thanks go to Adam Boardman, whose wonderful work let me focus on my own. Thanks to my parents, Kent and Franceen. Their support and longstanding obsession with movies of all kinds inspired me in ways that still catch me off guard. Thanks to my sister, Nora, for her patience and advice as she listened to me talk about this for years. My greatest thanks go to Kara Wittman, who followed this book's development at every step and improved its arguments, its language, and its sense of the world with her grace, intelligence, and generosity. As with so much else, I couldn't have done it without her. And, although it's a heavy phrase to use in a book partly about *Henry V*, this is for Harry.

Notes

Preface

1. See Favret, *War at a Distance.*
2. Woloch, *Or Orwell*, 30.
3. MacKay, *Modernism and World War II*, 6.
4. Favret, *War at a Distance*, 10.
5. McLoughlin, *Authoring War*, 6.
6. MacKay, "Wartime Rise of *The Rise of the Novel*," 137.
7. Barthes, *S/Z*, 5.

8. Despite or rather because of the war, the cinema was more popular and successful in the 1940s than any other time in Britain, experiencing what Michael Balcon, head of Ealing Studios from 1938 into the 1950s, called a "marked renascence" ("British Film During the War," 66). Anthony Aldgate and Jeffrey Richards write: "The war was definitely to prove 'a golden age' as far as domestic films were concerned. In short, British films continued to play an important and necessary part in ensuring that cinemagoing in Britain remained, as it had been though out the 1930s, an 'essential social habit'" (*Britain Can Take It*, 3). Lant points to several "reasons for cinema's increased popularity, and the increased popularity of British films in particular. For one thing, higher wartime employment freed up spending money, while competing middle-class entertainments such as pleasure motoring and dining out were curtailed by rationing. Secondly, cinema fed the desire for news and information about the war for a wider selection of the population than any other medium" (*Blackout*, 24). See also Miller, *British Literature of the Blitz*, 152–88.

9. Trevor-Roper, *Wartime Journals*, 91. For more on the conceptual centrality of "the summer of 1940," see Gallagher, *Telling It Like It Wasn't* (Chicago: forthcoming).

10. Reeves, *Power of Film Propaganda*, 181.

11. For the relation between the residual, dominant, and emergent, see Williams, *Marxism and Literature.*

12. Formed in 1937 by Tom Harrisson, Humphrey Jennings, and Charles Madge and influenced by a number of diverse contemporary thinkers and intellectual currents (I. A. Richards, Bronisław Malinowski, and Surrealism among others), Mass Observation sought to develop tailored methodologies—

surveys, interviews, participant observation—that could help to account for the texture of everyday life in Britain. For more on Mass Observation's "autoethnographic" project, see Buzard, "Mass-Observation, Modernism, and Auto-ethnography," 93–122: "The persuasion that Britain stood in desperate need of auto-anthropologizing can be understood as deriving from the fear that the forces of unreason associated with humanity in the mass, and evidently on the march across the Channel, could overwhelm British people too, making it 'easy for others to set themselves up as their guardians.'" See also Hubble, *Mass Observation and Everyday Life.*

13. See Clark, "For a Left with No Future," 53–75.

Introduction

1. Despite its early success, *The Life and Death of Colonel Blimp* wasn't released in America until after the war. When Martin Scorsese first saw the film "as a child on daytime television . . . sometime in the fifties, . . . the 163-minute running time had been mercilessly cut, and, thanks to the original 'creative' distributor, the flashback structure had been unraveled to present a linear narrative" (Haskell, "*Life and Death of Colonel Blimp*"). Ian Christie offers as clear an account as one could of the film's several different edits ("Resurrection of 'Blimp,'" 37). I have here to thank Doug Pfeiffer, who lent me that tape almost two decades ago. I keep meaning to return it.

2. Lejeune, "The Films," *Observer*, June 13, 1943. With this, Powell and Pressburger seem to reproduce an ambivalence about reference, about *aboutness* that I discussed in the preface.

3. The phrase "Colonel Blimp" would have been very familiar to British audiences in 1943. The term, used to criticize an entrenched and reactionary old guard, comes from the political cartoons of David Low, which began to appear in the *Evening Standard* in 1934, and featured an aged and fulminating old officer, addressing current events while taking a Turkish bath. By the time Powell and Pressburger adopted it, the phrase had become a more general term of abuse, appearing for instance in Orwell's wartime essays. What's striking and complicated about *The Life and Death of Colonel Blimp* is its effort to add nuance to what Low and then Orwell intended as a more or less straightforward insult. See Low, *Years of Wrath.* I'll return to the tactical nuance of *Colonel Blimp* in chapter 1.

4. Durgnat, "Aiming at the Archers," in *The Essential Raymond Durgnat*, 219.

5. *Oxford English Dictionary*, 3rd ed., s.v. "eccentric": "Of orbital motion: Not referable to a fixed centre of revolution; not circular. Of a curve, an elliptic, parabolic, or hyperbolic orbit: Deviating (in greater or less degree) from a circular form."

6. Mark Wollaeger has shown that the British distrust of propaganda was—in addition to its widespread and primary association with Goebbels and the Nazis—a holdover from the Great War, which seemed in retrospect to have been

almost too willing to manage the message and, as a result, to have demanded too much from both writers and readers: "Revulsion on the part of propagandists and propagandees was reinforced by official disavowal. Speaking for the Foreign Office in 1935, Sir Samuel Hoare declared that government propaganda was 'one of the most pernicious features of modern life'" (*Modernism, Media, and Propaganda*, 222–23). As the war began, however, and the need to shape, share, and sometimes censor information became undeniable, the question of how to use propaganda in a democratic society without either duplicating Nazi methods or diluting a maybe decisive weapon became acute.

7. With this, we can see *Colonel Blimp* as an effort to realize the seemingly tautological promise of "democratic propaganda." In a short book he wrote for the Ministry of Information, the Cambridge psychologist Frederick Bartlett sought to draw a nuanced line between what he identified as "democratic propaganda" and "dictator propaganda," between what he, in other words, thought Britain should do and Goebbels was in fact doing. According to Bartlett, democratic propaganda "does not despise the intelligence of those whom it addresses, as the dictator propaganda does. It does not go all out to short-circuit reason, as the dictator propaganda does. It recognizes that men act where their affections, sentiments, and emotions are concerned, but that these must and can be led by intelligence without losing their strength. It knows that the stability of a social order does not depend upon everybody's saying the same things, holding the same opinions, feeling the same feelings, but upon a freely achieved unity which, with many sectional and individual differences, is nevertheless able to maintain an explaining and consistent pattern of life" (*Political Propaganda*, 153). See also Chapman, *British at War*, 44–46.

8. Sitwell, *English Eccentrics*, 22.

9. Ibid. It is, perhaps, worth noting that Sitwell's sense of eccentricity as gesture recalls an argument that the young Georg Lukács makes about Kierkegaard's doomed and eccentric effort to use the gesture as a kind of lived aesthetic form to manage the real complexities of his life: "Is it not self-delusion—however splendidly heroic—to believe that the essence of the gesture lies in an action, a turning towards something or a turning way: rigid as stone and yet containing everything immutably within itself?" (*Soul and Form*, 29).

10. Mill, *On Liberty*, 107.

11. Ibid.

12. Ibid. This sense of a healthy national culture as an internally differentiated whole persists from Mill's Victorian moment into World War II. We can see efforts to imagine Britain in just these terms with figures as different as George Orwell and T. S. Eliot. For Orwell, England was, at its best, "a nation," at once various, eccentric, and whole, "of flower-lovers, but also a nation of stamp-collectors, pigeon-fanciers, amateur carpenters, coupon-snippers, darts-players, crossword-puzzle fans" (*George Orwell: A Collection of Essays*, 255); and, for Eliot, the fact that Britain was a culture, which is to say a collection of real differences,

which together added up to a robust national whole, meant that it was best defined paratactically: "It includes all the characteristic activities and interests of a people: Derby Day, Henley Regatta, Cowes, the twelfth of August, a cup final, the dog races, the pin table, the dart board, Wensleydale cheese, boiled cabbage cut into sections, beetroot in vinegar, nineteenth-century Gothic churches and the music of Elgar" ("Notes Towards a Definition of Culture," in *Christianity and Culture*, 104). In both cases, the British national character was imagined more as a structure—differences held loosely suspended within a heterogeneous whole—than as any single characteristic or set of characteristics.

13. Sitwell, *English Eccentrics*, 20.

14. In what follows I move consciously between the terms *British* and *English*. When I use the term *British*, I'm usually referring to a set of historical, political, and geographical facts; when I use the term *English*, I'm usually referring to an ideological idea that was variously and incompletely deployed before and over the course of the war. Indeed, the concept of eccentricity can be seen as one difficult part of a larger tactical effort to reduce the complex geopolitical fact of Britain to a manageable and lovable if factitious idea of England.

15. Godard, "Woman in a Dressing-Gown," 86.

16. Lean, quoted in Wimmer, *Cross-Channel Perspectives*, 100.

17. Durgnat, "Michael Powell," in *The Essential Raymond Durgnat*, 34, 35.

18. Dyer, *Brief Encouter*, 55.

19. Macdonald, *Interviews with Dwight Macdonald*, 57.

20. Clark, *Farewell to an Idea*, 376.

21. Stephen Spender anticipated Clark's account in 1935; referring to Henry James, he writes, "as always with great aestheticians there is a certain vulgarity in his work, and this vulgarity found its expression in violence." Vulgarity erupts in James when style can no longer hold itself back. For Spender, the Jamesian style is a result of James's efforts to control his writing, to repress sexual contents or urges that would otherwise upset its sheer and lovely surface. As a result, when, as it must, that sexual repressed makes its return, it does so as a style that is itself the structural answer to and expression of the earlier repression. Vulgarity is, in other words, both a cause and an effect of style. For Spender, style is dialectical: although James's style is largely the negative impress of what he rejects or represses, that style also becomes both most and least itself when the repressed returns in the form of an unwilled vulgarity. For Spender, vulgarity is the unconscious truth of style; it is its antithesis and purest articulation. Spender, quoted in Connolly, *Enemies of Promise*, 9.

22. Valery, "Style," 19.

23. Barthes, *Writing Degree Zero*, 10–11.

24. Durgnat, *Films and Feelings*, 42.

25. In a sense, the lateral reappearance of red across the plotted surface of *Colonel Blimp* resembles a dialectical play between affect and narrative that Fredric Jameson has seen as necessary to realism; as he writes in relation to the

more or less untethered recurrence of certain sights and smells in Zola, "the very multiplication of these sensory onslaughts raises the question of their succession in time, where the gradual autonomization of the various affects slowly begins to release them from their relationship to plot as such and suggest whole new forms of temporal organization" (*Antinomies of Realism*, 65). As with the logic of affect in Zola, the chromatic irruption of red across *Colonel Blimp* threatens the sense of one totality while suggesting the conceptual possibility of another.

26. Lacan introduces the concept of the "anamorphic ghost" in his famous discussion of Hans Holbein's *The Ambassadors*, which features a death's head that can only be seen from a perspective that distorts the painting's putative subject, the well-heeled ambassadors themselves. As a result, the one painting includes or, rather, produces two wholly different but obscurely related worlds, the world of luxury and comfort and the world of death. The suspended skull serves, in that case, as a sort of hinge between worlds. As a result, the doubled presence of the perceived ghost forces the viewer to confront the essential doubleness of the perceiving self: "In *The Ambassadors* . . . [w]hat is this strange, suspended, oblique object in the foreground in front of these two figures? All this shows . . . Holbein makes visible for us here something that is simply the subject as annihilated. . . . But it is further still that we must seek the function of vision. We shall then see emerging on the basis of vision, not the phallic symbol, the anamorphic ghost, but the gaze as such, in its pulsatile, dazzling and spread out function, as it is in this picture" (*Four Fundamental Concepts of Psychoanalysis*, 89).

27. De Baecque, *Camera Historica*, 3.

28. Miller, *Hidden Hitchcock*, 4.

29. For more on the blurred beginnings and endings of war in general and of World War II in particular, see Dudziak, *War-Time*.

30. Thompson, "The Concept of Cinematic Excess," 132.

31. Heath, quoted in ibid., 130–31.

32. Eugenie Brinkema has recently called for a return to a poststructuralist model of cinematic excess as one way to think through the relation between affect theory and aesthetic form: "Exactly as 'affect' does for theorists such as Shaviro, what excess undoes is a certain approach to theory; it remains with the stubbornly contingent 'I,' and what it 'disturbs, sterilizes is metalanguage (criticism)'" (*Forms of the Affects*, 42).

33. Michael Powell to Sir James Grigg, in Powell and Pressburger, *Life and Death of Colonel Blimp*, 28.

34. Ibid., 33. Rather than make its own feature films, the Ministry of Information sought rather to influence production, offering advice, materials, and support: "It controlled the allocation of film stock, it could secure the release of film technicians from the Services, and sanction the supply of scarce materials" (Drazin, *Finest Years*, 182). The Ministry of Information in fact offered direct financial support to only one feature, Powell and Pressburger's *49th Parallel* (1941), and although that film worked well, people within and beyond the Films

Division felt that more distance between the film industry and government was advisable: "Though *49th Parallel,* the costs of which had been underwritten by the MOI, had turned out to be a great success, the giving of state funds to a private company had become too controversial to repeat" (MacKenzie, *British War Films,* 50). See also Chapman, *British at War,* 13–160; and Reeves, *Power of Film Propaganda,* 136–194.

35. For more on the history, theory, and practice of total war, see Aron, *Century of Total War*; Bell, *First Total War*; Black, *Age of Total War*; Chickering and Forster, "Are We There Yet?"; Gat, *War in Human Civilization*; Hobsbawm, *Age of Extremes*; Joxe, *Empire of Disorder*; Paret, Craig, and Gilbert, *Makers of Modern Strategy*; Marwick, Emsely, and Simpson, *Total War and Historical Change*; Wright, *Ordeal of Total War.*

36. Saint-Amour, *Tense Future,* 56.

37. Saint-Amour suggests that the idea of total war functioned for Britain less as a real state of affairs than as an ideological screen behind which to manage local, limited but no less pernicious forms of imperial violence: "A study of total war, then, must be a study of its partiality as an idea—of its prejudicial functions and its implications in an imperial world-system" (ibid., 9).

38. Mieszkowski, *Watching War,* 147–48.

39. Chickering and Forster, "Are We There Yet?," 3.

40. Miller, *British Literature of the Blitz,* 1.

41. Hobsbawm, *Age of Extremes,* 49.

42. Bowen, quoted in Stonebridge, *Writing of Anxiety,* 3.

43. Mieszkowski, *Watching War,* 192.

44. Saint-Amour, *Tense Future,* 184.

45. Barthes, "Introduction to the Structural Analysis of Narratives," in *Image, Music, Text,* 79.

46. Lord Beaverbrook's "Great Aluminum Scare" is a key example of the way the thrift and sentiment came together to support morale in the early days of the war. Faced with shortages of materials to produce fighter planes in 1940, Beaverbrook called upon the British to donate their domestic metals to the war effort: "We will turn your pots and pans into Spitfires and Hurricanes." Of course, he knew that the metal salvaged from the tons and tons of kitchenware and knick-knacks collected "would not yield much high-grade aluminum," a fact that points to the stunt's real and brilliant value as almost pure, lived propaganda (Calder, *People's War,* 149).

47. Piette, *Imagination at War,* 1. In thinking of this embodied "war in the mind," we might turn to Althusser's great account of an ideology of actions and practices: "This ideology talks of actions: I shall talk of actions inserted into *practices.* And I shall point out that these practices are governed by the *rituals* in which these practices are inscribed, within the *material existence of an ideological apparatus,* be it only a small part of that apparatus: a small mass in a small church, a funeral, a minor match at a sports' club, a school day, a political

party meeting, etc. Besides, we are indebted to Pascal's defensive 'dialectic' for the wonderful formula which will enable us to invert the order of the notional schema of ideology. Pascal says more or less: 'Kneel down, move your lips in prayer, and you will believe'" ("Ideology and Ideological State Apparatuses," 168).

48. Saint-Amour, *Tense Future*, 185.

49. Priestley, *Postscripts*, 2–3.

50. Calder, *People's War*, 138.

51. On the *Englishness* of eccentricity, see Dickison, "Ken Russell, National Culture, and Experimental TV," 79–81; and Aymes-Stokes and Mellet, *In and Out*. See also Gill, *Eccentricity*.

52. Forster, "The English Eccentrics," 18.

53. Barker, "Some Constants of the English Character," 61.

54. Connolly, *Enemies of Promise*, 12, 261.

55. Schneider, *Loving Arms*, 27.

56. Esty, *Shrinking Island*, 3, 165.

57. MacKay, *Modernism and World War II*, 2.

58. Piette, *Imagination at War*, 179.

59. Stewart, *Second World War*, 30.

60. Havardi, *Projecting Britain at War*, 21.

61. Snow, *Science and Government*, 46–47.

62. Priestly, *Postscripts*, 2.

63. For an account of how a baldly manipulative version of this tactical eccentricity has been mobilized in the service of British austerity from Thatcher to the present, see Hatherly, *Ministry of Nostalgia*. He looks, for instance, at the recent and frankly weird ubiquity of the phrase, "Keep Calm and Carry On": "The power of 'Keep Calm and Carry On' comes from a yearning for an actual or imaginary English patrician attitude of stiff upper lips and muddling through. This is, however, something that largely survives only in the popular imaginary, in a country devoted to services and consumption, and where elections are decided on the basis of house price value, and given to sudden, mawkish outpourings of sentiment. The poster isn't just a case of the return of the repressed, it is rather the return of repression itself. It is a nostalgia for the state of being repressed—solid, stoic, public-spirited, as opposed to the depoliticised, hysterical and privatised reality of Britain over the last thirty years" (*Ministry of Nostalgia*, Kindle location 267).

64. To many, Jennings seemed to embody the same spirit of energetic, irrepressible, and yet comfortable quiddity that he sought to capture in his films: "Jennings," writes his friend Jacob Bronowski, "was not at all a conformist; he was the most wonderful eccentric that I have ever met; he was totally unaware of the fact that every gesture that he made was outrageous." And another friend, Gerald Noxon, writes, "To say that Humphrey Jennings was a typical Englishman is, of course, a contradiction in terms, for the most characteristic quality of the English is their untypicalness, their eccentricity. In fact he was most English in

his eccentricity" (Noxon, quoted in Aldgate and Richards, *Britain Can Take It*, 229). In terms of the relation and difference between Jennings and Grierson, Alan Lovell writes that, although apparent, their different commitments weren't given a chance to come to light: "In fact, the conflict between the positions the two men represented never took place. It was prevented from doing so by the Second World War, which . . . stopped the debate by giving overwhelming support to the use of the cinema as a vehicle for propaganda. In the context of the war it was impossible to argue against the need for the 'grim and desperate education of propaganda'" ("The British Cinema," 44).

65. Synthetically influenced by a number of figures—Kant, Hegel, Eisenstein, Walter Lippman, and others—John Grierson had developed an idealist theory of documentary realism that he saw as commensurate with the goals of a strong, centralized, and progressive state. In practice this meant adapting Eisenstein's theory of "overtonal montage" in order to stitch together disparate "actualities" (both bits of film and bits of the world) and to get at and dialectically present the difficult ideal "reality" of particular institutions and ultimately the whole state. Ian Aitken writes, "Grierson argued that the empirical content (the actual) of [a film's] documentary images was organized so as to express general truths (the real), which existed at a level of abstraction beyond the empirical, and which could not be directly represented" (*European Film Theory and Cinema*, 166). The way one spliced two pieces of film together could and should produce a larger, "third" idea, something that was properly in neither but that somehow really sat between both. One can see this at work in Grierson's *Drifters* (1929), where cuts and dissolves between ocean waves, North Sea herring fishermen, crowds bustling at a local market, and trains crisscrossing the country work to suggest a larger and largely invisible institutional network—a seaport sublime—that brought producer and consumer, country and city, nature and culture together as part of a more capacious and synthetically whole reality. "His technique," writes Dan Blanton, "is explicitly dialectical, suspending character and narrative to render labor visible in a pure gesture" (*Epic Negation*, 266). Also see Evans, *John Grierson*.

66. As Jennings understood and sought to capture on film, the London Blitz was experienced not only as a hugely destructive event but also as a chance to imagine a necessary kind of national unity, a fact that the Queen registered when she remarked, after the bombing of Buckingham Palace on September 13, 1940, that she could now "look the East End in the face" (Stansky, *First Day of the Blitz*, 125). According to Kristine A. Miller: "The Blitzkrieg on the United Kingdom during the Second World War was the most direct attack on civilians in British history. As London and other British cities came under siege beginning in September 1940, the common cause of national defense seemed to reduce distance between soldiers and civilians, to resolve differences between men and women, and to repair divisions between leisured and working classes" (*British Literature of the Blitz*, 1).

67. Madge, "A Note on Images," 78.

68. Hubble, *Mass Observation and Everyday Life*, 228.

69. Martin Hunt argues that what might seem like an insoluble tension between "stylistic flamboyance"—what I'm calling cinematic eccentricity—and social conservatism in wartime and postwar British cinema in fact represents one version of a distinctively British effort to negotiate the politics of reformist consensus: "'Our mild revolution,' 'Conservative by nature, Labour by experience,' continuity and change—the sentiments are interchangeable and evidence of a common culture founded on progressive consensus. The films of Ealing and The Archers [Powell and Pressburger's company] generally, and *Pool of London* and *A Matter of Life and Death* in particular, are a product and articulation of these values" ("New Labour, New Criticism," 268).

70. Jennings, quoted in Wendy Webster, "*The Silent Village*," 266.

71. Piette, *Imagination at War*, 5.

72. Orwell, "Prevention of Literature," in *George Orwell: In Front of Your Nose*, 60.

73. Orwell, quoted in Hatherley, *Ministry of Nostalgia*, Kindle location 1536.

74. Forster, *Two Cheers for Democracy*, 54.

75. Waugh, *Put Out More Flags*.

76. Calder, *People's War*, 468.

77. Churchill, quoted in Hastings, *Winston's War*, 72.

78. Walzer, *Just and Unjust Wars*, 253.

79. Churchill, *Never Give In!*, 171.

80. Walzer, *Just and Unjust Wars*, 251.

81. This helps also to explain Churchill's unwillingness to articulate war aims: "What this meant was, not that the coalition had no war aims, but that willynilly its aims were Churchill's" (Calder, *People's War*, 98).

82. Agamben, *State of Exception*, 1.

83. Ibid., 3.

84. Ibid., 23.

85. Empson, quoted in Piette, *Imagination at War*, 155.

86. *Penguin Hansard*, 1:36.

87. Nicolson, *Why Britain Is at War*. Calder writes that, "Like the Germans, the British devised 'black propaganda'—the creation of fake 'underground radios,' the forgery of documents, the fabrication of rumors—justifying this on the grounds that such lies were necessary of a Nazi regime based on lies was to be defeated" (*People's War*, 502).

88. Nicolson, *Diaries and Letters*, 2:105.

89. Connolly, quoted in MacKay, *Modernism and World War II*, 12. Elsewhere, Connolly writes, "To have to dispense with their ideals and thus support a cynical policy in which they do not believe is a humiliating position for idealists. They therefore cannot be said to remain spiritually alive and this necessity of choosing between the perils of war and physical extermination and the dangers of an

ostrich peace and spiritual stagnation, between physical death and moral death, is another predicament" (*Enemies of Promise*, 5).

90. Orwell, "Prevention of Literature," 67.

91. Forster, *Two Cheers for Democracy*, 23. After the war, Orwell captured what it might have meant if one had to live with this logical dilemma once the supreme emergency of total war had ended; *1984* indeed imagines a state permanently built on just this kind of doubled, fractured logic: "DOUBLETHINK means the power of holding two contradictory beliefs in one's mind simultaneously, and accepting both of them" (*1984*, 176).

92. Esty, *Shrinking Island*, 80.

93. Powell and Pressburger, "Memorandum from the Archers," in *Life and Death of Colonel Blimp*, 37.

94. Powell, "The Week's Films."

95. Churchill, quoted in Hastings, *Winston's War*, 97–98.

96. Although the war began with an attempt to forget the nation's shared culpability, it is important to recognize that the avoidance of war at almost any cost was never merely craven; the will to appease was also an ultimately misguided effect of some of what was best if most unrealistic about British culture between the wars. As A. J. P. Taylor puts it: "The settlement at Munich was a triumph for British policy, which had worked precisely to this end; not a triumph for Hitler, who had started with no such clear intention. Nor was it merely a triumph for selfish or cynical British statesmen, indifferent to the fate of far-off peoples or calculating that Hitler might be launched into war with Soviet Russia. It was a triumph for all that was best and most enlightened in British life; a triumph for those who had preached equal justice between peoples; a triumph for those who had courageously denounced the harshness and short-sightedness of Versailles" (*Origins of the Second World War*, 189). For all its obvious and subsequent shame, the deal Chamberlain managed at Munich should not in that case be seen simply as a sell-out; rather, it was a bad compromise that emerged out of a field of sentiments, virtues, and values that were revealed as foolish and ultimately disastrous only after the fact. At the time, Chamberlain's willingness to negotiate and to avoid the waste of war seemed to many like an eminently sensible, humane, and grown-up response to the maybe empty saber-rattling of an unhinged dictator.

97. Allport, *Demobbed*, 179.

98. Bersani and Dutoit, *Forms of Being*, 127.

99. Miller, "An Introduction to Seminars I and II," 21.

100. Burgess, quoted in Piette, *Imagination at War*, 78.

101. Woolf, "Thoughts on Peace in an Air Raid," 218.

102. Storr, *Churchill's Black Dog*, 34.

103. Cole, *At the Violet Hour*, 43.

104. Ibid., 24.

105. Forster, *Two Cheers for Democracy*, 68.

106. For work from anthropology, archaeology, and evolutionary biology on the idea that violence and war come before and not after civilization, see Burkert, *Homo Necans*; Keeley, *War Before Civilization*; Gat, *War in Human Civilization*; and Pinker, *Better Angels of Our Nature*.

107. Adorno, "The Late Style (I)," 121.

108. Ibid., 125.

109. Ibid.

110. Ibid.

111. Said, *On Late Style*, 10.

112. Huizinga, *Homo Ludens*, 101.

113. Favret, *War at a Distance*, 1.

114. Mannock, "We Critics Have Our Uses," quoted in Lant, *Blackout*, 162. Other films that use the structure include *In Which We Serve* (1942), *The First of the Few* (1942), *Went the Day Well* (1944), and *The Way to the Stars* (1945).

115. Benjamin, *Arcades Project*, 474.

116. Clark, "For a Left with No Future," 66–67. See also Susan Watkins's trenchant response to Clark for a clear statement of reservations about the idea that any war could be reduced to an essential "hankering after evil" ("Presentism?," 77–102). That said, I'm less interested in the reality of that innate capacity for badness than I am in the fact that some sense of something like it seems to have haunted people living in the midst of World War II.

117. Adorno, "The Late Style (I)," 125.

118. Clark, *Sight of Death*, 174.

119. Jarman, quoted in Christie, *Arrows of Desire*, 99.

1. "But what is it about?": *The Life and Death of Colonel Blimp*

1. "The Life and Death of Colonel Blimp," *Monthly Film Bulletin*, no. 114 (1943): 10.

2. Quoted in Powell and Pressburger, *Life and Death of Colonel Blimp*, 59–60.

3. A. D., "The Life and Death of Colonel Blimp."

4. G. Ward Price, "Blimp Film Must NOT Go Abroad," quoted in Havardi, *Projecting Britain at War*, 77.

5. Haskell, "The Life and Death and Life of Colonel Blimp." Similar notes of pleasant confusion appear in Mass Observation's "1943 Directive Replies on Favorite Films": "Life and Death of Colonel Blimp was both in color and was 'different.' I liked it—why I cannot say." "Col. Blimp. In spite of technicolor, and the glamourising of that pest, the Colonel, it was an amusing film" (Richards and Sheridan, *Mass-Observation at the Movies*, 228, 252).

6. Christie, *Arrows of Desire*, 17; Chapman, "Cinema, Propaganda, and National Identity," 194.

7. Lejeune, "The Films," *Observer*, June 13, 1943.

8. Powell and Pressburger, *Life and Death of Colonel Blimp*, 42.

9. Ibid., 33.

10. Christie, "*Colonel Blimp* File," 14.

11. Powell later described how he and Pressburger managed to get material for their film: "The answer is quite simple: we stole them. Any prop man worth his salt—and we had one of the best—would laugh at the question. There may have been one or two forged passes too. Who knows? It was all part of the war effort" (quoted in Murphy, *British Cinema and the Second World War*, 70, 69).

12. Ibid., 28.

13. Quoted in Chapman, *British at War*, 193.

14. Powell, quoted in Chapman, *British at War*, 83.

15. Mitchell, *Picture Theory*, 45.

16. In a sense, the condition I'm describing amounts to something like a state of pragmatic suspension, an internally divided conceptual disposition that would allow one to hold pragmatically on to two incommensurate but necessary ideas at one and the same time. This is something like the ability pragmatically to suspend what is referred to in formal logic as *the principle of bivalence*, which states that propositions must be either true or false and not both at once.

17. Observers tended to cast the question of British propaganda in relation to Goebbels in particular as opposed to Germans in general, a tactic that implicitly tied the specific ugliness of bad or "black" propaganda to a single reprehensible and thus disavowable individual; if, in the nature of conflict, it is hard to be absolutely unlike one's enemy, it was or should have been something else to be unlike Goebbels. In a 1941 essay for *Horizon*, Peter Cromwell wrote that "the tragedy of all our propaganda" was that we "have such a first-rate story to tell, the truth is so much on our side, yet it is told so badly that Goebbels can get away with practically any concoction he wants to" (quoted in Piette, *Imagination at War*, 145). On September 31, 1940, a House Member wondered if the Emergency Powers Act wouldn't put the government in a "position by no means inferior, as regards the scope of [its] powers over newspapers, to that occupied by the distinguished Dr. Goebbels in Germany" (*Penguin Hansard*, 3:135). And Nicolson, who worked at the Ministry of Information in 1940 and was an early casualty of one of its early purges, reflected on the ministry's situation in these terms: "At present the Ministry is too decent, educated and intellectual to imitate Goebbels. It cannot live by intelligence alone. We need crooks. Why I hate Hitler so much is that he has coined a new currency of fraudulence which he imposes by force. I am prepared to see the old world of privilege disappear. But as it goes, it will carry with it the old standards of honour" (*Diaries and Letters*, 2:105).

18. Bartlett, *Political Propaganda*, 153. See also Chapman, *British at War*, 44–46.

19. The political theorist J. L. Talmon refers to this potential bind as "the paradox of freedom": "Is human freedom compatible with an exclusive pattern of social existence, even if this pattern aims at the maximum of social justice and security?" (*Origins of Totalitarian Democracy*, 2).

20. Kant, "What Is Enlightenment?," 5.

21. Ellul, *Propaganda*, 241. See also Marlin, "Jacques Ellul's Contribution to Propaganda Studies," 361: "either a democracy does not engage in propaganda, in which case it will be overcome from without or subverted from within by those who do make use of propaganda, or a democracy does engage in propaganda, defeating the threatening powers, but in the process becoming itself undemocratic in its methods."

22. Wollaeger, *Modernism, Media, and Propaganda*, 3.

23. Although they stray significantly from their model, Powell and Pressburger based their character on David Low's acidly satirical comic strip, which appeared first in the *Evening Standard* in 1934. However, whereas Low's character exhibited an out-of-date, reactionary, and, dangerous complacency, Clive Candy is something altogether more sympathetic, a figure whose stubbornness is balanced by his sentiment, humor, and sense of honor (he is, as his ATS driver and third great love, Angela "Johnny" Cannon says, "an old darling"). Raymond Durgnat writes: "It's of the essence of Low's Blimp that he's not only inefficient and pompous, but mean and vicious. As played by Roger Livesy . . . he's a forlorn old boy, touchingly gallant in his Edwardian prime, but far too gentlemanly for this modern world" (*A Mirror for England*, 32).

24. Powell and Pressburger, *Life and Death of Colonel Blimp*, 91. I have checked quotations from the film against Christie's excellent interpolated edition of the written and shooting scripts.

25. Ibid., 92.

26. Ibid., 93.

27. Ibid., 94.

28. Ibid.

29. The inspiration for the flashback structure of *Blimp* came from a single line that had been cut from Powell and Pressburger's earlier war film, *One of Our Aircraft Is Missing* (1942): "Sir George, the old gentleman, tells one of the younger members of the crew: 'I was just like you thirty years ago and you'll be just like me thirty years from now.' Emeric liked the paradox, but David Lean persuaded him to drop it, saying: 'It's got nothing to do with the plot. It's the sort of idea you could make a whole film about'" (Macdonald, *Emeric Pressburger*, 206).

30. Bordwell, Staiger, and Thompson, *Classical Hollywood Cinema*, 62.

31. Daniel Morgan has seen a similar effect at work in Michelangelo Antonioni's *The Passenger* (1975), in which the camera pans away from Jack Nicholson's character musing in the present only to land moments later on his own remembered image in the past: the film, he writes, shows David Locke "'looking' into the past," where he "unexpectedly sees scenes from his earlier life in adjacent spaces" (*Late Godard and the Possibilities of Cinema*, 249). In *The Passenger*, the move is understood as an effect of Locke's appropriately associative memory; because the film's perspective has already been clearly linked to his point of view, we understand that the pan from present to past follows the associative drift of his thinking. The move is all the more appropriate given the existential

dispersal of subjectivity that stands behind Locke's inexplicably ready willingness to take up another identity, a dead man's identity, leaving his own behind. Because, however, *Colonel Blimp* has not by this early point established Clive as any kind of a focalizing presence, we can't easily understand the move from one end of the pool to the other as a similar fall into or drift through an individual's memory.

32. For Grierson, documentary realism's ability to imagine the totality of a society in order to encourage the total participation of that society's citizens served a softly but nonetheless coercive function that he understood as a form of "good totalitarianism": "I am not going to pretend that I do not realize how 'totalitarian' some of my conclusions seem. . . . You can be 'totalitarian' for evil and you can also be 'totalitarian' for good" (quoted in Ellis, *John Grierson*, 158).

33. Bazin, *What Is Cinema?*, 1:62.

34. Durgnat, "Montage Rides Again!," in *The Essential Raymond Durgnat*, 154.

35. To track and not to cut was also a costly choice in *Colonel Blimp*. Although it would have been simple and cheap to cut from old Clive to young Clive, and to use some clear editorial effect to signal the reverse passage of time, Powell and Pressburger instead opted for a more elaborate set-up that required a body double for Livesy as well as at least two days of shooting for only a few seconds of film. Because we need to see the double fall into the water with Spud before the younger Clive can emerge from the water, it would have been necessary to call back all of the actors and extras from the first shot in order to stage the second. And because Livesy shaved his head to create the effect of aging into the older role, the later shot of him emerging from the pool as young would had to have been filmed *before* the earlier shots of him arguing with Spud as an old man. This gets all the more complicated when we consider the film's several overlapping chronologies: there is its plot, which runs from 1902 to 1942; there is its formal arrangement into narrative discourse, which begins in 1942 and goes back to 1902 before taking the long way back to a narrative present that is both the film's beginning and its end; and there is the more obscure, but nonetheless significant chronology of the film's production where young Clive with his full head of hair would have to be filmed before its artificial but real loss to the make-up artist's razor. All of which is to say that the choice to track instead of to cut was expensive in terms of time, planning, and money.

36. Powell and Pressburger, *Life and Death of Colonel Blimp*, 87.

37. Ibid., 80–81.

38. Ibid., 80.

39. Chickering and Forster, "Are We There Yet?," 3.

40. Saint-Amour, *Tense Future*, 59.

41. Ibid.

42. Fuller, quoted in Marwick, Simpson, and Emsley, *Total War and Historical Change*, 261.

43. Williams, quoted in Saint-Amour, "Air War Prophecy and Interwar Modernism," 135.

44. Powell and Pressburger, *Life and Death of Colonel Blimp*, 92.

45. Ibid., 107.

46. Ibid., 101.

47. Critic, quoted in Lacombe, *Keys to French Opera*, 116.

48. Powell and Pressburger, *Life and Death of Colonel Blimp*, 133.

49. Ibid.

50. Ibid., 140.

51. Moor, "Bending the Arrow," 213.

52. Looking back to the Turkish bath scene with which this chapter and the film begin, we can see there, too, the close combination of military aggression (between Candy and Spud) and the erotic charge that comes with a roomful of barely dressed men. Although I am finally more interested here in how a formal similarity in the way in which these scenes are shot contributes to the film's larger theoretical argument about the nature of war, that there is a suggestion of *something more* than aggression, *something more* than war at stake in these scenes points to an important aspect of the way in which *Colonel Blimp* thinks about and possibly beyond the limited terms of total war.

53. McAleer, *Dueling*, 46.

54. Ibid., 5.

55. Elias, *Civilizing Process*, 161–62.

56. Huizinga, *Homo Ludens*, 95.

57. Powell and Pressburger, *Life and Death of Colonel Blimp*, 140.

58. Powell and Pressburger, "Analysis of the Idea behind the Story of *Blimp*," in *The Life and Death of Colonel Blimp*, 309.

59. Clausewitz, *On War*, 75.

60. Ibid., 80.

61. Wills, "Critical Inquiry in Clausewitz," 284.

62. Clausewitz, *On War*, 605.

63. Wills, "Critical Inquiry in Clausewitz," 294.

64. Mieszkowski, *Watching War*, 22. See also ibid., 184–91, for an analysis of the logical, semantic, and stylistic path taken by Clausewitz's famous axiom, "war is a continuation of politics by other means," as it passes through the pages of Michael Walzer, Gilles Deleuze and Felix Guattari, Michel Foucault, Michael Hardt and Antonio Negri, and Hannah Arendt: "For authors of all ideological stripes, coming to terms with this canonical proposition is never simply a matter of deciding whether Clausewitz 'got it right.' Whether seeking to applaud the truth of his insight or to correct his errors, Clausewitz's readers consistently aim to rival his stylistic virtuosity by recasting his elemental formula in even more striking terms" (185).

65. Powell and Pressburger, *Life and Death of Colonel Blimp*, 147.

66. Taken by itself, Powell and Pressburger's use of a dissolve to move from one space into another is, of course, not unique. Dissolves of this sort are common enough in narrative cinema. We might think here of another shot that seems to

have influenced Powell: the dissolve Orson Welles uses in *Citizen Kane* to track from the stormy exterior into the seamy interior of the El Rancho nightclub, where the reporter Jerry Thompson first meets an inebriated Susan Alexander Kane. The difference, underscored by the *Blimp* script's emphasis on the camera's moving "without a break," comes with the dissolve's particular relation to the content of the scene. Because the theory of war as duel depends explicitly on a number of conceptual breaks, dissolving where the film could have cut takes on a specific thematic and formal significance.

67. Fuller, *First of the League Wars*, 167.

68. Hilgers, *War Games*, 114.

69. We can track the waning of Clausewitz's influence in several ways. The rise of militarism across Europe and particularly in Wilhelmine Germany led some to question what authority civilians and diplomats ought to have over soldiers. Colmar Freiherr von der Goltz's *The Nation in Arms* (1883, rev. in 1906) exploited contradictions within Clausewitz's thinking in order to argue that the military could best serve political ends by wholly ignoring them: "War will on that account be in no way lowered in importance nor restricted in its independence, if only the commander in chief and the leadings statesmen are agreed that, under all circumstances, war serves the end of politics best by a complete defeat of the enemy. By attention to this maxim the widest scope is allowed in the employment of fighting forces" (quoted in Howard, "Influence of Clausewitz," 32). In 1903, the French military strategist, Ferdinand Foch, argued: "You must henceforth go to the very limits to find the aim of war. Since the vanquished party now never yields before it has been deprived of all means of reply, what you have to aim at is the destruction of those very means of reply" (*Principles of War*, 38). The disappointed World War I general and early Hitler crony Erich Ludendorff was most explicit in his bitter 1935 pamphlet, *Der Totale Krieg*: "All the theories of Clausewitz should be thrown overboard. Both warfare and politics are meant to serve the preservation of the people, but warfare is the highest expression of the national 'will to live,' and politics must, therefore, be subservient to the conduct of the war" (quoted in Handel, *War, Strategy and Intelligence*, 76). In Britain after World War I, there was a different but related reaction to Clausewitz's legacy. As a result of the horrific losses of that war, losses that seemed the result of having come all too close to war's absolute limit, B. H. Liddel Hart recommended imposing strategic limits on the scope of war, limits made possible by the development of increasingly mobile military technologies, especially fast-moving armored tanks (Bond and Alexander, "Liddell Hart and de Gaulle," 600).

70. Bell, *First Total War*, 5.

71. Moretti, *Bourgeois*, 115.

72. Huizinga, *Homo Ludens*, 11.

73. Puckett, *Bad Form*, 150–62.

74. Powell and Pressburger, *Life and Death of Colonel Blimp*, 257.

75. Fuller, quoted in Sheftall, *Altered Memories*, 13.

76. Powell and Pressburger, *Life and Death of Colonel Blimp*, 105.

77. Fuller, *Military History*, 145.

78. Sheftall, *Altered Memories*, 14.

79. Judd and Surridge, *Boer War*, 194.

80. For more on how the British sought and often failed to maintain a tenuous difference between the imagined tactics of total war and the violence of colonial "small wars," see Saint-Amour, *Tense Future*, 49–55.

81. Powell and Pressburger, *Life and Death of Colonel Blimp*, 192.

82. Faber, *Munich, 1938*, 37–38.

83. Quoted in ibid., 39.

84. Reiter, *How Wars End*, 102.

85. Quoted in Powell and Pressburger, *Life and Death of Colonel Blimp*, 295.

86. McLoughlin, *Authoring War*, 98–99.

87. Empson, *Some Versions of Pastoral*, 22.

88. Mellor, *Reading the Ruins*, 166.

89. Elias, *The Germans*, 308–9.

90. Huizinga, *Homo Ludens*, 101.

91. Powell and Pressburger, *Life and Death of Colonel Blimp*, 278.

92. Ibid., 181–82.

93. Rattigan, *This Is England*, 216.

94. Spenser, *Faerie Queene*, 201.

95. Huizinga, *Waning of the Middle Ages*, 1.

96. Welles and Bogdanovich, *This Is Orson Welles*, 100.

97. Saler, *Avant-garde in Interwar England*, 61–62.

98. The war's fantasy of the late Middle Ages was one invested in the structuring force of chivalric play, what Mark Girouard describes as a "code of conduct evolved for the knights of the middle ages, that is to say for an elite and increasingly hereditary class of warriors; it accepted fighting as a necessary and indeed glorious activity, but set out to soften its potential barbarity by putting it into the hands of men committed to high standards of behavior" (*Return to Camelot*, 16).

99. Justice, "Did the Middle Ages Believe in Their Miracles?," 9.

100. *A Canterbury Tale* (1944) begins with one of the more remarkable sequences in all of Powell and Pressburger's work. A voiceover moves through the opening lines of *The Canterbury Tales* while a familiar cast of characters—the clown, the scholar, the shrew, the knight—make their way, eating, flirting, and cutting capers along the Pilgrim's Road. This brief sketch again resembles the freedom, the contrasts, the violence, and the play of order and disorder that Huizinga saw in his Middle Ages. Powell and Pressburger then bring their film suddenly into the present with a startling match cut: a falconer's bird is released, arcs into the sky, and is cut suddenly into a matching image of a fighter plane flying overhead. And, while the cut draws a contrast between the past and the present (a bird is not a plane), it also reveals—cinematically—the possibility that

something of the medieval spirit might survive in an age of mechanized war. See Christie, "History Is Now and England," 75–94.

101. Eliot, "East Coker," 12.

102. Woolf, *Between the Acts*, 81, 76.

103. We might also think of Guild Socialists such as S. G. Hobson and Alfred Orage, who looked to the example of Morris, Ruskin, and the Fabian Society for the basis of a renewed twentieth-century politics; or of Frank Pick, the designer responsible for much of the London Underground who developed a design philosophy and aesthetic that owed its marriage of form and function to an idea of what premodern life might have felt like: "Given the horrors that mechanisation and 'locomotion' were creating," writes Owen Hatherly, "it is unsurprising that Pick's project became ever more obviously an attempt to fuse modernity with a deep English nostalgia" (*Ministry of Nostalgia*, Kindle location 1139).

104. Esty, *Shrinking Island*, 61.

105. We might in these terms compare *Colonel Blimp* with H. G. Wells's 1936 film, *Things to Come*, which offers a less subtle but no less related example: as a result of decades of bombing and germ warfare that began with the fictional World War II of 1940, British society has been thrown back into an explicitly medieval state. Although the film ultimately supports the smooth, scientific utopia represented by Raymond Massey's character, John Cabal, the feudal society that emerges before utopia but after years of disease, violence, and deprivation is nonetheless a mostly cheerful relief. Despite the vulgarity of Everytown's warlord (played beautifully against type by Ralph Richardson), our first look at early modern Britain is one of craft, honest labor, simplicity, and ruddy physical health. And, despite, the ultimate victory of science over nationalism and force, the techno-future represented in the film's third and final act remains dangerously susceptible to the seductions of the past: the peace and prosperity of the future is temporally disrupted when a charismatic sculptor, Theotocopulos ("I am a craftsman!"), successfully encourages the people to revolt against progress itself; that they fail is mostly a matter of chance. Medievalism is thus presented both as a cause of and a cure for the violence at the heart of war.

106. Powell and Pressburger, *Life and Death of Colonel Blimp*, 210.

107. Ibid., 256.

108. Arnold, "Preface to the First Edition of *Poems (1853)*," 1.

109. Babbington and Evans, "Matters of Life and Death in Powell and Pressburger's *The Tales of Hoffman*," 167.

110. Freud, *Civilization and Its Discontents*, 144.

111. "The sentimental poet is thus always involved with two conflicting representations and perceptions—with actuality as a limit and with his idea as infinitude; and the mixed feelings that he excites will always testify to the dual source" (Schiller, "On Naive and Sentimental Poetry," 196).

112. Powell and Pressburger, *Life and Death of Colonel Blimp*, 257.

113. Plomer, quoted in Piette, *Imagination at War*, 62.

114. Saint-Amour, *Tense Future*, 9. *Colonel Blimp* in fact figures its ironic relation to epic when Clive attends (but doesn't much attend to) a performance of Stephen Phillips's 1902 verse drama, *Ulysses*. The care with which Powell and Pressburger register what Edgar Allan Poe might call the "the cock's feathers, the red paint and the black patches" at work behind Phillips's Edwardian epic suggests the degree to which they understood what was essentially ironic about their own "very British epic" (Poe, "Philosophy of Composition," 14; Christie, introduction to Power and Pressburger, *Life and Death of Colonel Blimp*, 1). For more on Phillips's *Ulysses*, see Kershner, "Joyce and Stephen Phillips' 'Ulysses,'" 194–201.

115. Rattigan, *This Is England*, 221.

116. Powell and Pressburger, *Life and Death of Colonel Blimp*, 237.

117. The difference between the cut and the no-cut in *Colonel Blimp* recalls a distinction recently made by Saint-Amour between the epic and the encyclopedic fiction: "I understand epic as constellating war, form, and totality in a particular way—and encyclopedic fiction as departing most emphatically from epic in how it reconstellates the same terms" (*Tense Future*, 10).

2. Pistol's Two Bodies: *Henry V* at War

1. Agee, "Masterpiece," 351–52.

2. "Arthur Rank, who'd gained control of Filippo del Giudice's production company in return for the money to finish the film, told me I should have cut the 'unimportant' scenes like Henry's wooing of Katherine—played with delicious humor by Renee Asherson, and part of the delicate balance of the play—and I said, 'All right. But the film would have seemed twice as long. I'll show you!' I did, and it did" (Olivier, *On Acting*, 283).

3. Canby, "*Henry V*," 445.

4. Buzacott, *Death of the Actor*, 110.

5. Holderness, *Shakespeare Recycled*, 190.

6. Rabkin, "Rabbits, Ducks, and *Henry V*," 285.

7. Stone, "For God and Country."

8. Taylor, introduction to *Henry V*, 7.

9. See Altman, "Vile Participation," 1–32.

10. Hazlitt, *Characters of Shakespeare's Plays and Lectures*, 126.

11. Quoted in Schoch, *Shakespeare's Victorian Stage*, 138.

12. Gould, "A New Reading of *Henry V*," 42.

13. Rabkin, "Rabbits, Ducks, and *Henry V*," 285. One might suggest that Rabkin's own double-talking, ethically gray version of the play is perhaps less about war than about Watergate, about a seemingly novel and horrible political situation that appeared to have put the truth or falsity of statements into a state of ideological suspension.

14. Barber and Wheeler, *Whole Journey*, 221.

15. McEachern, introduction to *Henry V*, 1124.
16. Rabkin, "Rabbits, Ducks, and *Henry V*," 286.
17. Ibid., 296.
18. Hastings, *Winston's War*, 403.
19. Shakespeare, *Richard II*, in *The Complete Pelican Shakespeare*, 973–74.
20. Barker, "Shakespeare, Stratford, and the Second World War," 199–217.
21. Olivier, *On Acting*, 66.
22. Knight, *Olive and the Sword*, 3.
23. Ibid., 31–32.
24. Ibid., 28.
25. Donnelly, *Britain in the Second World War*, 45.
26. MacKay, *Modernism and World War II*, 4.
27. Donnelly, *Britain in the Second World War*, 46.
28. *Penguin Hansard*, 1:36.
29. *Penguin Hansard*, 3:135.
30. Wilson, *Fortunes of Falstaff*, 11.
31. Ibid., 128.
32. Ibid., 40.
33. Holderness, "Agincourt 1944," 191–92.
34. Ibid., 190.
35. Tillyard, *Shakespeare's History Plays*, 296.
36. Aldgate and Richards, *Britain Can Take It*, 138.
37. Oliver, *On Acting*, 273.
38. Tillyard, *Elizabethan World Picture*, 10.
39. Ibid., 99.
40. Ibid., 4.
41. Ibid., 7.
42. Ibid., 8.
43. Ibid., 108.

44. Tillyard imagines the medieval period as a large, slightly absurd, but nonetheless effective game, a system that might both allow and contain violence. He imagines the Elizabethan age as the moment where cracks begin to show in that earlier edifice, cracks that in Shakespeare reveal not the ordered stability of the social world but rather its native tendency toward repetition, aggression, betrayal, and violence. In this regard, Tillyard's world picture comes to look presciently, oddly, and disturbingly like Jan Kott's "Grand Mechanism": "Feudal history is like a great staircase on which there treads a constant procession of kings. Every step upwards is marked by murder, perfidy, treachery. Every step upwards is marked by murder, perfidy, treachery. Every step brings the throne nearer. Another step and the crown will fall" (*Shakespeare Our Contemporary*, 10–11). If we want to understand Tillyard as offering the Elizabethan world picture as a thinly veiled account of his present, we should see it not as a naive wish fulfillment but instead as a historical diagnosis based in a recognition

that modern war had unbalanced a social relation between order and disorder, between violence and civilization that had once been seemed given. And it is this darker, paranoid version of the Elizabethan world picture that we must look to in order to understand the political complexity of Olivier's exactly contemporary reading of *Henry V*. In a sense, this is to argue for Olivier's film as itself a version of Kott's topsy-turvy history, one in which the catastrophes of the twentieth century somehow authored Shakespeare or at least lately revealed him as what he always already was: our contemporary. Olivier's experience of World War II similarly allowed him to see *Henry V*'s inherent ambivalence about war, an ambivalence that had, as Olivier seems to intuit and as Joel Altman explicitly argues, a precedent in Shakespeare's late fifteenth century. Altman suggests that *Henry V* is shot through with historical ambivalence about "the penultimate phase of the Elizabethan struggle to subdue Ireland": "One of my aims in this essay is to [show] that the contrariety we have come to admire in *Henry V* is closely related to the complexity of response that the Irish struggle was evoking in Shakespeare's audience, forced to lend themselves, materially and spiritually, after for years of dearth and more than a decade of war in the Low Countries, France, and Ireland, to a vast new military undertaking." In Olivier's film, the ambivalence of the present situation helped both to reveal the ambivalence of the past and to use that rediscovered history to explain and the enliven that present. In the complex, circular terms of Olivier's war historiography, Shakespeare appears, indeed, as our contemporary ("Vile Participation," 8).

45. I have checked quotations from the film as opposed to the play against Olivier's shooting script. See Shakespeare, *Henry V*, ed. Laurence Olivier, in *Masterworks of the British Cinema*, 202.

46. Olivier, *On Acting*, 271.

47. Ibid., 280–81.

48. Shakespeare, *Henry V*, ed. Laurence Olivier, in *Masterworks of the British Cinema*, 210.

49. This effect is one that Deleuze sees at work in the weaving together of the real and the theatrical in Renoir: "If we consider the relations between theatre and cinema in general, we no longer find ourselves in the classical situation where the two arts are two different ways of actualizing the same virtual image. . . . The situation is quite different: the actual image and the virtual image coexist and crystalize; they ender into a circuit which brings us constantly back rom one to the other; they form one and the same 'scene' where the characters belong to the real and yet play a role. In short, it is the whole of the real, life in its entirety, which has become spectacle" (*Cinema 2*, 83–84).

50. Shakespeare, *Henry V*, ed. Laurence Olivier, in *Masterworks of the British Cinema*, 263.

51. Santner, *Royal Remains*, 34–35.

52. Kantorowicz, *King's Two Bodies*, 29; Shakespeare, *Henry V*, 1151.

53. Quoted in Coleman, *Olivier*, 112.

54. Ibid., 121.

55. Quoted in Holderness, "Agincourt 1944," 173.

56. Ibid., 192–93.

57. "Perspective subjects the artistic phenomenon to stable and even mathematically exact rules, but on the other hand, makes that phenomenon contingent upon human beings, indeed upon the individual: for these rules refer to the psychological and physical conditions of the visual impression, and the way they take effect is determined by the freely chosen position of a subjective 'point of view'" (Panofsky, *Perspective*, 67).

58. Blair, *Henry of Navarre*, 127; Tolstoy, *War and Peace*, 779. Lévi-Strauss writes in *The Origin of Table Manners* that cup-and-ball not only passes the time but also alters the way time passes: cup-and-ball is one among several "magical devices which act sometimes as accelerators, sometimes as brakes, but are always intended to obtain seasonal equality: over a vast territory stretching from the Arctic circle to California, string games are used to slow down the sun's course, or may be in danger of prolonging the winter months, which must then be shortened by cup-and-ball games" (173). As in those other contexts, the Duke of Orleans's game suggests that the French inhabit a temporality experienced as distinct from the rest of the film.

59. Shakespeare, *Henry V*, in *The Complete Pelican Shakespeare*, 1133.

60. Powell and Pressburger, *Life and Death of Colonel Blimp*, 130.

61. Quoted in Henricks, *Disputed Pleasures*, 60.

62. Van Doren, *Shakespeare*, 151

63. Shakespeare, *Henry V*, in *The Complete Pelican Shakespeare*, 1142.

64. Lenoir and Lowood, "Theaters of War," 429.

65. Bond and Alexander, "Liddell Hart and De Gaule," 600.

66. H. G. Wells, *Little Wars*, 152–53.

67. Van Doren, *Shakespeare*, 151. For more on the wartime limits of abstraction, see Mieszkowski, *Watching War*, 144: "How can a diagram capture the horrific physical and emotional trials that compose the traumas of combat? Surely this is the fantasy of someone condemned to a perpetual childhood of waging wars with chessboards of various sizes and colors. In fact, war's uniqueness among human endeavors has to do with the way in which it demands a new understanding of the concrete consequences that abstractions have in the physical world."

68. Keegan, *Face of Battle*, 110.

69. Ibid.,104.

70. Ibid.

71. Wiles, *Shakespeare's Clown*, 119

72. Shakespeare, *Henry IV*, part 2, 1122.

73. On these questions see Wiles, *Shakespeare's Clown*; Gurr, *Shakespearean Stage*; and Shapiro, *Year in the Life of William Shakespeare*, and Knapp, *Shakespeare Only*.

74. Bradley, "The Rejection of Falstaff," 712.

75. Knight, *Olive and the Sword*, 27.

76. Wilson, *Fortunes of Falstaff*, 120.

77. Tillyard, *Shakespeare's History Plays*, 296.

78. Wilson, *Fortunes of Falstaff*, 88.

79. Shakespeare, *Henry IV*, part 1, 1074. The wartime analysis of Hal and Falstaff needs in that case to be seen in the context of wider anxieties about the psychic effects of combat on soldiers, as part of a larger effort to differentiate between healthy and unhealthy responses to war. While there were efforts to understand and anticipate trauma in the light of World War I, World War II nonetheless saw the coinage of a new and humiliating technical term with which to describe troops unwilling or unable to fight, "lack of moral fiber." Put forward in a 1940 RAF memo, the phrase was intended to shame soldiers into action: those designated "'LMF' were deliberately stigmatized; they lost their flying badges and were sent to a network of 'not yet diagnosed, neuropsychiatric' centers for assessment and treatment" (Jones and Wessely, *Shell Shock to PTSD*, Kindle location 2394). For more on LMF, see English, *Cream of the Crop*.

80. Shakespeare, *Henry V*, ed. Laurence Olivier, in *Masterworks of the British Cinema*, 219.

81. Shakespeare, *Henry IV*, part 1, 1074.

82. Bradley, "Rejection of Falstaff," 714.

83. Ibid., 725. Harold Nicolson almost seemed to have this characterological phrase in mind when he wrote in his journal: "Yet through all this regret and dread pierces a slim clean note of pride. 'London can take it.' I believe that what will win us this war is the immense central dynamo of British pride. The Germans have only assertiveness to put against it. That is transitory. Our pride is permanent, obscure and dark. It has the nature of infinity" (*Diaries and Letters*, 145).

84. Quoted in Behler. *Irony and the Discourse of Modernity*, 74.

85. Empson, *Some Versions of Pastoral*, 109–10.

86. Quoted in Welles and Bogdanovich, *This Is Orson Welles*, 101.

87. Ibid., 114.

88. Ibid., 100.

89. Coleridge, *Shakespeare and the Elizabethan Dramatists*, 71.

90. Danson, *Shakespeare's Dramatic Genres*, 98.

91. Marx, "Shakespeare's Pacifism," 67.

92. Shapiro, *Year in the Life of William Shakespeare*, 32.

93. Shakespeare, *Henry IV*, part 2, 1122.

94. Ibid.,

95. Ibid., 39–40.

96. Welles and Bogdanovich, *This Is Orson Welles*, 16.

97. Shakespeare, *Henry IV*, part 1, 1058.

98. Quoted in Anderegg, *Orson Welles, Shakespeare, and Popular Culture*, 140.

99. Quoted in Schuchard, *Eliot's Dark Angel*, 108.

100. Faulk, "Modernism and the Popular," 618.

101. Calder, *People's War*, 138.

102. Bate, *Genius of Shakespeare*, 122.

103. Samuel Johnson offers a survey of the carnage: "The comic scenes of the history of Henry the fourth and fifth are now at an end, and all the comic personages are now dismissed. Falstaff and Mrs. Quickly are dead; Nym and Bardolph are hanged; Gadshill was lost immediately after the robbery; Poins and Peto have vanished since, one knows not how; and Pistol is now beaten into obscurity. I believe every reader regrets their departure" (*Johnson on Shakespeare*, 173–74).

104. Shakespeare, *Henry V*, in *The Complete Pelican Shakespeare*, 1134.

105. Coleridge, *Lectures upon Shakespeare*, 187.

106. Hazlitt, *Characters of Shakespeare's Plays and Lectures*, 132.

107. Shakespeare, *Henry IV*, part 2, 1099.

108. Shapiro, *Rival Playwrights*, 101.

109. Woloch, *One vs. the Many*, 25.

110. Ibid.

111. Shakespeare, *Henry IV*, part 2, 1099.

112. Bukatman, *Poetics of Slumberland*, 21.

113. Taylor, introduction to Shakespeare, *Henry V*, 65.

114. Davies, *Filming Shakespeare's Plays*, 32

115. Arnheim, "In Praise of Character Actors," 205.

116. Sharp, "Newton, Robert Guy"; McGillivray, "Now You Know," 6; Crowdus, "Films of David Lean," 49.

117. "Andronocles and the Lion," *Sight and Sound*, 148.

118. Quoted in McFarlane, *Lance Comfort*, 34.

119. Crowther, "*Odd Man Out*," 710.

120. Nemerov, *Icons of Grief*, 80.

121. Ibid., 74.

122. Thomson, "Lives of Supporting Players," 207.

123. Nemerov, *Icons of Grief*, 68.

124. Farber, quoted in Nemerov, *Icons of Grief*, 68.

125. Woloch, *One vs. the Many*, 4.

126. Ibid., 5.

127. Nemerov, *Icons of Grief*, 71. For more on the Thersites's structural and critical position in *The Iliad*, see Bell, "Homer's Humor: Laughter in *The Iliad*": "Thersites is a disgraceful, ridiculous caricature of the hero's tragic grandeur, greater stature and complexity. To regard Thersites as a conventional foil makes sense but begs the question: why does Homer make Thersites so eerily like Achilles in several minute particulars?" (105). See also, McLoughlin, *Authoring War*: "The function in war and war representation of the *gelotopoios* or laughter-maker is to neutralise the pervading hyperlogic by matching or exceeding it.

This figure—from Homer's Thersites to Shakespeare's 'fool and jester' Falstaff to Hašek's Schweik to Heller's Yossarian to Spike Milligan as he appears in his own memoirs to Tim O'Brien's Cacciato—is the (often self-appointed) creator and butt of jokes, described by Robert H. Bell (in the case of Thersites) as 'an avatar of comic energy that disrupts events, complicates issues, eludes closure, and generates inquiry'"(178).

128. Shakespeare, *History of Troilus and Cressida*, 492.

129. Homer, *Iliad*, 108.

130. Shakespeare, *Henry V*, ed. Laurence Olivier, in *Masterworks of the British Cinema*, 292.

131. Ibid.

132. MacKenzie, *British War Films*, 71. "Invalided out of the Army in 1916, divorced and living apart from his children, at a low moment he was reduced to selling his paintings on street corners, so ashamed of his failure that he pretended to be disabled, and wore a mask to disguise his identity. By the time he was 40, he had long been familiar with what the 19th-century critics Jules and Edmond de Goncourt described as 'the bohemia that embitters'" (Dormant, "The Peculiarity of Algernon Newton").

133. Neame, *Straight from the Horse's Mouth*, 80.

134. Ibid., 112.

135. Griffith, quoted in McFarlane, *Autobiography of British Cinema*, 255.

136. Brownlow, *David Lean*, 141.

137. Sellers, *Hellraisers*, 31.

138. Niven, *Moon's a Balloon*, 308.

139. Connolly, *Enemies of Promise*, 106.

140. Burnett, *Liquid Pleasures*, 133.

141. Orwell, *As I Please*, 43.

142. Ibid., 136.

143. Nicholls, "Drink the British Disease?"

144. Shakespeare, *Henry V*, ed. Laurence Olivier, in *Masterworks of the British Cinema*, 294.

145. Ibid., 294–95.

146. Altman, "Vile Participation," 12.

147. Shapiro, *Year in the Life of William Shakespeare*, 100.

148. Rabkin, "Rabbits, Ducks, and *Henry V*," 293.

149. Gill Plain writes of the commando, "This liminal bogeyman is beyond re-domestication: a figure curiously both ancient and modern, a skilled warrior who fights outside the rules" (*Literature of the 1940s*, 210).

150. Allport, *Demobbed*, Kindle location 3255.

151. James Hodson, quoted in Allport, *Demobbed*, Kindle location 3475. Joanna Bourke, quoting deputy minister of National Health and president of the National Committee for Mental Hygiene, Canada (1944): "[T]he whole object of [the serviceman's] existence and the focus of all endeavor about him is killing.

Effective and wholesale killing for years has been given precedence as the highest moral value and the most admirable of virtues. . . . Aggressive urges which have been carefully nurtured and developed over a period of years are supposed to disappear overnight, leaving a peaceful civilian with no such pressures and consequently no need of outlet. . . . With the memory . . . of his friends or relatives who have been killed or maimed or even tortured by the enemy, fresh in his experience and kept alive as a spur to his aggressions, this changeover in attitude may be very difficult indeed" (*Intimate History of Killing*, 340).

152. T. S. Eliot, "The Waste Land," 67.

3. Celia Johnson's Face: Before and After *Brief Encounter*

1. Lant, *Blackout*, 158–59. Coward's screenplay specifies the film's setting as "the winter of 1938–39" (*Brief Encounter*, 119).
2. Brownlow, *David Lean*, 196.
3. Thomson, *Big Screen*, 194
4. Fleming, *Celia Johnson*, 137.
5. Dyer, *Brief Encounter*, 18.
6. Barr, "Amnesia and Schizophrenia," 63.
7. Schaefer and Salvato, *Masters of Light*, 278.
8. Genette, *Narrative Discourse*, 84.
9. Benjamin, *Arcades Project*, 462.
10. Fleming, *Celia Johnson*, 140.
11. Johnson, quoted in Brownlow, *David Lean*, 200.
12. Manvell, *Film and the Public*, 157.
13. Lean, "Brief Encounter," 30.
14. Phillips, *Beyond the Epic*, 86.
15. Place and Peterson, "Some Visual Motifs of *Film Noir*," 66.
16. Ibid., 67.
17. Lant, *Blackout*, 176.
18. Kracauer, "Hollywood's Terror Films," 45.
19. Thomson, *Big Screen*, 193.
20. Coward, *Brief Encounter*, 132. This excerpt and those that follow are from Coward's screenplay, which differs slightly from what appears in the film and thus from what I have reproduced in the text. I offer these notes as assistance to readers who might like to compare lines from the finished film to what appears in the screenplay.
21. Bazin, "Bicycle Thief," in *What Is Cinema?*, 2:49.
22. Queval, quoted in Wimmer, *Cross-Channel Perspectives*, 100.
23. Thomson, *Big Screen*, 195.
24. Ibid., 194.
25. Lant, *Blackout*, 153–57.
26. Quoted in Lant, *Blackout*, 168.
27. Brownlow, *David Lean*, 196.

28. Taylor, introduction to *Masterworks of the British Cinema*, 113.
29. Kosseleck, *Futures Past*, 105.
30. Ibid., 106.
31. Laplanche, *Life and Death in Psychoanalysis*, 40.
32. Lacan, "Desire and the Interpretation of Desire in *Hamlet*," 46.
33. Benjamin, *Arcades Project*, 476.
34. Bell, *F. R. Leavis*, 4.
35. Saint-Amour, *Future Tense*, 7.
36. Benjamin, *Arcades Project*, 461.
37. Benjamin, *Illuminations*, 236.
38. Pudovkin, quoted in Nichols, *Movies and Methods*, 409.
39. Bloch, quoted in de Baecque, *Camera Historica*, 17.
40. Bloch, *Historian's Craft*, 38.
41. De Baecque, *Camera Historica*, 6.
42. *Book of Common Prayer*, 189.
43. Whereas British war films often focus on good relations between socio-economic classes, American films take pains to imagine the military as a racial and ethnic "melting pot." See Basinger, "The World War II Combat Film," 30–49. For more on the float as a figure for the suspension of class differences, see Chapman, *British at War*, 185–86: "The image of the men clinging to the float becomes a powerful and irresistible metaphor for class leveling."
44. Brownlow, *David Lean*, 154.
45. Cardulo, *In Search of Cinema*, 280.
46. Ibid.
47. Young, quoted in Brownlow, *David Lean*, 437.
48. Miller, *Hidden Hitchcock*, 15.
49. Anderson, *Lawrence in Arabia*, 5.
50. Clausewitz, *On War*, 119.
51. Saint-Amour, *Tense Future*, 185; Franco Moretti also sees the modern epic as a text that reveals "a discrepancy between the totalizing will of the epic and the subdivided reality of the modern world" (*Modern Epic*, 5).
52. For more on the relation between the development of aerial warfare between the wars and the idea of total war, see Harrison, *Living Through the Blitz*, 19–43; Mellor, *Reading the Ruins*, 11–47; Grayzel, *At Home and Under Fire*; and Saint-Amour, *Tense Future*.
53. Douhet, *Command of the Air*, 9–10.
54. MacKay, *Modernism and World War II*, 6.
55. Churchill, quoted in Lindqvist, *History of Bombing*, 84.
56. Harris, quoted in Bellamy, *Massacres and Morality*, 142.
57. Schlosser, *Command and Control*, 119.
58. O'Connell, *Of Arms and Men*, 284. Referring to Frederick Lindemann's notorious "de-housing" memo, C. P. Snow writes, "It is possible, I suppose, that some time in the future people living in a more benevolent age than ours may

turn over the official records and notice that men like us, men well-educated by the standards of the day, men fairly kindly by the standards of the day, and often possessed of strong human feelings, made the kind of calculation I have just been describing. Such calculations, on a much larger scale, are going on at this moment in the most advanced societies we know. What will people of the future think of us? Will they say, as Roger Williams said of some of the Massachusetts Indians, that we were wolves with the minds of men?" (*Science and Government*, 42).

59. Schlosser, *Command and Control*, 120.

60. Fussell, *Great War*, 64; quoted in Harrison, *Living Through the Blitz*, 78.

61. Orwell, *Lion and the Unicorn*, 9; we might also think of Fussell's account of how the diurnal patterns of trench warfare had ironized even sunrise and sunset: "It was a cruel reversal that sunrise and sunset, established by over a century of Romantic poetry and painting of tokens of hope and peace and rural charm, should now be exactly the moments of heightened ritual anxiety" (*Great War*, 52).

62. Nossack, *The End*, 12.

63. Deer, *Culture in Camouflage*, 106.

64. Bloch, *Strange Defeat*, 54.

65. Glover, quoted in Stonebridge, *Writing of Anxiety*, 19.

66. Runia, "Into Cleanness Leaping," 6.

67. Genette, *Narrative Discourse Revisited*, 88.

68. Thomson, *Big Screen*, 191.

69. Nicolson, *Diaries and Letters*, 163.

70. Dickens, *Great Expectations*, 507.

71. For much more on the image and idea of the ruin, see Mellor, *Reading the Ruins*.

72. Lean, "Brief Encounter," 130.

73. Coward, *Brief Encounter*, 160.

74. Ibid.

75. Neal Gabler, *Walt Disney*, 151.

76. Bukatman, *Poetics of Slumberland*, 22. Part of Donald's appeal is that, unlike other Disney characters, his distinctive speech seems to put him on either side of the animal and the human. Whereas Mickey speaks with a recognizably human, if highly pitched, voice and Pluto is a dog who barks and barks alone, Donald's moist half-man/half-duck squawk seems to put him on both sides of that divide: "Voice-man Clarence 'Duck' Nash's Donald has a special speech impediment for this talking animal. It is not stuttering . . . nor does it involve a lisp like Daffy Duck's *dethpicable*. . . . Rather, Donald Duck has a speech impediment closely tied to breathing" (Shell, *Stutter*, 100). Both the frustration and the joy of his character stems from the fact that unlike other characters, his impeded speech frees and disqualifies him from Disney's otherwise rigorous system of species being (some animals talk, some don't). This is a source of both

his freeing anger and, in the nature of things, his comic frustration; his speech is the sound of air pushed against a physical constraint.

77. Gabler, *Walt Disney*, 202.

78. Coward, *Brief Encounter*, 161.

79. Leslie, *Hollywood Flatlands*, 171.

80. Schatz, *Boom and Bust*, 222.

81. Wartime Donald was immensely popular. Throughout the forties, he surpassed Mickey as the most important and recognizable Disney character. His propaganda message was one that resonated widely both in and out of the military. Spike Jones's version of the theme song to "Der Fuehrer's Face," "sold 1.5 million copies and provided an anthem for the war"; and Donald's image became one of the most frequently painted images on both bombs and military bombers, maybe most famously on the nose of the "Ruptured Duck," the doomed B-25 featured in Mervyn LeRoy's *Thirty Seconds over Tokyo* (1944). Disney's next major wartime production was the 1943 animated adaptation of Alexander P. de Seversky's polemic, *Victory Through Air Power* (1942).

82. Rachmaninoff, quoted in Ross, *Rest Is Noise*, 160.

83. Williams, *British Theatre in the Great War*, 51.

84. Eliot, quoted in Schuchard, *Eliot's Dark Angel*, 108.

85. Brownlow, *David Lean*, 200.

86. Coward, *Brief Encounter*, 159.

87. Ibid., 132.

88. Ibid., 129–30.

89. Ibid., 147.

90. Ibid., 150–51.

91. Ibid., 156.

92. Ibid., 177.

93. Lant, *Blackout*, 155.

94. Alton, *Painting with Light*, 97.

95. Manvell, "Lunch with Carl Dreyer," 67. Although close-ups are important to all of Lean's films, the influence of Dreyer feels particular to *Brief Encounter*. In *In Which We Serve*, *Lawrence of Arabia*, and *Doctor Zhivago* his faces are as striking but seem more influenced by the polemic of Eisenstein than the mysticism of Dreyer.

96. Bazin, *Cinema of Cruelty*, 20.

97. Deleuze, *Cinema 1*, 107.

98. Deleuze, *Cinema 2*, 47.

99. De Baecque, *Camera Historica*, 45.

100. Ibid., 32.

101. *The Third Man*, directed by Carol Reed (London Film Productions, 1949).

102. De Baecque, *Camera Historica*, 62.

103. T. S. Eliot, "The Waste Land," 67.

104. Welles and Bogdanovich, *This Is Orson Welles*, 182.

105. Brownlow, *David Lean*, 195.

106. Bordwell, *Poetics of Cinema*, 67.

107. Allport, *Demobbed*, Kindle location 1066.

108. Ibid., Kindle location 1675.

109. Smart, "Good Wives and Moral Lives," 93; Allport, *Demobbed*, Kindle location 1594.

110. See Hall, *Policing the Crisis*.

111. Allport, *Demobbed*, Kindle location 1767.

112. Ibid., Kindle location 1659.

113. Brownlow, *David Lean*, 205.

114. Gazeley, "Women's Pay in British Industry," 653.

115. Mazower, *Dark Continent*, 208

116. Lant, *Blackout*, 155.

117. For more on the effects of World War II on gender and ideology, see Schneider, *Loving Arms*: "the culturally sanctioned definitions of gender continuously threatened to implode as the necessities and cruel mechanisms of war revealed radical disjunctions between the discourse of gender and actual experience" (21).

118. Johnson had appeared as a major in an ATS training film directed by Carol Reed in 1942.

119. *In Which We Serve*, directed by Noël Coward and David Lean (Two Cities Films, 1949).

120. For more on the representation of women in *In Which We Serve* and *Mrs. Miniver*, see Grayzel, *At Home and Under Fire*, 301–14. See also Miller, *British Literature of the Blitz*, 176–78.

121. See Schneider, *Loving Arms*: "Because of the war's double threat to the stability and legitimacy of its own sex-gender system, Britain's patriarchal hegemony made every attempt to (re)assert its political and narrative authority over the feminine (feminized) Other" (26).

122. Coward, *Brief Encounter*, 161.

123. Ibid., 180.

124. Dyer, *Brief Encounter*, 25.

125. Ibid., 177–78.

126. Ibid., 178.

127. Peter Ackroyd characterizes the period of postwar social retrenchment in this way: "This air of mild oppression, like a hangover after the excitement of war, was intensified by a concerted if unspoken desire to redefine sexual and social mores which had been considerably relaxed during the conflict. The relative sexual freedom of women, and the chummy egalitarianism of enforced contact between the classes, were phenomena strictly of the past" (*London*, Kindle location 13226–28).

128. Coward, *Brief Encounter*, 188.

129. Cavell, *Pursuits of Happiness*, 2.
130. Quoted in Lant, *Blackout*, 182.
131. Nossack, *The End*, 29.
132. Nemerov, *Icons of Grief*, 20.
133. Coward, *Brief Encounter*, 188.
134. See Jones and Wessely, *Shell Shock to PTSD*, Kindle location 4526.
135. Chippington, quoted in Allworth, *Demobbed*, Kindle location 3855.
136. Ibid., Kindle location 3927.
137. Ibid., Kindle location 3920.
138. Dyer, *Brief Encounter*, 33.
139. Coward, *Brief Encounter*, 151.
140. Lean, *Interviews*, 5.
141. Thomson, *Big Screen*, 195.
142. Marcus, *History of Rock 'n' Roll*, 52.
143. Lant, *Blackout*, 161.

Epilogue: Derek Jarman's War

1. Quoted in Hastings, *Winston's War*, 61.
2. Martin, *Father Figures*, 200.
3. Connolly, quoted in MacKay, *Modernism and World War II*, 12.
4. Christie, *Arrows of Desire*, 84–85.
5. Jarman, *Kicking the Pricks*, 107.
6. Jarman, quoted in Christie, *Arrows of Desire*, 99.
7. Benjamin, *Arcades Project*, 474.
8. Jarman, *Jubilee*, 44.
9. O'Pray, introduction to Jarman, *Jubilee: Six Film Scripts*, x.
10. Jarman, *Last of England*, 178.
11. Ibid., 14.
12. Wymer, *Derek Jarman*, 6.
13. Ibid.
14. Cooke, *Britten*, 16.
15. Wiebe, *Britten's Unquiet Pasts*, 208.
16. Wymer, *Derek Jarman*, 125.
17. Ibid.

Works Cited

A. D. "The Life and Death of Colonel Blimp." *Manchester Guardian.* June 10, 1943.

Ackroyd, Peter. *London: The Biography.* London: Chatto and Windus, 2000. Kindle edition.

Adorno, Theodor W. "The Late Style (I)." In *Beethoven: The Philosophy of Music,* edited by Rolf Tiedemann and translated by Edmund Jephcott, 123–38. Stanford, CA: Stanford University Press, 1998.

Agamben, Giorgio. *State of Exception.* Translated by Kevin Attell. Chicago: University of Chicago Press, 2005.

Agee, James. "Masterpiece." In *Agee on Film: Criticism and Comment on the Movies.* 347–54. New York: Modern Library, 2000.

Aitken, Ian. *European Film Theory and Cinema: A Critical Introduction.* Bloomington: Indiana University Press, 2001.

Aldgate, Anthony, and Jeffrey Richards. *Britain Can Take It: British Cinema in the Second World War.* London: I. B. Taurus, 2007.

Allport, Alan. *Demobbed: Coming Home after the Second World War.* New Haven, CT: Yale University Press, 2009. Kindle edition.

Althusser, Louis. *Lenin and Philosophy, and Other Essays.* Translated by Ben Brewster. New York: Monthly Review Press, 1971.

Altman, Joel B. "'Vile Participation': The Amplification of Violence in the Theater of *Henry V.*" *Shakespeare Quarterly* 42, no. 1 (Spring 1991): 1–32.

Alton, John. *Painting with Light.* Berkeley: University of California Press, 2013.

Amad, Paula. "Film as 'the Skin of History': André Bazin and the Specter of the Archive and Death in Nicole Védrès's Paris 1900 (1947)." *Representations* 130, no. 1 (Spring 2015): 84–118.

Anderegg, Michael A. *Orson Welles, Shakespeare, and Popular Culture.* New York: Columbia University Press, 1999.

Anderson, Scott. *Lawrence in Arabia: War, Deceit, Imperial Folly, and the Making of the Modern Middle East.* New York: Doubleday, 2013.

Arnheim, Rudolph. "In Praise of Character Actors." In *Movie Acting: The Film Reader,* edited by Pamela Robertson Wojcik, 205–7. Florence, KY: Psychology Press, 2004.

Arnold, Matthew. "Preface to the First Edition of Poems (1853)." In *On the Classical Tradition,* 1–16. Ann Arbor: University of Michigan Press, 1960.

Aron, Raymond. *The Century of Total War.* Boston, MA: Beacon Press, 1966.

Aymes-Stokes, Sophie, and Laurent Mellet. *In and Out: Eccentricity in Britain.* New Castle upon Tyne: Cambridge Scholars Publishing, 2012.

Babbington, Bruce, and Peter Evans. "Matters of Life and Death in Powell and Pressburger's *The Tales of Hoffman.*" In *A Night at the Opera: Media Representations of Opera,* edited by Jeremy Tambling, 145–69. London: John Libbey and Company, 1994.

Balcon, Michael. "The British Film during the War." In *The Penguin Film Review 1946–1949.* Vol. 1. 66–74 London: Penguin Books, 1977.

Barber, C. L., and Richard Paul Wheeler. *The Whole Journey: Shakespeare's Power of Development.* Berkeley: University of California Press, 1986.

Barker, Ernest. "Some Constants of the English Character." In *Writing Englishness, 1900–1950: An Introductory Sourcebook,* edited by Judy Giles and Tim Middleton, 55–63. London: Routledge, 2003.

Barker, Simon. "Shakespeare, Stratford, and the Second World War." In *Shakespeare and the Second World War: Memory, Culture, Identity,* edited by Irena R. Makaryk and Marissa McHugh, 199–218. Toronto: University of Toronto Press, 2012.

Barr, Charles. "Amnesia and Schizophrenia." In *British Cinema: Critical Concepts in Media and Cultural Studies,* vol. 3, ed. Robert Murphy, chapter 58. London: Routledge, 2014.

Barthes, Roland. "Introduction to the Structural Analysis of Narratives," *Image-Music-Text.* Translated by Stephen Heath. 79–125. New York: Hill and Wang, 1977.

———. *S/Z: An Essay.* Translated by Richard Howard. New York: Hill and Wang, 1974.

———. *Writing Degree Zero.* Translated by Annette Lavers and Colin Smith. New York: Hill and Wang, 1967.

Bartlett, F. C. *Political Propaganda.* Cambridge: Cambridge University Press, 1940.

Basinger, Jeanine. "The World War II Combat Film: A Definition." In *The War Film,* edited by Robert Eberwein, 30–53. New Brunswick, NJ: Rutgers University Press, 2006.

Bate, Jonathan. *The Genius of Shakespeare.* Oxford: Oxford University Press, 1998.

Bazin, André. *The Cinema of Cruelty.* New York: Arcade Publishing, 2013.

———. *What Is Cinema?* Vol. 1. Berkeley: University of California Press, 2005.

———. *What is Cinema?* Vol. 2. Berkeley: University of California Press, 2009.

Bazin, André, and Bert Cardullo. "On *Why We Fight*: History, Documentation, and the Newsreel (1946)." *Film and History: An Interdisciplinary Journal of Film and Television Studies* 31, no. 1 (2001): 60–62.

Behler, Ernst. *Irony and the Discourse of Modernity.* Seattle: University of Washington Press, 1990.

Bell, David A. *The First Total War.* Boston, MA: Houghton Mifflin Co., 2007.

Bell, Michael. *F. R. Leavis*. London: Routledge, 1988.

Bell, Robert H. "Homer's Humor: Laughter in *The Iliad*." *Humanitas* 20, nos. 1–2 (2007): 96–116.

Bellamy, Alex J. *Massacres and Morality: Mass Atrocities in an Age of Civilian Immunity*. Oxford: Oxford University Press, 2012.

Benjamin, Walter. *The Arcades Project*. Translated by Howard Eiland and Kevin McLaughlin. Cambridge, MA: Harvard University Press, 1999.

———. *Illuminations*. Edited by Hannah Arendt, Translated by Harry Zohn. New York: Random House, 1968.

Bersani, Leo, and Ulysse Dutoit. *Forms of Being: Cinema, Aesthetics, Subjectivity*. London: BFI, 2004.

Black, Jeremy. *The Age of Total War: 1860–1945*. Lanham, MD: Rowman and Littlefield, 2010.

Blair, Edward Tyler. *Henry of Navarre and the Religious Wars*. Philadelphia: J. B. Lippincott, 1895.

Blanton, Dan. *Epic Negation: The Dialectical Poetics of Late Modernism*. New York: Oxford University Press, 2015.

Bloch, Marc. *The Historian's Craft*. Manchester: Manchester University Press, 1992.

———. *Strange Defeat: A Statement of Evidence Written in 1940*. New York: W. W. Norton, 1999.

Bond, Brian, and Martin Alexander. "Liddell Hart and de Gaulle: The Doctrines of Limited Liability and Mobile Defense." In *Makers of Modern Strategy from Machiavelli to the Nuclear Age*, edited by Peter Paret, Gordon A. Craig, and Felix Gilbert, 598–624. Princeton, NJ: Princeton University Press, 1986.

The Book of Common Prayer and Administration of the Sacraments and other Rites and Ceremonies of the Church. London: H. and S. Raynor, 1842.

Bordwell, David. *Poetics of Cinema*. London: Routledge, 2012.

Bordwell, David, Janet Staiger, and Kristin Thompson. *The Classical Hollywood Cinema: Film Style and Mode of Production to 1960*. New York: Columbia University Press, 1985.

Bourke, Joanna. *An Intimate History of Killing*. New York: Basic Books, 2000.

Bradley, A. C. "The Rejection of Falstaff." *The Living Age: A Weekly Magazine of Contemporary Literature and Thought* 15, no. 3024 (June 21, 1902): 711–25.

Brinkema, Eugenie. *The Forms of the Affects*. Durham, NC: Duke University Press, 2014.

Brownlow, Kevin. *David Lean: A Biography*. London: Macmillan, 1996.

Bukatman, Scott. *The Poetics of Slumberland: Animated Spirits and the Animating Spirit*. Berkeley: University of California Press, 2012.

Burkert, Walter. *Homo Necans: The Anthropology of Ancient Greek Sacrificial Ritual and Myth*. Translated by Peter Bing. Berkeley: University of California Press, 1983.

Burnett, John. *Liquid Pleasures: A Social History of Drinks in Modern Britain.* London: Routledge, 1999.

Buzacott, Martin. *The Death of the Actor: Shakespeare on Page and Stage.* London: Routledge, 1991.

Buzard, James. "Mass-Observation, Modernism, and Auto-ethnography." *Modernism/Modernity* 4, no. 3 (1997): 93–122.

Calder, Angus. *The People's War: Britain, 1939–1945.* London: Pimlico, 1992.

Canby, Vincent. "*Henry V.*" In *The New York Times Guide to the Best 1,000 Movies Ever Made,* edited by Peter M. Nichols. New York: St. Martin's Griffin, 2004.

Cardulo, Bert. *In Search of Cinema: Writings on International Film Art.* Montreal: McGill-Queens Press, 2004.

Cavell, Stanley. *Pursuits of Happiness: The Hollywood Comedy of Remarriage.* Cambridge, MA: Harvard University Press, 1981.

Chapman, James. *The British at War: Cinema, State, and Propaganda, 1939–1945.* London: I. B. Tauris Publishers, 1998.

———. "Cinema, Propaganda, and National Identity: British Film and the Second World War." In *British Cinema Past and Present,* edited by Justine Ashby and Andrew Higson, 193–207. London: Routledge, 2000.

Chickering, Roger, and Stig Forster. "Are We There Yet? World War II and the Theory of Total War." In *A World at Total War: Global Conflict and the Politics of Destruction, 1937–1945,* edited by Roger Chickering, Stig Forster, and Bernd Greiner, 1–19. Cambridge: Cambridge University Press, 2005.

Christie, Ian. *Arrows of Desire: The Films of Michael Powell and Emeric Pressburger.* London: Faber and Faber, 1994.

———. "The *Colonel Blimp* File." *Sight and Sound* 48, no. 1 (Winter 1978–79): 13–14.

———. "History Is Now and England." In *The Cinema of Michael Powell: International Perspectives on an English Film-Maker,* edited by Ian Christie and Andrew Moor, 75–94. London: BFI, 2005.

———, ed. "The Resurrection of 'Blimp': A Note on the Script and Film." In *The Life and Death of Colonel Blimp* by Michael Powell and Emeric Pressburger. 67–71. London: Faber and Faber, 1994.

Churchill, Winston. *Never Give In! Winston Churchill's Speeches.* London: A. and C. Black, 2014.

Clark, T. J. *Farewell to an Idea: Episodes from a History of Modernism.* New Haven, CT: Yale University Press, 1999.

———. "For a Left with No Future." *New Left Review,* no. 74 (March–April 2012): 53–75.

———. *The Sight of Death: An Experiment in Art Writing.* New Haven, CT: Yale University Press, 2006.

Clausewitz, Carl von. *On War.* Edited and translated by Michael Eliot Howard and Peter Paret. Princeton, NJ: Princeton University Press, 1989.

Cole, Sarah. *At the Violet Hour: Modernism and Violence in England and Ireland.* New York: Oxford University Press, 2012.

Coleman, Terry. *Olivier.* New York: Macmillan, 2006.

Coleridge, Samuel Taylor. *Lectures upon Shakespeare and Other Dramatists.* New York: Harper, 1884.

———. *Shakespeare and the Elizabethan Dramatists.* Edinburgh: John Grant, 1905.

Connolly, Cyril. *Enemies of Promise.* Chicago: University of Chicago Press, 2008.

Cooke, Mervyn. *Britten: War Requiem.* Cambridge: Cambridge University Press, 1996.

Coward, Noel. *Brief Encounter.* In *Masterworks of the British Cinema.* London: Faber and Faber, 1990.

Crowdus, Gary. "The Films of David Lean." *Cineaste* 22, no. 2 (1996): 48–51.

Crowther, Bosley. "*Odd Man Out.*" In *The New York Times Guide to the Best 1,000 Movies Ever Made*, edited by Peter M. Nichols and A. O. Scott. New York: Macmillan, 2004.

Danson, Lawrence. *Shakespeare's Dramatic Genres.* Oxford: Oxford University Press, 2000.

Davies, Anthony. *Filming Shakespeare's Plays: The Adaptations of Laurence Olivier, Orson Welles, Peter Brook, and Akira Kurosawa.* New York: Columbia University Press, 1990.

De Baecque, Antoine. *Camera Historica: The Century in Cinema.* New York: Columbia University Press, 2012.

Deer, Patrick. *Culture in Camouflage: War, Empire, and Modern British Literature.* Oxford: Oxford University Press, 2009.

Deleuze, Gilles. *Cinema 1: The Movement-Image.* Translated by Hugh Tomlinson and Barbara Habberjam. Minneapolis: University of Minnesota Press, 1986.

———. *Cinema 2: The Time-Image.* Translated by Hugh Tomlinson and Robert Galeta. Minneapolis: University of Minnesota Press, 2003.

Dickens, Charles. *Great Expectations.* London: Penguin 2002.

Dickison, Kay. "Ken Russell, National Culture, and Experimental TV." In *Experimental British Television*, edited by Laura Mulvey and Jamie Sexton, 75–88. Manchester: Manchester University Press, 2007.

Donnelly, Mark. *Britain in the Second World War.* London: Routledge, 1999.

Dormant, Richard. "The Peculiarity of Algernon Newton." *Telegraph*, November 27, 2012.

Douhet, Guilio. *The Command of the Air.* Birmingham: University of Alabama Press, 2009.

Drazin, Charles. *The Finest Years: British Cinema of the 1940s.* London: I. B. Tauris, 2007.

Dudziak, Mary L. *War-Time: An Idea, Its History, Its Consequences.* Oxford: Oxford University Press, 2012.

Durgnat, Raymond. *The Essential Raymond Durgnat.* Edited by Henry K. Miller. London: Palgrave Macmillan, 2014.

———. *Films and Feelings.* London: Faber and Faber, 1967.

———. *A Mirror for England: British Movies from* Austerity *to* Affluence. London: Palgrave Macmillan, 2011.

Dyer, Richard. *Brief Encounter.* London: Macmillan, 1993.

Elias, Norbert. *The Civilizing Process.* Translated by Edmund Jepbcott. Oxford: Blackwell Publishers, 1994.

———. *The Germans: Power and Struggles and the Development of Habitus in the Nineteenth and Twentieth Centuries.* Edited by Michael Schröter. Translated by Eric Dunning and Stephen Mennell. New York: Columbia University Press, 1996.

Eliot, T. S. "East Coker." In *Four Quartets.* New York: Harcourt, Brace and Company, 1943.

———. *Notes Towards a Definition of Culture.* New York: Read Books, 1962.

———. "The Waste Land." In *Collected Poems, 1909–1962,* 51–76. New York: Harcourt, 1963.

Ellis, Jack C. *John Grierson: Life, Contributions, Influence.* Carbondale: Southern Illinois University Press, 2000.

Ellul, Jacques. *Propaganda: The Formation of Men's Attitudes.* Translated by Konrad Kellen and Jean Lerner. New York: Vintage Books, 1973.

Empson, William. *Some Versions of Pastoral.* New York: New Directions Publishing, 1935.

English, Allan Douglas. *Cream of the Crop: Canadian Aircrew, 1939–1945.* Montreal: McGill-Queen's University Press, 1996.

Esty, Jed. *A Shrinking Island: Modernism and National Culture in England.* Princeton, NJ: Princeton University Press, 2004.

Evans, Gary. *John Grierson and the National Film Board: The Politics of Wartime Propaganda.* Toronto: University of Toronto Press, 1984.

Faber, David. *Munich, 1938: Appeasement and World War II.* New York: Simon and Schuster, 2009.

Faulk, Barry J. "Modernism and the Popular: Eliot's Music Halls." *Modernism/Modernity* 8, no. 4 (November 2001): 603–21.

Favret, Mary. *War at a Distance: Romanticism and the Making of Modern Wartime.* Princeton, NJ: Princeton University Press, 2010.

Fleming, Kate. *Celia Johnson: A Biography.* London: Weidenfeld and Nicolson, 1991.

Foch, Ferdinand. *The Principles of War.* Translated by Hilaire Belloc. New York: H. Holt, 1920.

Forster, E. M. "The English Eccentrics." *Spectator* (London), May 18, 1933: 716.

———. *Two Cheers for Democracy.* New York: Harcourt, Brace, 1951.

Freud, Sigmund. *Civilization and its Discontents.* Translated and edited by James Strachey. New York: W. W. Norton, 1961.

Fuller, J. F. C. *The First of the League Wars: Its Lessons and Omens*. London: Eyre and Spottiswoode, 1936.

———. *A Military History of the Western World: From the American Civil War to the End of World War II*. New York: Da Capo Press, 1987.

Fussell, Paul. *The Great War and Modern Memory*. Oxford: Oxford University Press, 2013.

Gabler, Neal. *Walt Disney: The Triumph of the American Imagination*. New York: Random House, 2007.

Gallagher, Catherine. "The Fictions of Nazi Britain." In *Telling It Like It Wasn't: The Counterfactual Imagination in History and Fiction*. Chicago: University of Chicago Press (forthcoming).

Gat, Azar. *War in Human Civilization*. Oxford: Oxford University Press, 2006.

Gazeley, Ian. "Women's Pay in British Industry During the Second World War." *Economic History Review* 61, no. 3 (August, 2008): 651–71.

Genette, Gérard. *Narrative Discourse: An Essay in Method*. Translated by Jane E. Lewin. Ithaca, NY: Cornell University Press, 1983.

———. *Narrative Discourse Revisited*. Translated by Jane E. Lewin. Ithaca, NY: Cornell University Press, 1988.

Gill, Miranda. *Eccentricity and the Cultural Imagination in Nineteenth-Century Paris*. Oxford: Oxford University Press, 2009.

Girouard, Mark. *The Return to Camelot: Chivalry and the English Gentleman*. New Haven, CT: Yale University Press, 1981.

Godard, Jean-Luc. "Woman in a Dressing-Gown." In *Godard on Godard: Critical Writings by Jean-Luc Godard*, edited by Jean Narboni and Tom Milne, 85–86. New York: Da Capo Press, 1986.

Gould, Gerald. "A New Reading of *Henry V*." *English Review*, no. 128 (July–December 1919): 42–55.

Grayzel, Susan R. *At Home and Under Fire: Air Raids and Culture in Britain from the Great War to the Blitz*. New York: Cambridge University Press, 2012.

Gurr, Andrew. *The Shakespearean Stage 1574–1642*. Cambridge: Cambridge University Press, 2009.

Hall, Stuart. *Policing the Crisis: Mugging, the State, and Law and Order*. London: Palgrave Macmillan, 2013.

Handel, Michael. *War, Strategy and Intelligence*. London: Frank Cass, 1989.

Harrison, Tom. *Living Through the Blitz*. London: Faber and Faber, 2010.

Haskell, Molly. "The Life and Death and Life of Colonel Blimp." Current (blog). March 20, 2013. http://www.criterion.com/current/posts/2699-the-life-and-death-and-life-of-colonel-blimp.

Hastings, Max. *Winston's War: Churchill, 1940–1945*. New York: Vintage Books, 2011.

Hatherley, Owen. *The Ministry of Nostalgia: Consuming Austerity*. London: Verso, 2016. Kindle edition.

Havardi, Jeremy. *Projecting Britain at War: The National Character in British World War II Films*. Jefferson, NC: McFarland, 2014.

Hazlitt, William. *Characters of Shakespeare's Plays and Lectures on the English Poets.* London: Macmillan, 1920.

Henricks, Thomas S. *Disputed Pleasures: Sport and Society in Preindustrial England.* Westport, CT: Greenwood Publishing Group, 1991.

Hilgers, Philipp von. *War Games: A History of War on Paper.* Cambridge: MIT Press, 2012.

Hobsbawm, Eric. *The Age of Extremes: A History of the World, 1914–1991.* New York: Vintage, 1996.

Holderness, Graham. "Agincourt 1944: Readings in the Shakespeare Myth." In *Popular Fictions,* edited by Peter Humm, Paul Stigant, and Peter Widdowson, 173–95. London: Routledge, 2013.

———. *Shakespeare Recycled: The Making of Historical Drama.* New York: Harvester Wheatsheaf, 1992.

Homer. *The Iliad.* Translated by Robert Fagels. London: Penguin, 1998.

Howard, Michael. "The Influence of Clausewitz." In *On War* by Carl von Clausewitz, edited and translated by Michael Eliot Howard and Peter Paret, 27–45. Princeton, NJ: Princeton University Press, 1989.

Hubble, Nick. *Mass Observation and Everyday Life: Culture, History, Theory.* London: Palgrave, 2010.

Huizinga, Johan. *Homo Ludens: A Study of the Play-Element in Culture.* Boston, MA: Beacon Press, 1970.

———. *The Waning of the Middle Ages.* Mineola, NY: Dover Publications, 1999.

Hunt, Martin. "New Labour, New Criticism: A Contemporary Re-Assessment of Ealing and The Archers." *Quarterly Review of Film and Video* 19, no. 3 (2002): 261–69.

Jameson, Fredric. *The Antinomies of Realism.* London: Verso, 2013.

Jarman, Derek. *Jubilee: Six Film Scripts.* Minneapolis: University of Minnesota Press, 2011.

———. *Kicking the Pricks.* Minneapolis: University of Minnesota Press, 2010.

———. *The Last of England.* London: Constable and Robinson, 1987.

Johnson, Samuel. *Johnson on Shakespeare.* Andhra Pradesh, India: Orient Blackswan, 1985.

Jones, Edgar, and Simon Wessely. *Shell Shock to PTSD: Military Psychiatry from 1900 to the Gulf War.* London: Taylor and Francis, 2005. Kindle edition.

Joxe, Alain. *Empire of Disorder.* Translated by Ames Hodges. Los Angeles: Semiotext(e), 2002.

Judd, Denis, and Keith Surridge. *The Boer War: A History.* London: I. B. Tauris, 2013.

Justice, Steven. "Did the Middle Ages Believe in Their Miracles?" *Representations* 103, no. 1 (Summer 2008): 1–29.

Kant, Immanuel, "What is Enlightenment?" In *On History,* edited by Lewis White Beck, 3–10. New York: Macmillan, 1963.

Kantorowicz, Ernst H. *The King's Two Bodies: A Study in Mediaeval Political Theology*. Princeton, NJ: Princeton University Press, 1997.

Keegan, John. *The Face of Battle: A Study of Agincourt, Waterloo, and the Somme*. London: Penguin Group, 1978.

Keeley, Lawrence H. *War Before Civilization: The Myth of the Peaceful Savage*. New York: Oxford University Press, 1996.

Kemp, William. *Kemp's Nine Days' Wonder*. In *The Broadview Anthology of Sixteenth-Century Poetry and Prose*, edited by Marie Loughlin, Sandra Bell, and Patricia Brace. 1042–51. Peterborough, CA: Broadview Press, 2012.

Kershner, R. B. "Joyce and Stephen Phillips' 'Ulysses.'" *James Joyce Quarterly* 13, no. 2 (1976): 194–201.

Knapp, Jeffrey. *Shakespeare Only*. Chicago: University of Chicago Press, 2009.

Knight, G. Wilson. *The Olive and the Sword: A Study of England's Shakespeare*. London: Oxford University Press, 1944.

Koselleck, Reinhart. *Futures Past: On the Semantics of Historical Time*. New York: Columbia University Press, 2004.

Kott, Jan. *Shakespeare Our Contemporary*. Translated by Boreslaw Taborski. Garden City, NY: Anchor Books, 1966.

Kracauer, Siegfried. "Hollywood's Terror Films: Do They Reflect an American State of Mind?" In *Siegfried Kracauer's American Writings: Essays on Film and Popular Culture*, 41–46. Berkeley: University of California Press, 2012.

Lacan, Jacques. "Desire and the Interpretation of Desire in Hamlet." *Yale French Studies*, nos. 55–56 (1977): 11–52.

———. *The Four Fundamental Concepts of Psychoanalysis*. Edited by Jacques-Alain Miller. Translated by Alan Sheridan. New York: W. W. Norton, 1998.

Lacombe, Hervé. *The Keys to French Opera in the Nineteenth Century*. Berkeley: University of California Press, 2001.

Lant, Antonia. *Blackout: Reinventing Women for Wartime British Cinema*. Princeton, NJ: Princeton University Press, 1991.

Laplanche, Jean. *Life and Death in Psychoanalysis*. Baltimore, MD: Johns Hopkins University Press, 1985.

Lean, David. "*Brief Encounter*." In *The Penguin Film Review 1946–1949*. Vol. 4. 27–36 London: Penguin Books, 1977.

———. *Interviews*. Edited by Steven Organ. Jackson: University of Mississippi Press, 2009.

Lejeune, C. A. "The Films." *Observer*, June 13, 1943.

Lenoir, Timothy, and Henry Lowood. "Theaters of War: The Military-Entertainment Complex." In *Collection, Laboratory, Theater: Scenes of Knowledge in the 17th Century*, edited by Ludger Schwarte Schramm and Jan Lazardzig, 427–57. Berlin: Walter de Gruyter, 2005.

Leslie, Esther. *Hollywood Flatlands: Animation, Critical Theory, and the Avant-Garde*. London: Verso Books, 2002.

Levi-Strauss, Claude. *The Origin of Table Manners.* Chicago: University of Chicago Press, 1990.

Lindqvist, Sven. *A History of Bombing.* New York: New Press, 2003.

Lovell, Alan. "The British Cinema: The Unknown Cinema." In *British Cinema: Critical Concepts in Media and Cultural Studies,* vol. 3, edited by Robert Murphy, chapter 56. London: Routledge, 2014.

Low, David. *Years of Wrath: A Cartoon History: 1931–1945.* New York: Simon and Schuster, 1946.

Lukács, Georg. *The Theory of the Novel: A Historico-Philosophical Essay on the Forms of Great Epic Literature.* Translated by Anna Bostock. Cambridge, MA: MIT Press, 1971.

———. *Soul and Form.* Translated by Anna Bostock. London: Merlin Press, 1974.

Macdonald, Dwight. *Interviews with Dwight Macdonald.* Edited by Michael Wreszin. Jackson: University Press of Mississippi, 2003.

Macdonald, Kevin. *Emeric Pressburger: The Life and Death of a Screenwriter.* London: Faber and Faber, 1994.

MacKay, Marina. *Modernism and World War II.* Cambridge: Cambridge University Press, 2007.

———. "The Wartime Rise of *The Rise of the Novel.*" *Representations* 119, no. 1 (Summer 2012): 119–43.

MacKenzie, S. P. *British War Films: 1939–1945: The Cinema and the Services.* London: Hambledon Continuum, 2006.

Madge, Charles. "A Note on Images." In *Humphrey Jennings: Film-Maker, Painter, Poet,* edited by Mary-Lou Jennings, 78–83. London: BFI, 2014.

Manvell, Roger. *The Film and the Public.* London: Penguin Books, 1955.

———. "Lunch with Carl Dreyer." In *The Penguin Film Review 1946–1949.* Vol. 3. 67–68. London: Penguin Books, 1977.

Marcus, Greil. *The History of Rock 'n' Roll in Ten Songs.* New Haven, CT: Yale University Press, 2014.

Marlin, Randal. "Jacques Ellul's Contribution to Propaganda." *The Oxford Handbook of Propaganda Studies.* Oxford: Oxford University Press, 2013: 348–365.

Martin, Kingsley. *Father Figures: A First Volume of Autobiography, 1897–1931.* London: Hutchinson, 1966.

Marwick, Arthur, Clive Emsley, and Wendy Simpson. *Total War and Historical Change: Europe, 1914–1955.* Buckingham: Open University Press, 2001.

Marx, Steven. "Shakespeare's Pacifism." *Renaissance Quarterly* 45, no. 1 (Spring 1992): 49–95.

Mazower, Mark. *Dark Continent: Europe's Twentieth Century.* New York: A. A. Knopf, 2009.

McAleer, Kevin. *Dueling: The Cult of Honor in Fin-de-siècle Germany.* Princeton, NJ: Princeton University Press, 1994.

McEachern, Claire. Introduction to *Henry V*. In *The Complete Pelican Shakespeare* by William Shakespeare, edited by Stephen Orgel and A. R. Braunmuller, 1123–27. London: Penguin, 2002.

McFarlane, Brian, ed. *An Autobiography of British Cinema by the Actors and Filmmakers Who Made It*. London: Methuen, 1997.

———. *Lance Comfort*. Manchester: Manchester University Press, 1999.

McGillivray, David. "Now You Know." In *Films and Filming*. 42–43. New York: Hansom Books, 1984.

McLoughlin, Kate. *Authoring War: The Literary Representation of War from the Iliad to Iraq*. Cambridge: Cambridge University Press, 2011.

Mellor, Leo. *Reading the Ruins: Modernism, Bombsites and British Culture*. Cambridge: Cambridge University Press, 2011.

Mieszkowski, Jan. *Watching War*. Stanford, CA: Stanford University Press, 2012.

Mill, J. S. *On Liberty*. Peterborough, Canada: Broadview Press, 1999.

Miller, D. A. *Hidden Hitchcock*. Chicago: University of Chicago Press, 2016.

Miller, Jacques-Alain. "An Introduction to Seminars I and II." In *Reading Seminars I and II: Lacan's Return to Freud*, edited by Richard Feldstein, Bruce Fink, and Maire Jaanus, 3–39. Albany: State University of New York Press, 1996.

Miller, Kristine A. *British Literature of the Blitz: Fighting the People's War*. Basingstoke, England: Palgrave Macmillan, 2009.

Mitchell, W. J. T. *Picture Theory: Essays on Verbal and Visual Representation*. Chicago: University of Chicago Press, 1995.

Monthly Film Bulletin. "The Life and Death of Colonel Blimp." 10, no. 114 (1943).

Moor, Andrew. "Bending the Arrow: The Queer Appeal of The Archers." In *The Cinema of Michael Powell: International Perspectives on an English Filmmaker*, edited by Ian Christie and Andrew Moor, 209–24. London: BFI, 2005.

Moretti, Franco. *The Bourgeois: History and Literature*. London: Verso, 2013.

———. *Modern Epic: The World-System from Goethe to Garcia Marquez*. London: Verso Books, 1996.

Morgan, Daniel. *Late Godard and the Possibilities of Cinema*. Berkeley: University of California Press, 2013.

Murphy, Robert. *British Cinema and the Second World War*. London: Continuum, 2000.

Neame, Ronald. *Straight from the Horse's Mouth: Ronald Neame, an Autobiography*. Blue Ridge Summit, PA: Scarecrow Press, 2003.

Nemerov, Alexander. *Icons of Grief: Val Lewton's Home Front Pictures*. Berkeley: University of California Press, 2005.

Nicholls, James. "Drink the British Disease?" *History Today* 60, no. 1 (2010): 10–17.

Nichols, Bill. *Movies and Methods: An Anthology*. Vol. 1. Berkeley: University of California Press, 1976.

Nicolson, Harold. *Diaries and Letters*. Vol. 2, *The War Years: 1939–1945*. Edited by Nigel Nicolson. New York: Atheneum, 1967.

———. *Why Britain Is at War.* London: Penguin, 2010.

Niven, David. *The Moon's a Balloon.* New York: G. P. Putnam and Sons, 1972.

Nossack, Hans Erich. *The End: Hamburg 1943.* Chicago: University of Chicago Press, 2004.

O'Connell, Robert L. *Of Arms and Men: A History of War, Weapons, and Aggression.* Oxford: Oxford University Press, 1989.

Olivier, Laurence. *On Acting.* New York: Simon and Schuster, 1986.

Orwell, George. *1984.* New York: New American Library, 1961.

———. *As I Please: 1943–1945.* Edited by Ian Angus and Sonia Orwell. Boston, MA: Nonpareil Books, 1968.

———. *George Orwell: A Collection of Essays.* New York: Harvest, 1981.

———. *The Lion and the Unicorn: Socialism and the English Genius.* London: Secker and Warburg, 1940.

———. "The Prevention of Literature." In *George Orwell: In Front of Your Nose: 1945–1950*, edited by Ian Angus and Sonia Orwell, 59–72. Boston, MA: Nonpareil Books, 1968.

Owen, Wilfred. "Strange Meeting." In *The Poems of Wilfred Owen*, edited by Owen Knowles, 95. Ware, England: Wordsworth Classics, 1994.

Panofsky, Erwin. *Perspective as a Symbolic Form.* Translated by Christopher S. Wood. New York: Zone Books, 1997.

Paret, Peter, Godron A. Craig, and Felix Gilbert, eds. *Makers of Modern Strategy: from Machiavelli to the Nuclear Age.* Princeton, NJ: Princeton University Press, 1986.

The Penguin Hansard. Vol. 1, *From Chamberlain to Churchill.* Harmondsworth, England: Penguin, 1940.

The Penguin Hansard. Vol. 3, *Britain Gathers Strength.* Harmondsworth, England: Penguin, 1941.

Phillips, Gene D. *Beyond the Epic: The Life and Films of David Lean.* Louisville: University Press of Kentucky, 2006.

Piette, Adam. *Imagination at War: British Fiction and Poetry, 1939–1945.* London: Papermac, 1995.

Pinker, Steven. *The Better Angels of Our Nature: Why Violence Has Declined.* London: Penguin, 2011.

Place, Janey, and Lowell Peterson. "Some Visual Motifs of *Film Noir*." In *The Film Noir Reader*, edited by Alain Silver and James Ursini. New York: Hal Leonard, 1996.

Plain, Gill. *Literature of the 1940s: War, Postwar and "Peace."* Edinburgh: Edinburgh University Press, 2013.

Poe, Edgar Allan. "The Philosophy of Composition." In *Essays and Reviews*, 13–25. New York: Library of America, 1984.

Powell, Dilys. *The Golden Screen: Fifty Years of Films.* Edited by George Perry. London: Pavilion Books, 1989.

———. "The Week's Films." *Sunday Times*, June 13, 1943.

Powell, Michael, and Emeric Pressburger. *The Life and Death of Colonel Blimp.* Edited by Ian Christie. London: Faber and Faber, 1994.

Price, G. Ward. "Blimp Film Must NOT Go Abroad." *Daily Mail*, June 11, 1943.

Priestley, J. B. *Postscripts.* London: William Heinemann, 1940.

Puckett, Kent. *Bad Form: Social Mistakes and the Nineteenth-Century Novel.* New York: Oxford Press, 2011.

Rabkin, Norman. "Rabbits, Ducks, and *Henry V*." *Shakespeare Quarterly* 28, no. 3 (Summer 1977): 279–96.

Rattigan, Neil. *This Is England: British Film and the People's War, 1939–1945.* Madison, WI: Fairleigh Dickinson University Press, 2001.

Reeves, Nicholas. *The Power of Film Propaganda: Myth or Reality?* London: Continuum Books, 1999.

Reiter, Dan. *How Wars End.* Princeton, NJ: Princeton University Press, 2009.

Richards, Jeffrey, and Dorothy Sheridan, eds. *Mass-Observation at the Movies.* London: Routledge and Kegan Paul, 1987.

Ross, Alex. *The Rest Is Noise: Listening to the Twentieth Century.* London: Macmillan, 2007.

Runia, Eelco. "Into Cleanness Leaping: The Vertiginous Urge to Commit History." *History and Theory* 49, no. 1 (2010): 1–20.

Said, Edward. *On Late Style: Music and Literature Against the Grain.* New York: Vintage Books, 2007.

Saint-Amour, Paul K. "Air War Prophecy and Interwar Modernism." *Comparative Literature Studies* 42, no. 2 (2005): 130–61.

———. *Tense Future: Modernism, Total War, Encyclopedic Form.* New York: Oxford University Press, 2015.

Saler, Michael T. *The Avant-Garde in Interwar England: Medieval Modernism and the London Underground.* Oxford: Oxford University Press, 1999.

Santner, Eric L. *The Royal Remains: The People's Two Bodies and the Endgames of Sovereignty.* Chicago: University of Chicago Press, 2011.

Schaefer, Dennis, and Larry Salvato. *Masters of Light: Conversations with Contemporary Cinematographers.* Berkeley: University of California Press, 2013.

Schatz, Thomas. *Boom and Bust: American Cinema in the 1940s.* Berkeley: University of California Press, 1999.

Schiller, Friedrich. "On Naive and Sentimental Poetry." In *German Aesthetic and Literary Criticism*, edited by H. B. Nisbet, 177–233. Cambridge: Cambridge University Press, 1985.

Schlosser, Eric. *Command and Control: Nuclear Weapons, the Damascus Accident, and the Illusion of Safety.* London: Penguin, 2013.

Schneider, Karen. *Loving Arms: British Women Writing the Second World War.* Lexington: The University Press of Kentucky, 1997.

Schoch, Richard W. *Shakespeare's Victorian Stage: Performing History in the Theatre of Charles Kean.* Cambridge: Cambridge University Press, 1998.

Schuchard, Ronald. *Eliot's Dark Angel: Intersections of Life and Art.* Oxford: Oxford University Press, 1999.

Sellers, Robert. *Hellraisers: The Life and Inebriated Times of Richard Burton, Richard Harris, Peter O'Toole, and Oliver Reed.* New York: St. Martin's Press, 2011.

Shakespeare, William. *Henry IV.* Part 1. In *The Complete Pelican Shakespeare,* edited by Stephen Orgel and A. R. Braunmuller. London: Penguin, 2002.

———. *Henry IV.* Part 2. In *The Complete Pelican Shakespeare,* edited by Stephen Orgel and A. R. Braunmuller. London: Penguin, 2002.

———. *Henry V.* In *The Complete Pelican Shakespeare,* edited by Stephen Orgel and A. R. Braunmuller. London: Penguin, 2002.

———. *Henry V.* Edited by Laurence Olivier. In *Masterworks of the British Cinema.* London: Faber and Faber, 1990.

———. *The History of Troilus and Cressida.* In *The Complete Pelican Shakespeare.* Edited by Stephen Orgel and A. R. Braunmuller. London: Penguin, 2002.

———. *Richard II.* In *The Complete Pelican Shakespeare,* edited by Stephen Orgel and A. R. Braunmuller. London: Penguin, 2002.

Shapiro, James. *Rival Playwrights: Marlowe, Jonson, Shakespeare.* New York: Columbia University Press, 1991.

———. *1599: A Year in the Life of William Shakespeare.* New York: HarperCollins Publishers, 2005.

Sharp, Robert. "Newton, Robert Guy." In *Oxford Dictionary of National Biography.* http://www.oxforddnb.com.

Sheftall, Mark David. *Altered Memories of the Great War: Divergent Narratives of Britain, Australia, New Zealand, and Canada.* London: I. B. Tauris, 2009.

Shell, Marc. *Stutter.* Cambridge, MA: Harvard University Press, 2005.

Sight and Sound. "Andronocles and the Lion." 22, no. 4 (April/June 1953): 148.

Sitwell, Edith. *English Eccentrics.* London: Dobson Books, 1958.

Smart, Carol. "Good Wives and Moral Lives: Marriage and Divorce 1937–51." In *Nationalizing Femininity: Culture Sexuality, and British Cinema in the Second World War,* edited by Christine Gledhill and Gillian Swanson, 91–109. Manchester: Manchester University Press, 1996.

Snow, C. P. *Science and Government.* Cambridge, MA: Harvard University Press, 2013.

Spenser, Edmund. *The Faerie Queene.* In *The Broadview Anthology of British Literature,* edited by Joseph Black et al. London: Broadview Press, 2010.

Stansky, Peter. *The First Day of the Blitz: September 7, 1940.* New Haven, CT: Yale University Press, 2007.

Stapleton, Julia. "Ernest Barker: Classics, England-Britain, and Europe, 1906–1960." *Polis* 23, no. 2 (2006): 203–21.

Stewart, Victoria. *The Second World War in Contemporary British Fiction: Secret Histories.* Edinburgh: Edinburgh University Press, 2011.

Stone, Alan A. "For God and Country." *Boston Review: A Political and Literary Forum*, February 1, 2005. http://bostonreview.net/stone-god-and-country.

Stonebridge, Lyndsey. *The Writing of Anxiety: Imagining Wartime in Mid-Century British Culture*. Basingstoke, England: Palgrave Macmillan, 2007.

Storr, Anthony. *Churchill's Black Dog and Other Phenomena of the Human Mind*. New York: Harper Collins, 1997.

Talmon, J. L. *The Origins of Totalitarian Democracy*. New York: Frederick A, Praeger, 1960.

Taylor, A. J. P. *The Origins of the Second World War*. London: Penguin Books, 2001.

Taylor, Gary. Introduction. In *Henry V* by William Shakespeare, edited by Gary Taylor, 1–72. Oxford: Oxford University Press, 1982.

Taylor, John Russell. Introduction to *Masterworks of the British Cinema*. 111–15. London: Faber and Faber, 1990.

Thomson, David. *The Big Screen: The Story of the Movies*. London: Macmillan, 2012.

———. "The Lives of Supporting Players." In *Movie Acting: The Film Reader*, edited by Pamela Robertson Wojcik, 207–11. Florence, KY: Psychology Press, 2004.

Thompson, Kristin. "The Concept of Cinematic Excess." In *Narrative, Apparatus, Ideology: A Film Theory Reader*, edited by Philip Rosen, 130–43. New York: Columbia University Press, 1986.

Tillyard, E. M. W. *The Elizabethan World Picture: A Study of the Idea of Order in the Age of Shakespeare, Donne, and Milton*. New York: Vintage Books, 1960.

———. *Shakespeare's History Plays*. London: Penguin Books, 1991.

Tolstoy, Leo. *War and Peace*. Translated by Richard Pevear and Larissa Volokhonsky. New York: Knopf, 2011.

Trevor-Roper, Hugh. *The Wartime Journals*. London: I. B. Tauris, 2012.

Tribune. "The Life and Death of Colonel Blimp." June 18, 1943.

Valery, Paul. "Style." In *The Problem of Style*, edited by J. V. Cunningham, 18–19. Greenwich, CT: Fawcett Publications, 1966.

Van Doren, Mark. *Shakespeare*. New York: New York Review of Books, 2005.

Walzer, Michael. *Just and Unjust Wars: A Moral Argument with Historical Illustrations*. New York: Basic Books, 2006.

Watkins, Susan. "Presentism? A Reply to T. J. Clark." *New Left Review*, no. 74 (March–April 2012): 77–102.

Waugh, Evelyn. *Put Out More Flags*. New York: Little, Brown, and Company, 2012.

Webster, Wendy. "*The Silent Village*: The GPO Film Unit Goes to War." In *The Projection of Britain: A History of the GPO Film Unit*, edited by Scott Anthony and James G. Mansell, 263–71. London: British Film Institute, 2011.

Weil, Simone. "*The Iliad*, or the Poem of Force." In *War and the Iliad*, edited by Christopher Benfey, 1–39. New York: New York Review of Books, 2005.

Welles, Orson, and Peter Bogdanovich. *This Is Orson Welles*. New York: Da Capo Press, 1998.

Wells, H. G. *Little Wars*. Boston, MA: Small, Maynard, and Company, 1913.

Wiebe, Heather. *Britten's Unquiet Pasts: Sound and Memory in Postwar Reconstruction*. Cambridge: Cambridge University Press, 2012.

Wiles, David. *Shakespeare's Clown: Actor and Text in the Elizabethan Playhouse*. Cambridge: Cambridge University Press, 1987.

Williams, Gordon. *British Theatre in the Great War: A Reevaluation*. London: Continuum, 2003.

Williams, Raymond. *Marxism and Literature*. Oxford: Oxford University Press, 1977.

Wills, Gary. "Critical Inquiry in Clausewitz." *Critical Inquiry* 9, no. 2 (December 1982): 281–302.

Wilson, J. Dover. *The Fortunes of Falstaff*. Cambridge: Cambridge University Press, 1979.

Wimmer, Leila. *Cross-Channel Perspectives: The French Reception of British Cinema*. Oxford: Peter Lang, 2009.

Wollaeger, Mark. *Modernism, Media, and Propaganda: British Narrative from 1900 to 1945*. Princeton, NJ: Princeton University Press, 2006.

Woloch, Alex. *The One vs. the Many: Minor Characters and the Space of the Protagonist in the Novel*. Princeton, NJ: Princeton University Press, 2009.

———. *Or Orwell: Writing and Democratic Socialism*. Cambridge, MA: Harvard University Press, 2016.

Woolf, Virginia. *Between the Acts*. New York: Harcourt, 1941.

———. "Thoughts on Peace in an Air Raid." In *Selected Essays*, edited by David Bradshaw, 216–20. Oxford: Oxford University Press, 2008.

Wright, Gordon. *The Ordeal of Total War: 1939–1945*. New York: Harper and Row, 1968.

Wymer, Rowland. *Derek Jarman*. Manchester: Manchester University Press, 2005.

Index

WORLD WAR II: THE GLOBAL, HUMAN, AND ETHICAL DIMENSION

G. Kurt Piehler, series editor

Lawrence Cane, David E. Cane, Judy Barrett Litoff, and David C. Smith, eds., *Fighting Fascism in Europe: The World War II Letters of an American Veteran of the Spanish Civil War*

Angelo M. Spinelli and Lewis H. Carlson, *Life behind Barbed Wire: The Secret World War II Photographs of Prisoner of War Angelo M. Spinelli*

Don Whitehead and John B. Romeiser, *"Beachhead Don": Reporting the War from the European Theater, 1942–1945*

Scott H. Bennett, ed., *Army GI, Pacifist CO: The World War II Letters of Frank and Albert Dietrich*

Alexander Jefferson with Lewis H. Carlson, *Red Tail Captured, Red Tail Free: Memoirs of a Tuskegee Airman and POW*

Jonathan G. Utley, *Going to War with Japan, 1937–1941*

Grant K. Goodman, *America's Japan: The First Year, 1945–1946*

Patricia Kollander with John O'Sullivan, *"I Must Be a Part of This War": One Man's Fight against Hitler and Nazism*

Judy Barrett Litoff, *An American Heroine in the French Resistance: The Diary and Memoir of Virginia d'Albert-Lake*

Thomas R. Christofferson and Michael S. Christofferson, *France during World War II: From Defeat to Liberation*

Don Whitehead, *Combat Reporter: Don Whitehead's World War II Diary and Memoirs*, edited by John B. Romeiser

James M. Gavin, *The General and His Daughter: The Wartime Letters of General James M. Gavin to His Daughter Barbara*, edited by Barbara Gavin Fauntleroy et al.

Carol Adele Kelly, ed., *Voices of My Comrades: America's Reserve Officers Remember World War II*, Foreword by Senators Ted Stevens and Daniel K. Inouye

John J. Toffey IV, *Jack Toffey's War: A Son's Memoir*

Lt. General James V. Edmundson, *Letters to Lee: From Pearl Harbor to the War's Final Mission*, edited by Dr. Celia Edmundson

John K. Stutterheim, *The Diary of Prisoner 17326: A Boy's Life in a Japanese Labor Camp*, Foreword by Mark Parillo

G. Kurt Piehler and Sidney Pash, eds., *The United States and the Second World War: New Perspectives on Diplomacy, War, and the Home Front*

Susan E. Wiant, *Between the Bylines: A Father's Legacy*, Foreword by Walter Cronkite

Deborah S. Cornelius, *Hungary in World War II: Caught in the Cauldron*

Gilya Gerda Schmidt, *Süssen Is Now Free of Jews: World War II, The Holocaust, and Rural Judaism*

Emanuel Rota, *A Pact with Vichy: Angelo Tasca from Italian Socialism to French Collaboration*

Panteleymon Anastasakis, *The Church of Greece under Axis Occupation*

Louise DeSalvo, *Chasing Ghosts: A Memoir of a Father, Gone to War*

Alexander Jefferson with Lewis H. Carlson, *Red Tail Captured, Red Tail Free: Memoirs of a Tuskegee Airman and POW, Revised Edition*

Kent Puckett, *War Pictures: Cinema, Violence, and Style in Britain, 1939–1945*